THE UNMAKING OF A WHIG
And Other Essays in Self-Definition

THE UNMAKING OF A WHIG

And Other Essays in Self-Definition

EDWIN M. YODER, JR.

GEORGETOWN UNIVERSITY PRESS
Washington, D.C.

Library of Congress Cataloging-in-Publication Data

Yoder, Edwin.
  The unmaking of a Whig and other essays in self-definition / Edwin
M. Yoder, Jr.
    p. cm.
  ISBN 0-87840-496-1
    1. United States—Politics and government. 2. United States—
Constitutional history. 3. United States—History I. Title.
JK21.Y63   1990   89-71493
320.973—dc20   CIP

For Jane

Contents

viii *CONTENTS*

Foreword

In volume 4 of Arnold J. Toynbee's *A Study of History,* which appeared in London in 1939, we are of a sudden transported across the Atlantic to

> ... make a comparative study of the *post-bellum* histories of the several states in 'the Old South' which were members of the Confederacy in the Civil War of 1861–5 and were involved in the Confederacy's defeat, we shall notice a marked difference between them in the extent to which they have since recovered respectively from that common disaster; and we shall also notice that this difference is the exact inverse of an equally well marked difference which had distinguished the same states from one another in the *ante-bellum* period.

These were once serene Virginia, with an aristocracy not unlike that of Oxonian Britain's with their "tranquil sense of effortless superiority"; proud, impetuous South Carolina, with the coursing blood of Hotspurs in its veins, now both brought low to a lotus land of nostalgia and lassitude. And there between them a "'hustling', 'boosting'" North Carolina, chock-a-block with distinguished personalities and burgeoning life. In the ante-bellum era North Carolina had been "socially barren while Virginia and South Carolina were . . . bursting with social vitality." With poor soil and no port it was an in-between state, a place to slink off, when you failed in others, to "a hard life in a blind alley." But no longer!

> It will be seen that the *ante-bellum* contrast between North Carolina and her two neighbours was the natural outcome of historical and geographical circumstance. It is the *post-bellum* inversion of this natural situation that has to be explained; and, here again, the explanation is not to be found in any inborn merits of the community which has achieved an eventual eminence, but rather in its freedom from the incubus that has weighed its fallen neighbours down. The former exaltation of Virginia and South Carolina is the veritable cause of their abasement now. They have failed to rise again from their prostration in the Civil War because they have never succeeded in forgetting the height from which that fearful catastrophe once hurled them, whereas North Carolina, who lost so much less because she had so little to lose, has found it relatively easy to recover from a slighter shock. "For whosoever exalteth himself shall be abased; and he that humbleth himself shall be exalted."

As with much in Toynbee, we never know whether what we are getting is a real history or a series of Bible stories in modern (or medieval) dress; or yet, in the manner of Sir James G. Frazier in *his* multivolume *Golden Bough,* some good pagan stuff prettified by High Church propriety. It doesn't matter. Toynbee was right this time. Witness Edwin M. Yoder, Jr., author of the sparkling collection, *The Night of the Old South Ball,* and now of this stunning set of essays in *The Unmaking of a Whig, And Other Essays in Self-Definition.*

It would be a joy to read Yoder *on* Toynbee; only a true Southern writer would know how to handle all that "Macbeth v, iii, 23; Luke, xvii, 214; Matthew, xxii, 12," all in two pages on The Nemesis of Creativity in South Carolina. But he has more pressing work. The Whig historians have a stronger hold on the American mind, and that, not world history, is Yoder's more limited subject. Is it the mark of a Southern writer to keep his subject within some bounds? Regardless, it is surely a Southerner who would write: "In the inexact sciences labels can be as treacherous as they are useful. . . ." Thus also propositions concerning the improbability of precision. That, too, could be wrong! Melbourne wished that he could be as certain of anything as Macaulay was of everything. Yoder would agree but with mild perplexity: *why* did Melbourne strive so for detachment? Was it aversion to pleasure that led him so to disdain the agreeable orthodoxies of his time? A concealed Calvinist? Yoder is the Augustinian: Lord make me infallible, but not yet. He is, after all, a Southerner and was born to ambiguity.

Is it late in our national experience to identify a writer as a *Southerner?* I suppose. All that is going quickly, if not gone. But we ought, even so, to treasure a writer of great gifts and national eminence, a Rhodes Scholar, a Pulitzer Prize winner, a distinct and inimitable voice in the counsels of the nation's capital who never once loses touch with that small town in central North Carolina in which he was raised, nor the memory of his schoolmaster father, "a seventh-generation Carolina Lutheran," much drawn to subjects such as geometry, of which he would observe that "proofs are not a matter of opinion. They are either right or wrong," the while abidingly aware that there are few proofs of anything.

This is only half our sage's inheritance—"the sober, learned, admirable, always serious and decorous Yoders." Mother came from livelier stock, the Logues and Laseters, Bruces and Rivieres and Warthens of central Georgia— "places of spacious landscape and big airy houses in the country, filled with merry, laughing, tippling, fun-loving people, cavaliers in their southern way." With *that* Southern history. Sherman's men "swatting and slashing" their way through the family dining room; a great-grandfather dead at Deep Bottom on the James River.

Inasmuch as Yoder is forever turning to poets to explain politics, let me turn to Yeats to explain, to try to explain, just a little bit of Yoder. That telling line from "The Fiddler of Dooney": "For the good are always merry/Save by an evil chance." That evil chance had come to Southerners, good and bad. He cites C. Vann Woodward, "The experience of evil and the experience of tragedy are parts of the Southern heritage that are as difficult to reconcile with the American legend of innocence and social felicity as the experience of poverty and defeat are to reconcile with the legends of abundance and success."

Each of these essays reaches this topic; at one or more removes may be but soon or late, there it is. Herbert Butterfield's *The Whig Interpretation of History* introduces the young man, on his way now to Oxford, to the idea that memory must not consist solely of the views of the victors; that losers need to have a say; that they may have been right. We read on and learn much of those for whom we have previously had a mixed, or at most an unfinished regard. Yoder's long opening essay, "Black v. Jackson, A Study in Judicial Enmity," is a masterwork of psychological writing, that has no equal among histories of the Supreme Court. On the one hand Hugo Black, a populist radical from the deep South, and the deep poverty of the deep South, and the deep culture also. Those who knew him found him closest of any modern justice to the thinking of the Founders for the elemental reason that he knew what they knew, and not all that much more. He had read the same books; the only ones at hand: Tacitus, Thucydides, Gibbon, Carlyle, Macaulay. And then finding this intellectual world pleasing, he stayed with the authors the rest of his life. This was a wholly different personal formation from that of Robert Houghwout Jackson of Jamestown, New York. Both men were New

Dealers, of "the strictest sect," Yoder writes, both appointed by Franklin D. Roosevelt. Jackson had a spare education, one year at Albany Law School (which happens, however, to be the oldest in the nation). He read law, as they said in those days, rather than being taught it, and at an age when Black was joining the Klan, joined instead the Chautauqua County Democratic Committee which brought him in touch with Roosevelt, the Assistant Secretary of the Navy in the Wilson administration. Hence his return to the capital in the 1930s and thereafter the Court. Black was from the red clay hills of the deep South. The hills around Jamestown are low, and lovingly green. A gentle portage of some twenty miles or so makes its way up from Lake Erie to Lake Chautauqua, and thereafter through the city of Jamestown. This is no less Protestant country than southern Alabama (although I must confess that my grandfather made his way there from the County Kerry). But it was abolitionist country; one of the few regions outside the South where the Civil War memorial tends to occupy the most prominent site in town. It appears to me that only a Southerner of Yoder's range could see how the two men differed and give us the full range and import of the feud that still echoes in that Greek Temple across the park from where I write.

The Unmaking of a Whig should not dispose us to think that Yoder is any the less Whiggish for knowing the faults of that persuasion. What is the point of being a Southern writer, if not to be able to entertain with ease and generosity a houseful of attitudes and inclinations? The one thing he is not, however, is sentimental. He cites John M. Evans on Butterfield, " . . . The simplest version of Butterfield's argument drifts toward *tout comprendre, c'est tout pardonner. . . .* " A maxim with some truth about it. But—may I?—an eighteenth century maxim. A twentieth century version might be nearer *tout pardonner, c'est tout comprendre.* Not on your life with Yoder. Empathy helps you get to a subject; it does not help you think once you arrive. Thus we learn at the outset of "The Madisonian Persuasion":

> It is impossible to venture far into the writings of James Madison without suspecting, to understate the situation, that in what is perhaps the most crucial of all debates about government Madison clearly stands with the Augustinians, not the Pelagians.

No enticing visions of "potential human perfection." Yoder's eyes look up more often for signs of rain than signs of celestial approval. Arriving at the end of this marvelous collection, my own thoughts turned to a Yankee, of all things. That Yankee poet of ours, Robert Frost. He gets this book perfectly in that wonderful opening stanza of "The Pasture."

> I'm going out to clean the pasture spring;
> I'll only stop to rake the leaves away
> (And wait to watch the water clear, I may):
> I sha'n't be gone long.—You come too.

Watch the water clear. It won't take long. Y'all come!

DANIEL PATRICK MOYNIHAN

September 13, 1989

Author's Note

This collection is a true omnium gatherum, covering everything from judicial history to literature to religion, with a bit of autobiographical reminiscence thrown in. The thread that unites these pieces may seem elusive, but I have adopted the conceit—it may be no more—that the common theme is a search for self-definition. Writing about nearly anything involves the deployment of one's personal sonar, to put it metaphorically, and the bouncing echoes are points of reference for oneself as for the subject.

The collection was first suggested by Timothy S. Healy, S.J., then president of Georgetown University and now president of the New York Public Library. His generous friendship has been among the blessings of my sojourn in Washington. When I began gathering these stray pieces, the collection seemed an appropriate home for a longer manuscript I had been working on for years, about the Black-Jackson "feud" within the U.S. Supreme Court in 1946. This "Study in Judicial Enmity" forms Part I of the collection and appears in print here for the first time.

In the Black-Jackson study, I have omitted such warning phrases as, "it may be argued that . . . " and "one gathers that . . . " This study is not guesswork, nor is it that fictionalized history which is now often called "faction" or, in its film forms, "docudrama." But like all historical studies it is a construct, selective to a degree, and built of many pieces from many sources. It is my hope to achieve pace and coherence, and to tell an intriguing story as it deserves to be told, without pedantic clutter. The reader who has questions may consult the notes; but there will be little prompting by rhetorical hand-signals.

There is a precedent for this procedure, which some have regarded as a bit disreputable. In his *Eminent Victorians,* Lytton Strachey claimed—not altogether persuasively—that he had taken only one liberty with the historical facts. He had guessed, without actually knowing, that Dr. Thomas Arnold's legs were short. What Strachey actually wrote is that "[Arnold's] legs, perhaps, were shorter than they should have been." There being no regulation length for the legs of a Victorian schoolmaster, Strachey even here meets any conceivable objection that he has falsified history. Indeed, that conditional "perhaps" makes the case airtight. This is not to claim that my "Study in Judicial Enmity" rivals Strachey's for art or wit; only that like *Eminent Victorians,* a model any writer must envy, it claims to be true, but strives for narrative flow without distracting cautionary road signals.

Many friends helped with this book. Some of them read all or parts of the manuscript and saved me from errors and inelegances. They include my editor, John Breslin, S.J., and his friendly staff at the Georgetown University press, especially Eleanor Waters, an exacting copy and proof editor; William Dickinson and Anna Karavangelos, my editors at The Washington Post Writers Group and a constant source of good counsel; Jay Wilkinson, John Maurice and Martha Noel Evans, and David McKenzie Clark Esq. I am grateful to the Hon. Daniel Patrick Moynihan, U.S. senator from New York, who borrowed time from the superhuman schedule he routinely keeps to read the manuscript and write a generous and entertaining foreword. Dick Howard lent me books from his personal law library, without so much as a chirp of alarm as they fell overdue by months and even years.

Some of these pieces, as the notes establish, began as lectures or talks at various institutions and seminars, where I was received with friendly hospitality and courtesy. My thanks to all their organizers and arrangers. Finally, my work, when it makes sense and when it is temperate and kind, reflects the wisdom and counsel of my wife and companion of three happy decades, Mary Jane Warwick Yoder. The book is dedicated to her, with love and gratitude.

EDWIN M. YODER, JR.

Alexandria, Virginia
October 1989

I

Black v. Jackson

Black v. Jackson: A Study in Judicial Enmity

April 22, 1946, was a brilliant day in Washington. When the eight present justices of the Supreme Court gathered in the East Conference Room for robing, just before noon, Chief Justice Harlan F. Stone seemed to be in high spirits. He introduced his guest Lord Wright, a senior British judge, who was on his way to Tokyo for the Japanese War Crimes Trials. Soon after the pleasantries the court crier called out the familiar "Oyez! Oyez! Oyez!" (the Supreme Court is one of the few American tribunals where the ancient words are given a French pronunciation and not sounded as "Oh yes! Oh yes!") and the Court seated itself, each justice settling into his own custom-made high-backed chair. Soon it was the chief justice's turn to read his dissent in a case involving the rights of resident aliens. Not far into his notes, Stone began to mumble inaudibly and shuffle the papers before him.

"What is this?" he was heard to ask Hugo Black, who as senior associate justice, sat immediately to his right. Both Black and Stanley Reed, to Stone's left, turned to help. The chief nodded, then seemed to rouse himself. "The case should be stayed," he murmured, and fell silent. Black and

3

Reed rose, and with each supporting a shoulder they helped the slumping chief justice behind the red curtains to the rear. Forty-five minutes later, Black reconvened the Court, "in the temporary absence and indisposition of the chief justice." One of the clerks soon handed Black a note. "The Chief Justice is sleeping," the senior associate justice read. "His doctor announced he had ordered him to rest for two or three days. No change on diagnosis of indigestion." A later note informed Black and the other anxious justices that Stone, now at home, "is still having a good sleep." But by nightfall, confounding these optimistic assurances, the chief justice was dead. He had never regained consciousness. The Court was now leaderless, and its last personal link with the pre-Roosevelt days, the days before the great court-packing storm of 1937, had been severed.

Someone in Washington, and doubtless more than one, had been telling unpleasant stories about Robert Houghwout Jackson and the fifty-four-year-old associate justice, the missing man from the scene described above, found himself increasingly annoyed. To his friends, Jackson usually appeared a cheerful man with a twinkling eye. But as the War Crimes Tribunal at the Palace of Justice amid the rubble of Nuremberg dragged on, Jackson seemed to be growing irascible—uncharacteristically so. He seemed irritated by picayune matters: whether, for instance, his deputies in the office of the U.S. chief of counsel might bring their wives across to stay while they served.

Just who the detractors and talebearers in Washington were, whom they were talking to (apart from newspaper columnists), and exactly what they were whispering against him, Jackson could not be sure. Four thousand long miles separated him from Court politics in Washington. The rumors had begun to reach him in late April, after the sudden death of Stone. It wasn't hard to guess who was behind them. The primary suspect was Hugo Lafayette

Black, 60, the senior New Deal justice, with whom Jackson had been very much at odds.

The distinguished old chief justice, who apart from Felix Frankfurter was Jackson's closest ally on the Court, had enjoyed a long career in American public life, stretching back to Calvin Coolidge's cabinet a quarter century earlier. Then, unexpectedly, Stone had faltered and died. Suddenly, as of this April 22, 1946, the coveted chair at the center of the nation's highest court stood vacant; and it was a seat that Robert Jackson had long had his eye on. Would the new president, Harry Truman, name him to succeed Stone? Washington expected it. So did most of the reporters who covered the Court and pretended to know what was going on there. Jackson's friends and admirers thought he had earned the post, and that his celebrated eloquence and wit would ornament it.

Yet here he was, helplessly stuck in the charnel house of Nuremberg, where the stench of corpses still buried in the rubble filled the air on certain days. Jackson was serving, to much sly criticism on the Court and in some legal circles, in the thankless role of chief prosecutor for the United States. He had leapt at the appointment when President Truman had offered it, a year earlier. The Nuremberg War Crimes Tribunal had seemed to him then a wonderful opportunity to escape the strife, the passivity, and the occasional triviality of the Court. He would never forget that at the time the Japanese bombed Pearl Harbor, the Court had been hearing arguments about taxes on golf green fees. Jackson thought it essential—perhaps the greatest mission a lawyer could undertake—that the monstrous crimes of the Nazi leaders should be brought home to them, and in a respectable judicial proceeding. But he had not expected the trials to drag on beyond the first summer, through the autumn and thence into another year, while his colleagues in Washington impatiently awaited his return. Important cases were stalled on tie votes; other justices had been forced to increase their writing chores. But Stone and Truman had refused to entertain any suggestion from Jackson that it would be better for him to resign from the Court, if his absence had intolerably baffled its work.

Now Jackson was very much out of touch with his friends and supporters in Washington. They had not been able to agree, for instance, whether he should suspend his work in Nuremberg to return for Stone's funeral. In the end, he had not. He had seen the eloquent photographs in *Life* magazine of the other justices entering the National Cathedral for the Chief's last rites, led by an immaculately dressed and bearded Charles Evans Hughes. He had told himself that it was not a good time to be away from the scene. But what could he do about it?

Scarcely had the mourning for Stone ended before the prince of journalistic gossip, Drew Pearson, was reporting an intrigue against him, to block his elevation to the chief justiceship. Pearson confided to his readers that several "liberal" members of the Court, Jackson's associates, had told Truman that they would quit outright, sooner than serve under Jackson. Since that initial shot across his bow, the Washington rumor mills had been busy—so much was clear from the letters and press clippings that reached him.

* * *

In 1945–46, the year of these events, the Second World War had come to a triumphant end and Americans were beginning to think a bit nervously about "reconversion"— shifting the economy back to a peacetime footing. It was, in a sense, uncharted terrain. The immediate prewar years had been a time of cruel economic depression, labor-management strife, and unemployment; and all three factors are pertinent to the dilemma that faced Robert Jackson that spring in Nuremberg. Once the stimulus of wartime spending disappeared, a replay of the 1930s seemed distinctly possible. There was nothing in the history of prior postwar eras to suggest otherwise. So it was natural in a way that an intense dispute over the meaning and legislative history of the Federal Wages and Hours Act of 1937 formed the immediate backdrop of what soon came to be called the Hugo Black-Robert Jackson "feud."

It was the classic "man bites dog" story of which journalists dream—the only open quarrel between two sitting members of the Supreme Court in its whole history. There has been bad blood between justices, before and since, but the combatants usually have managed to keep it out of the newspapers. This time the principals didn't and indeed made no effort to do so. Both Black and Jackson were figures of the first magnitude in the judicial history of this century. No justice exerted more influence upon it than Hugo L. Black, or was more resourceful in setting his personal and intellectual stamp on key areas of the law. And although early death, less than a decade after the events of the great feud, was to cut short the career of Robert H. Jackson, he had already established himself (in the eyes of Black, among others) as the most compelling courtroom advocate of his time. He was a man of storied eloquence whose pen contributed a stock of elegant apothegms to the law: "serpentine walls [separating church and state]" . . . "Not by the authority of our competence but by the force of our commissions" . . . "We are not final because we are infallible; we are infallible because we are final." Jackson was, among other things, a writer's writer.

On conventional assumptions about the Court and post-New Deal politics, it is and has been difficult to penetrate to the heart of their spectacular public disagreement. Both Black and Jackson were New Dealers of the strictest sect; both were among Franklin D. Roosevelt's appointees to the Court; both had been energetic and active in the judicial counterrevolution of 1937–38. The standard accounts, in standard biographies, tell the story well but are less than comprehensive or psychologically persuasive. Men of intellectual and political power are usually men of substantial ego; but they do not usually quarrel over trifles. And in Washington mere pique is carefully suppressed, even at times of tension and stress.

The usual explanation is that Jackson desperately wanted to succeed Harlan F. Stone as chief justice of the United States, and that Hugo Black was as doggedly determined to thwart that ambition. Why would anyone want to be chief justice? The short and obvious answer is prestige. It is no ignoble ambition for a great lawyer to covet the one great constitutionally designated judicial post; and at the time of the Black-Jackson donnybrook a succession of eminent men had been chief justice. They included one former president, William Howard Taft, who liked being chief justice much more than he had liked being president. There was the great Charles Evans Hughes, who could have posed persuasively for a Renaissance Jehovah. There was Stone, a bit less Olympian, but an imposing figure all the same.

Another factor in the public quarrel, less important than some accounts would have it but of some weight, was the dissension Jackson's year-long absence from the Court had caused. It was the longest leave of which we have record—much longer, for instance, than the most recent precedent: Justice Owen Roberts's departure of a few weeks to preside over the Pearl Harbor inquiry in 1942. And there was a philosophical dispute as well. Some of the other justices believed, or claimed to believe, that President Truman had flouted the intention of the Framers by giving a prosecutorial post, essentially executive, to a member of the judiciary; and some had even persuaded themselves that Jackson saw the task at Nuremberg as a stepping-stone to the presidency—or at least the governorship of New York. It was not yet, in those years, regarded as shocking for a Supreme Court justice to be "mentioned" for president or vice president, as William O. Douglas had been as recently as 1944. Finally, there were those who viewed the Nuremberg trials as an ex post facto proceeding, alien to Anglo-American legal traditions. Chief Justice Stone—not spitefully, for he was on good personal terms with Jackson—had privately called Nuremberg "Bob Jackson's lynching bee." But lynching bee or not, that was where Jackson was when he learned that April day that Stone was dead.

*   *   *

To Jackson, the campaign against him seemed as absurd as it was annoying. He obviously had his ambitions; everyone knew that. There was no point in denying that he would like to be chief justice. Supreme Court justices did not feel the need they would one day feel to disguise or hide political interests and ambitions. Hughes himself, who had served as chief justice in the stormy days of the fight with Roosevelt, had in his earlier career as a justice left the Court to run for president on the Republican ticket against Woodrow Wilson. And no judicial figure was now more widely respected. Only five years before, in 1942, James F. Byrnes had bolted from the Court after only a year to help Roosevelt run the war. Jackson's own eye, it was widely known, had recently fallen on the governorship of New York, his home state. That had been during his term as U.S. attorney general, just before FDR had appointed him to the Court. Roosevelt himself had suggested it. His poker table and breakfast levees were familiar Jackson haunts. The President had wagged his head in that curious way of his and told him he would make it all right with Jim Farley. But Farley, the Democratic Party boss whose influence was unrivaled in New York politics, had squelched Jackson's ambition. He had persuaded the incumbent, Herbert Lehman, to run for another term, blocking Jackson's tentative dip into politics. It had been an embarrassment and a warning, and a source of merriment to Jackson's critics and rivals.

Jackson was, and thought of himself as, an upstate New Yorker to the core. For a long time before coming to New Deal Washington in 1934, to be general counsel at the Internal Revenue Service, he had practiced law and raised show horses in the upstate hamlet of Jamestown. He often longed to go back. That was why he had responded to Roosevelt's blandishments about the governorship. But the truth was that Jackson lacked the patience for intrigue and logrolling by which one made his way in elective politics. He was too independent and took delight in being known to those who watched him closely as a maverick: a man who gloried in going against the grain of conventional opinion.

Now, in the spring of 1946, his colleagues on the Court, some of them anyway, suspected him of coveting the post of chief justice. Deny it as he might, they believed that Roosevelt had promised Jackson that he would have the position when Stone retired. Even Stone seemed to believe it. He had sheepishly explained to Jackson, one day during the war years, that he had decided to stay on for a while after the age of seventy, at which justices could now retire on full pay. In fact, as anyone who had been close to him knew, Roosevelt casually promised everything to everyone, with a shameless promiscuity of commitment. No Roosevelt associate who'd spent as much time in his company as Jackson would take such a "promise" at face value. Jackson knew well enough the late president's mastery of the arts of flattery: enough, in any case, to discount such talk heavily. What had happened then was known to no one else. FDR had summoned Jackson one day after Hughes announced his decision to retire and told him that the time was not quite opportune to make him, Jackson, Chief. Everyone had told him, the president said, that a chief justice is better off if he first gains some seasoning on the Court. As a gesture of national unity, and in deference to Hughes's advice, he was giving the post to Stone. But there was a clear implication that Jackson would be next in line.

It was only a hint, privately extended. But the liberals on the Court pretended to believe that Jackson had the job in his pocket. It was tiresome and undignified, Jackson had long since concluded, to deny it—it wasn't the sort of thing one openly discussed anyway. He was nonetheless persuaded now that much of the maneuvering and bickering he had witnessed as associate justice during the past five years expressed some veiled resentment of his heir-apparency. This, he thought, was especially clear in the demeanor of Hugo Black, Jackson's elder by six years and his senior on the Court by four.

Jackson would welcome the appointment if it came his way, but it was simply wrong to suppose that he thought he had been "promised" it, even by FDR, who was now dead. Jackson had seen enough of Stone's vexations in recent years, trying to bring some semblance of harmony to this "team of wild horses," to wonder if the leadership of so fiercely divided a body would be worth the effort. Harry Truman, whom Jackson knew only casually, was now in the White House; and Truman surely had his own ideas. Yet the rumors persisted, and so did the stories whispered to his discredit, some of which bordered on being vicious. Jackson could not be sure who the talebearers were. But his suspicions centered on three justices with whom he had often been at odds, both as to judicial procedure and philosophy and as to specific cases.

Frank Murphy, the ebullient Michigan Irishman who had preceded him as attorney general, was a minor suspect. Murphy had begun his career as mayor of Detroit and

Depression-years governor of Michigan. In political orienta-
tion he was an unswerving liberal, though a sufficiently
pliable one, Jackson thought, to bend often to the will of
Hugo Black, the liberal block's mastermind. Murphy's name
had appeared in the press among those who were said to be
scheming against Jackson, threatening to leave the Court.
But Murphy was restless; his friends knew that he hoped to
be sent back to the Philippines, where he had once been
governor-general. Besides, Murphy was—well, he was too
nice to be involved in an intrigue to undercut a colleague
with the new president.

A likelier suspect was William O. Douglas, who was not
very nice, and who had hardly bothered to conceal his
disapproval of Jackson's current mission in Nuremberg, and
on all sorts of scores too. Douglas had complained noisily
about the war crimes duties. A prosecutor, he pedantically
maintained, had to be an executive functionary, not a judicial
one; and so the role was inappropriate for a judge, even if
other things about it were right. Jackson's absence, moreover, would paralyze the Court, throttling it with an endless
succession of 4-4 deadlocks. Finally, like Harlan Stone,
Douglas had embraced the view that the Nuremberg tribunal was offensive to American constitutional traditions and
standards, an ex post facto proceeding, a necktie party
camouflaged as a trial. He had not gone quite as far as Stone,
had not confidentially called it a "high-class lynching bee."
But he was talking; one could be sure of that. Douglas,
indeed, made an unpleasant habit of suspecting colleagues
on the Court of political ambitions that were only too obvious
in his own case. He was a prime suspect.

But Jackson's suspicions had come mainly to focus on
Hugo Black, the slender, balding, chain-smoking sixty-year-
old Alabamian who had been, to much shock and surprise,
Roosevelt's first appointee in 1937. So far as rivalries could
be discerned from the outside, one of several, both sub-

stantive and personal, pitted Jackson against Black. Temperamentally, regionally, they came near being polar opposites. Black was a populist radical from the red clay hills of Alabama. Jackson was a settled, gregarious maverick from the farm country of upstate New York. People who did not know them well, who had no means of piercing the veil of secrecy behind which the Court worked, saw only the surface of the rivalry. It was revealing enough. In four collegial years, Jackson and Black had differed crisply over a number of important issues—the flag salute cases, the Japanese internment cases, and especially, as the war in Europe drew to a close and organized labor became more and more assertive, over union policy. That much was visible on the surface, in votes and opinions.

In the *Korematsu* case, for instance, one of three arising from the Army's removal and internment of West Coast citizens of Japanese ancestry, Jackson had written a blisteringdissent, attacking the court (meaning mostly Black, who wrote the majority opinion) for condoning military lawlessness. "Read this and perish!" the genial Murphy had exclaimed to his law clerk when he saw Jackson's preliminary draft. Ultimately, Jackson had softened his strictures a bit; but the fact remained that Black had found ways of upholding Fred Korematsu's internment, while Jackson had branded it as lawless. In some ways, that division echoed the earlier affair of the flag salute cases. Despite their usual (and highly advertised) sympathy with underdogs, Black and Douglas in a 1941 decision had embraced the astonishing view that Jehovah's Witness children might be compelled by law and school board regulations to salute the flag as a patriotic gesture, even though the children and their parents saw such gestures as idolatrous. Then Black and Douglas had recanted, and awaited a similar case to reverse the precedent. Joining the court between the two cases, Jackson had undertaken Stone's assignment and written a ringing freedom-of-conscience decision. Only Frankfurter had obstinately stood by his original view that compelling such patriotic exercises, however obnoxious to conscience, was within the legislative powers of the states.

Such differences occasionally caused irritation, but they were part of the ordinary routine of an appellate court. The real irritants lay more deeply hidden in the mysteries and rituals of the Court. Black, as Jackson viewed him, was beyond question the real leader of the Court's judicial activists. Clever, willful, courtly and ruthless, Black often reenacted in liberal causes the patterns of jurisprudence that had brought on the great backlash of 1937 between Roosevelt's New Deal and the Court's conservatives. When the political convictions of Black and the other liberals were engaged, they would in Jackson's view go quite far—stop at little or nothing—to press an advantage or even rewrite the law.

People seemed to assume that because he and Black were fellow New Deal Democrats, loyal followers of FDR, both sent to the Court by that president, they must be united by some deep if elusive affinity. The truth, Jackson often reflected, was almost directly to the contrary. As an Alabamian, as a political officeholder who had taken that route to the judiciary, Black seemed to Jackson to have paid whatever dues were asked to win preferment. He had joined the Ku Klux Klan when that was the required entree to public office in Alabama, then secretly resigned, no one knew for sure just when. For Black, as Jackson saw it, the Democratic Party had been a vehicle of conventional majority opinion and Black's deference to it had cost him nothing while rewarding him richly, with a seat in the U.S. Senate. How different, Jackson reflected, it was to be a Democrat in stalwartly Republican upstate New York, Jackson's home territory. His adherence to the Democrats, like his conscientious objection to World War I, had signaled his willingness to defy the conventional views of friends and neighbors.

Finally, there was a deeper difference, a subtle matter of temperament. Black seemed to Jackson to bear upon his mind, manner, and attitudes subtle scars of struggle, the marks of a man who had fought his way along in life. Beneath the quiet and courtly manner there stirred—Jackson had seen it—a certain fierceness and animus against the rich, the respectable, and the powerful. Black, to Jackson's dismay, took a strange satisfaction in denigrating the American Bar Association. He liked to tell friends that it was the only body he had ever regretted joining (not, it seemed, forgetting the Klan!) and this weird sentiment had cropped up constantly in magazine articles about him. Jackson sensed that in the core of Black there flamed the soul of a tribune of the people, a firebrand. Jackson had felt the heat of Black's muted passion more than once. But a single sharp and sour memory sealed Jackson's suspicion, now, that Black was probably masterminding the intrigue against his appointment as chief justice.

He and Black had parted, a year ago, on the worst possible terms. After assembling his skeleton staff, Jackson had headed for London the day after the Court adjourned to concert plans for the trials with the Allies. There had been a fearful wrangle right at the end of the Court session, a quarrel over proprieties so subtle, however, as to be little noticed outside. But it had been quite impassioned, behind the closed doors of the conference room.

It had begun with a labor law case, arising in the Virginia coal fields. To Jackson's dismay—and also to that of Stone and Frankfurter—the Court had reinterpreted the Federal Wages and Hours Act, ruling that coal miners were due "portal-to-portal" pay—compensation from the instant they entered the mine to the instant they left it. The rule would hold, no matter how much of that time was consumed by the sometimes lengthy travel to the coal faces where work actually began. From Jackson's perspective, and that of his fellow dissenters, there were all sorts of things wrong with this 5-4 decision of the *Jewell Ridge* coal case. For one thing, the legislative history of the Wages and Hours Act strongly indicated that it had been intended to protect the rights of *nonunion* workers, too feebly organized to win fair labor contracts. Clearly, Congress had not intended to help so powerful and well-organized a union as John L. Lewis's United Mine Workers—or suddenly to render coal mine operators liable for millions of dollars in back pay. Yet that was the effect of the ruling. Frank Murphy had written the opinion for the majority, acting, Jackson had no doubt, as cat's paw for Black. But Murphy's florid and emotional manifesto in favor of portal-to-portal pay for coal miners was hardly the worst of the matter. Not only had the Court overturned a universally held construction of the law; Black, in leading the way, had repudiated his own explanation of the intent of the Wages and Hours Act—the speech he had delivered as Senate floor leader for the bill eight years earlier. Black had been stung when Jackson dug this inconvenient speech, a sort of Banquo's Ghost, out of the Congressional Record and quoted it in a footnote. Black had stiffly protested, in a memorandum, that his words had been misread; that he had been describing an entirely different draft of the bill. But Jackson had refused to withdraw the nettlesome footnote, and the dissent had gone down intact on decision day.

But then the plot had thickened, and with it the tensions aroused by the decision. Arguing for the United Mine Workers in their appeal to the Court had been none other than Col. Crampton Harris of Birmingham, a seasoned Alabama labor lawyer who happened to be Hugo Black's onetime law partner. This connection had not gone un-noticed by the losing coal mine operators. When the decision went against them they petitioned for a rehearing of the case, arguing that Black should have withdrawn in view of his prior relationship with Harris. The rehearing petition, though polite in form, intimated bad judgment or worse on Black's part. Jackson privately agreed. But the reconsideration question was not in his hands. By longstanding custom, every justice is the keeper of his own conscience when a potential conflict of interest arises.

The question of disqualification faces every jurist more or less constantly; and there is no fixed standard. Often the arguments for sitting in a case in spite of some prior connection with one of the parties, or their counsel, is compelling. It may be, for instance, that otherwise the case will not be decided and the plaintiff will obtain no relief. After the portal-to-portal pay decision, Jackson had thought it ridiculous to pretend that Harris was in the courtroom because of his expertise in Virginia law or labor cases. But it was Black's decision. When it emerged that no one in the majority was willing to change his vote, and that the decision would therefore stand, Black suggested that the petition for a rehearing be denied "per curiam," that is, in an anonymous and otherwise unidentifiable opinion for the whole Court. Jackson, however, had insisted on writing a separate concurrence whose language would make it clear to the attentive that at least some members of the Court did not approve of Black's participation. In one of the last Saturday conferences of the term, almost a year before, Black had flared up. In what Jackson considered his most bullying and bellicose manner, Black had thrown down his challenge. If Jackson went forward with this telltale concurrence, it would mean "war." Jackson had stood his ground. Very well, he had responded, let there be war. He would not allow Black's threats to change his mind. Black might have every right to decide for himself whether to sit in a crucial case argued by his former law partner; but the parties should know that the practice was not unanimously approved within the Court. Frankfurter joined in the concurrence as well. Stone, though he shared their views on refusal, declined; he wanted no war at his age, he later commented privately.

Thus it had been amid such torrid scenes in the great classical building on Capitol Hill, the Court's home since Hughes had built it, that Jackson left for Nuremberg. Black was left steaming over what he deemed a personal insult. What could be more plausible, then, than to suppose that a resentful Hugo Black had seen Harry Truman, or sent a go-between to him, and had let it be known that he would never serve under Robert Jackson? To judge by what the papers said, the threat was now having its effect. The decision on Stone's successor had stalled back in Washington. Jackson had the distinct feeling that the prize, once within his grasp, was slipping away.

II

Drew Pearson was not the only Washington columnist reporting an intrigue against Jackson's promotion to the Court's center chair. Others, including well-connected New Deal officials like Harold Ickes, chimed in; and it all seemed to run to a pattern. Every writer had sources close to or within the liberal bloc at the Court. All were known to be sympathetic to the agenda of organized labor. In Nuremberg, however, Jackson's hands were much too full to permit much fretting over Washington intrigues, even when they vitally concerned his own fortunes. He headed a prosecution staff of more than six hundred at the U.S. chief of counsel's office. Its size was a source of astonishment to the British, French, and Russians, whose combined personnel at the trials did not equal Jackson's in number. Various duties had been parceled out to staff attorneys, with inevitable disagreements over trial strategy to be resolved, documents to be assembled and sorted, interrogations to be completed. The task was staggering.

The dimensions of Jackson's Nuremberg task had been unforeseen, and might, of course, have been avoided altogether. From the outset of the discussions of a war crimes tribunal, the British had wanted to round up the more egregious Nazis and hang them summarily, and without apology—a proceeding that would have evaded the tricky task of putting together an unprecedented legal process and giving it at least some color of due process. They had been dragged along under pressure, protesting all the while, into the elaborate Nuremberg enterprise. That project reflected the stubborn determination of Secretary of War Henry L. Stimson, his deputy John McCloy, and War Department lawyers in Washington. It was Stimson's view that a failure to punish "aggressive war" vigorously after 1918 had ultimately nurtured the far more lawless and murderous Hitler regime. Imperial Germany had been required, at Versailles, to sign a "war guilt" clause of the treaty, accepting blame for starting the war. But that admission, unattended by any legal consequences, had been a source of resentment rather than contrition. Such, at any rate, was Stimson's unshakeable belief.

Under the inspiration of an idealistic War Department lawyer, Murray Bernays, the war crimes trial idea had gone through many bureaucratic ups and downs, with little notice from Roosevelt or Churchill. But with the shocking Malmédy massacre in the Ardennes in December 1944, and most of all with the arrival of Harry S Truman in the White House the following April, the deadlock had been broken. Truman had speedily approved the policy and recruited Jackson to see it through.

From the first, Jackson had been among the War Department's top choices to undertake this experiment in the development of international law. As U.S. solicitor-general (1937–38), he had won for himself an unmatched reputation as a courtroom advocate. His appointment as

U.S. chief of counsel at Nuremberg had followed within three weeks Truman's decision to override British reservations and go ahead with the trials. At first, Jackson had approached the task with enthusiasm. It was his optimistic calculation that the trials could be taken in hand during the Supreme Court's long summer recess (late June to early October). He would prosecute Nazis throughout the summer, learn the verdict soon thereafter, and return to his seat at the court when the October 1945 term commenced. Alas, he had now found to his dismay that the difficulty and complexity of the task had been drastically underestimated.

From the perspective of Washington, that previous spring, it had all looked rather simple, a wonderful outlet for Jackson's celebrated powers of advocacy and his pent-up wish to break out of the passivity of the Court and undertake some great war-connected service. But that was not how it had turned out. He had woefully underestimated the administrative and bureaucratic toil. There was, for instance, the oddly paradoxical fact that the Hitler regime had saved almost every document, however fatally incriminating. Its mountainous archives were a monument of tidy bureaucratic self-indictment. But the great snowdrifts of paper had to be sorted, the relevant plucked from among the irrelevant.

The haste to get the trial on foot had been such that he and his son Bill, his secretary, Elsie Douglas, and a few others had dashed quickly through London for a preliminary conference with the Allies. A pair of the justice's trousers had been left hanging in a closet at Claridge's hotel. Later, the justice would also find himself without a suitable complement of underwear for the drab and chilly Nuremberg winter.

He and his party would not forget their entry into Nuremberg. The ancient city of the Meistersingers had been chosen for the trials, not because of its ironic association with the pagan excesses of Nazism but because the old Palace of Justice, alone among the relatively intact buildings left standing in the Reich, had the room to house them. Three-quarters of the central city lay in rubble. Robert E. Conot in *Justice at Nuremberg* describes the entry scene: "The Jackson convoy twisted through streets where rubble towered up like slag heaps, blackened girders contorted like frozen snakes . . . and a fine white dust sifted over everything. Shards of statuary and stained glass glinted jewellike in the sun. Here and there a German helmet perched atop a rock or a stake marked the grave of a Wehrmacht soldier buried where he had fallen. An estimated twenty thousand dead still entombed beneath the rubble wafted reminders of their presence up into the hot summer air."

Jackson and his son installed themselves behind a heavy guard (which Bill Jackson found absurd) in a roomy house, furnished, Bill wrote to his mother back at Hickory Hill, "in a rather tired Louis XIV style." It included a music room with a fine Steinway grand piano, a dining room "with a table big enough for a bowling alley," which seated twenty-five people. A stone wall conveniently enclosed the house and garden, with its fine trees and zinnias and asters. GIs cooked and served meals. A private bodyguard followed the justice as he came and went, and slept beside the front door "with his arsenal beside him." Despite these amenities, the trial had proved to be full of tedious vexations. Jackson and his son boiled at the judicial punctilio affected, for the occasion, by the American judge, Francis Biddle, a successor to Jackson as attorney general. The president had in effect kicked Biddle upstairs to his Nuremberg duties, and both Jacksons thought he exercised a bad influence on the presiding judge, Lord Lawrence. Meanwhile, the chief of the wartime Office of Strategic Services, General "Wild Bill" Donovan, had come to Nuremberg full of advice and exhortation, urging Jackson to make due allowance for the cooperation of some of the defendants (notably, the former economics minister, Dr. Heljemar Schacht) in the intrigues to overthrow Hitler.

For all these reasons, and no doubt others, by the time of Stone's death on April 22 Jackson's impatience had become visible to most of his coworkers at Nuremberg. The guile and craft of some of the defendants, unrestrained by American trial standards of relevance, upset him especially. His worst hours as chief prosecutor had come during his cross-examination of the exotic ex-commander of the Hitler Luftwaffe, the fat and epicene Hermann Goering. Goering, his cheeks rouged and his finger and toe nails painted, was a slippery quarry on the witness stand, launching into unchecked apologies for Nazism. Jackson had pleaded in vain with the judges to hold Goering to some standard of responsiveness. But Lawrence and Biddle seemed to think that he should be allowed to say whatever he wished, since he was on trial for his life. There was a different difficulty with Dr. Schacht, who did not regard himself as a war criminal (he was late acquitted) and matched a sense of self-righteousness with a ready tongue. One day when Jackson was pressing Schacht about the dismemberment of Czechoslovakia in 1938, "a wrong and reprehensible act," the quick-witted Schacht responded: "It is no 'wrong and reprehensible act committed by Hitler, but Hitler received the Sudeten German territory by a way of a treaty. There can be no talk of injustice." It was one of many occasions when the judges and Jackson's fellow prosecutors thought that Jackson had been incautious in his cross-examinations; and such embarrassments seemed to them to weigh on him. The lengthening trial, the unanticipated difficulty of sorting the documents, to say nothing of Jackson's own exacting postulate for the trial's credibility ("to pass these defendants a poisoned chalice is to put it to our lips as well," he had said, with his gift for aphoristic eloquence), frayed his patience. Now to all this difficulty had been added, with Stone's sudden death, a nagging anxiety and curiosity about affairs at the Court in Washington.

* * *

Jackson's friends at home continued to hold a watching brief for him. On May 17 one of them, Francis Shea, wrote from his law offices on Fifteenth Street that "for a few hours [the chief justiceship] seemed a sure thing for you. Then, Black got word to the President that there would be a row if you were appointed." Truman, Shea reported, then "began to make wide inquiries and to appreciate, perhaps exaggerate, the rifts in the Court." The outcome was now increasingly uncertain.

Shea's appraisal of the situation tallied with that of Joe and Stewart Alsop, the well-connected and widely read newspaper columnists. In a *New York Herald Tribune* column of May 18, the day after Shea had written his letter, the Alsops took the view that Truman's "backing and filling" over the chief justiceship illustrated in miniature the endemic confusion of the new and unseasoned administration. Jackson, they reported, had been the initial choice. But just as his selection was about to be announced, protests from Black and Murphy had signaled danger and the president had "faltered." According to the Alsop report, a great tug of war had ensued. It pitted organized labor and Postmaster General Robert Hannegan (the administration's chief political operative) against powerful New York state politicians who hoped to remove Jackson, once and for all, as a contender for the gubernatorial nomination in New York. Against this Byzantine background, the Alsops went on, a number of contenders for Stone's seat had now emerged. They even included—improbably—Secretary of Labor Lewis B. Schwellenbach, a liberal favorite, who "all but fell sick of desire from the moment when he learned of Stone's death." Truman's friend Fred Vinson, the highly regarded Kentuckian of vast governmental experience, now secretary of the treasury, was in the running as a dark horse.

Such reports were reaching Nuremberg in a flood by mid-May, tantalizing Jackson and titillating the transplanted legal community at the War Crimes Trials. But the jolting culmination of this transatlantic flow of speculation came in one explosive dose from Doris Fleeson, another columnist with close Court connections. In a front-page report in the *Washington Evening Star* of May 16, Miss Fleeson brought all the threads together; or so it seemed. Writing under the caption "Supreme Court Feud," she told a story that could only have come directly from some member of the Court. The secrecy of the conference room had clearly been breached. Miss Fleeson's views accorded with those of the Black wing of the Court; and there was no mistaking the flavor of her sympathies. For the first time she revealed the story of the tense battle over Black's role in the *Jewell Ridge* coal case—the portal-to-portal pay case in which the Court, over Jackson's dissent, had extended wage liability even where strong collective bargaining had been the rule. Miss Fleeson's column bore telltale marks of a briefing by someone with inside knowledge—one of the justices, it would seem. She dwelled, not altogether accurately, on such technicalities as the petition for a rehearing of the case, in which the mine operators had hinted at the impropriety of Crampton Harris's appearance in Court, or at least of Black's refusal to withdraw.

As Doris Fleeson framed the tale, there had been "a clash of strong wills" in the secrecy of the conference room; and Hugo Black had "reacted with fiery scorn to what he regarded as an open and gratuitous insult, a slur upon his personal and judicial honor. An already marked coolness [she continued] . . . froze into impenetrable ice." The quarrel among the justices, Miss Fleeson said, had been explained to the president, who as a "fellow southerner," felt, as if it had been an insult to himself, Black's sense of violated honor. This, then, was the hitherto undisclosed taproot of the tension on the Court, the strange dithering over the appointment of a successor to Harlan Stone, and the ultimate reason why Jackson's candidacy had slid into limbo.

Circumstantially, the Fleeson column seemed to confirm what Jackson had previously learned from his friend Shea and from other sources; and when copies of the piece reached Nuremberg, Jackson's puzzlement suddenly focused with a vengeance—especially on the charge that he had questioned Hugo Black's honor. He had, of course, done no such thing. The Fleeson account outrageously skewed the facts, in Jackson's view, and that was to say nothing of its casual breach of the confidentiality of the conference room. Fleeson's account was *ex parte*, incomplete, provocative, tendentious. From Jackson's perspective, it skirted many material factors in the unpleasant battle over the *Jewell Ridge* case and its querulous aftermath. Indeed, the issue of Crampton Harris, Black's old law partner, was far from the greatest of the difficulties. Jackson soon saw that he must somehow react. It must at least be made clear that more had been at stake the previous spring than harsh words or a piddling question of insulted honor. From Jackson's point of view the issues were far more serious. They went to the heart of the Court's integrity and the integrity of the judicial process, though how much of the story could now be publicly told was a question.

Some of it clearly must be. But here he was, far from Washington, wrestling with the maddeningly elusive Goering and Schacht, the Russians and their alien notions of legal process, and judges who seemed perversely bent on letting the Nazi defendants say anything that popped into their heads.

What might be done? Jackson decided to draft a response to the Fleeson column. It would probably be a public response, and it would deal directly with the challenge thrown down against him in Washington. Otherwise, the myth-making of his foes would come to dominate the record, would be accepted as the definitive version of the story, and that could not be tolerated. Black and his allies had overstepped themselves. It was one thing to lobby and intrigue at the White House, to send emissaries like Lister Hill and others with veiled threats of resignation. It was another to spill the Court's confidential business into the open in so partial and self-serving a manner. The other side of the story would have to be told.

Soon after reading and pondering Doris Fleeson's column—just when is uncertain—Jackson sat down at his desk and began to dissect the events of the previous spring, now rising to haunt him. His mind ran back—it was an inescapable accompaniment—to the curious history of his attitudes toward Hugo Black and the nature of their relationship both before and since both had sat on the Court. There could be no question of firing off this riposte while the choice of the new chief justice was pending. That would be self-defeating at best. It would also compound the impropriety. Nor would he seek advice on whether to respond and what to say. If he did, he would almost surely be urged to hold his tongue and it would be awkward to disregard advice once sought. Jackson resolved to draft a response and bide his time. But the story would be told from his perspective as well as Black's. Black would not, could not, have the public record to himself.

III

Harry Truman had acted with his usual decisiveness in deciding to stage the Nuremberg trials and in dispatching Robert Jackson to prosecute the Nazis. It was proving harder to decide whether to make him chief justice, as, he had been told, FDR had promised to do. The new president and the justice had been on friendly and mutually respectful terms since both had arrived in Washington in the mid-thirties, Jackson in 1934 and Truman in 1935. Later, when Truman put together what became the Special Committee to Investigate the National Defense Program in 1941, Jackson had done him an invaluable service. He had recommended a young lawyer named Hugh Fulton, and Fulton had served indispensably as legal adviser to what became known as the Truman Committee. The committee had provided Truman's springboard to larger note.

The Alsop brothers' faintly patronizing theory that all the dithering over the Stone vacancy reflected typical confusion at the Truman White House was a bit misleading, but not entirely so. At Stone's death on April 22, Harry Truman was completing a stormy first year in office. His hands were more than full with the problems of peacemaking in Europe and the "reconversion" of the American economy to a peacetime footing. He faced a bewildering menu of challenges. Famine stalked Europe, now as in 1918. Chiang Kai-shek's Nationalist government in China, which Roosevelt had inflated to the dimensions of a "power," seemed on the verge of collapse as the Japanese withdrew and Mao Tse-tung's communist forces broke off their de facto wartime alliance. There were gathering signs that the Soviet Union would not help restore democracy or prosperity in Europe, but attempt rather to feast on the ruins. In early March Winston Churchill had spoken under the President's auspices at Fulton, Missouri, and had seen an "iron curtain" descending across Europe. Truman, notwithstanding a preview of the speech, had partially disavowed Churchill's sentiments. Nevertheless, the self-styled "progressives" on Truman's left had squawked loudly that the president, by encouraging Churchill's gloomy sentiments, was needlessly provoking the Russians: the beginning shots of a feud that would ultimately materialize in Henry A. Wallace's third-party revolt in 1948.

Meanwhile, adding to Truman's burdens—and forming a material backdrop to this story—every major industry at home seemed to be either enduring a strike or recuperating from one. The list was staggering. In January, telephone workers, machinists, and steelworkers had walked out. In March, just as the United Auto Workers returned to General Motors after 113 days, 400,000 United Mine Workers had struck. As April turned to May and the cherry blossoms faded on the Tidal Basin, there were rumblings of a strike by railway trainmen and engineers that would stop the nation's transportation system literally in its tracks. The threat was especially embarrassing to the president, in that two of the union leaders, Alexander Whitney and Alvanley Johnson, had given Truman critical reelection help in his second senatorial campaign (1940) in Missouri. Nonetheless, Truman stood to his duty. In the Oval Office in mid-May he told Whitney and Johnson: "If you think I'm going to sit here and let you tie up this whole country, you're crazy as hell." Ten days later, even as Truman was laying a proposal before Congress that he be authorized to draft railway strikers into the Army, the unions capitulated. But before the end of this strife-worn year some 4.6 million U. S. workers would conduct some 5,000 strikes, at a loss of 116 million man-days of work time. The implacable attitudes of labor had sometimes stirred despair in the otherwise sympathetic Truman, who at times during this rocky year thought seriously of making a fighting speech and then quitting. (The president's "approval rating" in the Gallup Poll fell as low as 32 percent in the course of the year, and wits said, "To err is Truman.")

With Roosevelt's death, moreover, the great Democratic coalition brought together around his powerful personality had begun to dissolve. Progressive Democrats regarded Truman as unfit to wear FDR's mantle. In fact, the mounting struggle over the Court appointment reflected, in part, this factionalism within the Democratic Party. Truman's appointment of an eminent California oil tycoon and party contributor, Edwin Pauley, as undersecretary of the Navy had caused a typical brouhaha. As keeper of the old Progressive flame, the onetime Bull Mooser Harold Ickes, whom Truman had inherited as secretary of the Interior, publicly denounced the Pauley appointment, and charged that Pauley would no doubt surrender public rights on federal oil reserves (as in Teapot Dome days) in exchange for contributions to a Democratic campaign kitty for the 1946 off-year elections. This was too much and Ickes was soon gone from the Truman cabinet, the sixth FDR holdover to disappear within the year. He and the president would be on icy terms for two years.

Insofar as all this strife and political feuding allowed Truman to think about Court appointments, he had been made aware that Jackson's promotion to be chief justice would stir divisions within organized labor. He had been told of Jackson's largely nugatory ambitions in New York. He knew that some of Jackson's friends and foes viewed the Nuremberg assignment as a political buildup of some sort, possibly for a run at the New York governorship or even the presidency. What the president was only now learning, rather belatedly, was that turbulent and bitter factionalism had divided the Court over labor law and wage policy, now so critical an aspect of the national economy. For his part—as the famous suppressed draft of his speech against the railwaymen showed—Truman shared Jackson's suspicion that labor had now grown as grasping, as arrogant, as contemptuous of the larger public interest, as the business moguls had been in the Coolidge-Hoover era. Confronted with some evidence that Jackson's elevation might tear the Court apart, Truman drew back from his first resolve and sought counsel.

Over the spring weekend of April 27 and 28, the president and his staff boarded the presidential yacht *Williamsburg* for a brief holiday cruise down the Potomac and to the Virginia capes. Officially, the purpose was to view naval exercises. But Washington reporters were quick to connect the trip with the problem of finding a successor to Stone. The company on the cruise included Robert Hannegan, the postmaster general and chief political fixer of the administration. Hannegan was hearing a good bit from the anti-Jackson cabal, and indeed shared their sentiments. He had become the main conduit for the various protests against Jackson reaching the White House from within the Court. Disliking Jackson as he did, Hannegan was a willing listener.

Following the President's return from the cruise on April 29, it was soon clear in any event that the Supreme Court vacancy stood near the top of the list of pending business and must have been discussed in leisurely moments aboard the *Williamsburg*. That morning, the nation's senior jurist, retired Chief Justice Charles Evans Hughes, called at the White House. He conferred with the president for some thirty minutes. It was a scene made to order for the rumors that sprout so easily in the capital. One far-fetched speculation had Truman begging Hughes to return to the Court as "acting" chief justice until a permanent successor to Stone could be found. In fact, Hughes was ineligible, having already taken his retirement from the Court, and Truman almost certainly did not ask him to take on a third tour of Supreme Court duty in an "acting" capacity. That was indeed a figment of the reportorial imagination. After his chat with Truman, Hughes, always magnificent in his gleaming goatee, emerged from the White House, beamed courteously at the reporters and their questions, and with an affable "No comment. Thank you very much," vanished.

The exact nature of Hughes's advice to the president on this day would some years later become a subject of

controversy. When Merlo Pusey's biography of Hughes
appeared, Pusey's text and notes suggested that Hughes
recalled having urged Truman to ignore the political
clamor and appoint Jackson after all. Truman did not recall
having heard such advice. Whatever Hughes's counsel had
been, it clearly had not accelerated the march of delibera-
tion. It would be a long time—another thirty-seven days—
before the president acted. Other names continued to bob
up, not only that of Labor Secretary Schwellenbach (who was
being pushed by liberal lobbyists like journalist Irving
Brant), but also former assistant secretary of war, and
sometime appellate judge, Robert Patterson. Then there
was Vinson; his name continued to be heard. In addition to
his man-of-all-duties labors in the executive branch, Vinson
also had sat on the U. S. Court of Appeals for the federal
circuit in Washington. There were others, too, who would
prove to be less eligible.

This was how matters stood as May came on and the
suspense deepened. It was true that Jackson remained the
betting favorite. Fourteen of the twenty-one staff members
of the Scripps-Howard Washington bureau reported that
they were still expecting Jackson to be named. Five thought
the appointment would go to Hugo Black, who was not a
candidate and was telling friends that a sitting member of
the Court should never be made chief justice; it was bad
practice. Within the small community of tipster journalists
who liked to predict appointments, Jackson remained the
favorite. But Arthur Krock of the *New York Times*, usually the
best informed and certainly the most assertive of the press's
Court-watchers, had predicted on April 25 that the highest
judicial post would ultimately go to Vinson. Vinson, he said,
could be expected to exercise his celebrated diplomatic
talents, to smooth the Court's ruffled feathers. As a political
heir to Henry Clay, a son of the quintessential border state
of Kentucky, Vinson could make peace among the quarrel-

ing factions. If the Court was indeed on the verge of its own private civil war, over who knew just what, what could be more natural than the choice of a mediator? A man like Fred Vinson would keep the irrevocable shot from being fired.

IV

The disclosures of personal dissidence within the Court that broke out at Stone's passing were hardly news to those who followed the Court closely. A year earlier, for example, three historians of the Court had gathered one Sunday in Chicago around the radio microphones of the popular "University of Chicago Round Table." The topic of the day was, "Is The Supreme Court Becoming Unstable?" "From some of the newspaper articles," observed Herman Pritchett, "one gets the impression that the Hatfields and Coys [sic] have moved to the Supreme Court and are taking potshots at each other from behind the marble columns." Another panelist was Carl Brent Swisher, who would later write a distinguished biography of Chief Justice Roger B. Taney, the man who had presided over the Court from Marshall's death until well into the Civil War years, the chief justice who wrote the infamous *Dred Scott* opinion. Swisher knew, then, that there had been stormier days at the Court; yet he agreed with Pritchett that "personal or quasi-personal comments" were figuring in the news to an unusual degree. More cautiously, the third panelist, Walter Dodd, suggested that the press tended to magnify any institutional conflict. In any case, Dodd added, the disagreements of Supreme Court justices were usually not marked by "personal animosity." Had he known what was to transpire within twelve months, he might have spoken more guardedly.

But the Chicago radio round table discussion was only a symptom. Bickering within the Court's ornate halls was not exactly a secret, but even the best informed outsiders usually had to content themselves with fragmentary glimpses of an institution that by long tradition jealously guarded its confidences. At the time of Stone's death, the Court was only nine years removed from the era of the so-called "nine old men" whose obstruction of New Deal legislation Franklin Roosevelt had moved to push aside in 1937 with his "court-packing" plan. Ultimately, after a long summer battle, the Senate had balked at the centerpiece of Roosevelt's design, the power to appoint a new justice for every sitting justice (up to a total of fifteen) who chose at age seventy not to avail himself of the new and generous retirement incentives that were also to be added as a feature of the package. Notwithstanding the defeat of the FDR plan, some of the anti-New Deal justices had taken the hint. There had been a swift turnover in justices, the swiftest in the Court's history. By death or resignation, Roosevelt had been given the opportunity to transform the political tenor of the Court. Indeed, as soon as it was clear that Congress would not authorize a political expansion of the Court's numbers (as it had occasionally done before in U. S. history), Justice Willis Van Devanter had retired. FDR had given the vacant seat to Black, one of his faithful allies in the court-packing fight. The custom of senatorial courtesy made it certain that Black would be confirmed, without protest, by his colleagues. Soon, as other seats fell vacant, there had followed Murphy, Reed, Frankfurter, and, in 1941, Jackson himself. The new Court ceased to discover constitutional reasons for finding New Deal measures "unreasonable," that is, in disaccord with the economic predilections of a handful of justices. ("This is Nero at his worst!" one hostile justice had exclaimed, impromptu, when the Court barely upheld the government's constitutional power to alter the value and form of the currency.) But the great sea change had actually begun before Roosevelt filled a single vacancy. Justice Owen Roberts had discerned a distinction all but invisible to others between two apparently similar state minimum wage laws, finding reason to uphold the second. Wags had labeled it "the switch in time that saved nine." Now, less than a decade later, the nine old men had given way to a Court of "nine young men," the youngest on average in the nation's history.

Yet by the peculiar chemistry of lifetime appointment an old law of institutional dynamics had held true. The Court and the issues of the age do more to shape the views of justices than the views of justices do to shape the attitudes of the Court. New rivalries and alignments had soon emerged, causing those who disagreed to charge one another with infidelity to the New Deal faith.

And there was, of course, the issue of disqualification—the question of when, for the sake of appearances, a justice should withdraw from a case, the question central to the looming brawl between Jackson and Black. With three former U. S. attorneys general on the Court (Stone, Murphy, and Jackson) and two former solicitors general (Reed, and Jackson again), the justices regularly confronted controversies in whose origins they had played some sort of role before putting on the robes. Disqualification, never an easy decision, might conceivably strip the Court of a swing vote in some close case, depriving a worthy petitioner of justice. Many judges felt that the obligation to sit, if at all possible, usually outweighed the obligation to avoid unseemly appearances; but of course it all depended. It was difficult for men like Stone (who once had been a partner in the great New York firm of Sullivan and Cromwell) to avoid conflict. He would often peer down from the bench to the counsel's table and see before him the face of a former associate, or law partner, or friend. The same was true of Roberts and Reed. By longstanding custom, the decision on disqualification was not to be dictated by one justice to another. Yet every justice had sharp views, barely if at all concealed in private talk and correspondence, about the ethical standards of his brethren.

In early June, almost two months after Stone's death, Robert Jackson's explosive epistle from Nuremberg would thrust the disqualification issue into the national spotlight as never before. Hugo Black's old Senate colleague Sherman (Shay) Minton, now a federal judge, who would eventually join Black on the Supreme Court, would write in furious sympathy. The complaint about Colonel Crampton Harris's appearance in the *Jewell Ridge* case struck Minton as overwrought and hypocritical.

"Why the hullabaloo?" Minton demanded. "Did Owen J. Roberts get off the bench when Geo. Wharton Pepper came in to argue the Butler case, when everyone whose brains were thick as butter milk knew he was employed to bring Roberts in! He brought him with his voice filled with sobs & tears & Roberts wrote his opinion & Stone made him look like a justice of the peace & made himself immortal by his great dissent! Did Pierce Butler come down as his railroad pals argued? Hell no! He wrote the opinion usually—probably some of the railroads were his former clients." At that point in his fiercely scribbled letter Minton subsided—fearing, he said, that his indignation might bring on a heart attack. But it was in just such heated tones that, behind the facade of collegiality, opinions on the proprieties of recusal smoldered and occasionally flared.

Yet disqualification was not the only source of institutional tension that, under Stone's leadership, seemed to have made snarling foes of former New Deal allies. There were substantive issues, mainly though not exclusively economic. Had Congress intended, for example, to hand a charter of vast new power to labor unions? It was often a matter of reading disputed statutes; and when the Court did that there was vast room for differences over the appropriate role of judges in the construction of ambiguities in the letter of the law. Yet on the day of Stone's death the dissidence, in the view of several justices, including Felix Frankfurter, could be traced above all to Stone's clumsy administrative system. Elevated to the chief justiceship in 1941, Stone had followed Hughes, a man of vast experience and magisterial authority, whose early seasoning ran all the way back to the Teddy Roosevelt era. Hughes had been a consummate leader of the Court, a jurist of such exacting standards and unchallengeable command that no associate dared indulge in the schoolboyish bickering that began to ruffle the Court's deliberations after he retired. The professorial, loquacious Stone, once dean of the Columbia Law School, would be remembered as a man who combined "very great ability but also . . . very great vanity . . . great charm, but also . . . considerable testiness." The writer who found him so would write some years later that the Court under Stone had been the most frequently divided in history, the most strident in these many divisions, and productive of an uncommon proliferation of dissents and concurrences. "If success be measured by the Chief's ability to maintain the appearance of harmony," Stone's biographer Alpheus T. Mason would later write, "he certainly was a failure." Whereas under Hughes the Saturday conferences (at which the justices discussed and voted on pending cases) had usually required a martially disciplined four hours, under Stone they usually dragged on for days. A sometime Black clerk who watched it happen found this a "disastrous innovation." It meant, he recalled, that the justices staggered from these endless meetings "to pick up their opinion-writing duties in a spirit of physical exhaustion and emotional and intellectual exacerbation, with pride of opinion inflamed by oral emphasis."

Finally, there was sometimes a petty or spiteful edge to some decision or other. These matters could not be openly discussed, but their sour influence could be felt. So far as Jackson was concerned, the *Bethlehem Steel* case, a lingering holdover from World War I days, was typical. The steel company had reaped unconscionable wartime profits from

government shipbuilding contracts—"robbery in broad daylight," it had been called. As Coolidge's attorney general,
Stone had sued the company on the government's behalf,
seeking to force disgorgement of the excess profits. In a long
trial the government had lost. Years later, Jackson had
revived the suit and carried it to the Supreme Court, which
scheduled argument. By the time the case arose Stone and
Jackson, now justices, disqualified themselves as original
instigators. To their astonishment and disgust, Black led a
majority to hold in the steel company's favor, contrary, it
seemed, to all of Black's well-known predispositions. Jackson
suspected that Black's opinion was calculated to outrage
public opinion and provoke punitive congressional action,
not only against Bethlehem Steel but against profitable
business firms generally. Concealed in a case otherwise
disarming on the surface, there was to Jackson's mind
precisely the kind of personal irritation that strained personal feelings at the Court. Now Stone was dead, and Jackson
was far away in Nuremberg, and all eyes were on the
succession. Whoever now took Stone's chair, would he—
could he—subdue these "Hatfield and McCoy" feuds and
put an end to the rumors of internecine warfare? There was
as yet no answer, or even hint of one, from Truman's White
House.

V

Felix Frankfurter, the Court's best-informed gossip, did not
enjoy with Harry Truman the close friendship that had kept
him abreast of Roosevelt's innermost thoughts and purposes.
Like others, he could only guess at what was going on at the
White House. On May 16, Frankfurter sent his old friend
Charles Burlingham, of the New York Bar, a diary their idol
Oliver Wendell Holmes Jr. had kept during a journey to
England, "another rich Holmesian goldmine." As if by

afterthought, Frankfurter, who shared with Burlingham the hope that Jackson might succeed Stone, scrawled at the bottom of his letter: "Know nothin' of what's in the wind re C. J.'ship. Lots of dirty business going on against RHJ [Robert H. Jackson]."It was clear enough that Truman's deliberations had stalled, and that there was some sort of active intrigue against Jackson, probably involving politics more than "dirty business." In this as in other matters, Truman hoped to honor what he understood to be Roosevelt's commitments. Truman valued continuity and loyalty in government. But he had not expected Jackson's foes to dig in against him as they had done, pressing him with counter advice on all sides. At first, Truman had briefly considered the possibility of appointing James F. Byrnes, who had the double advantage of preeminence and experience on the Court. He had mixed feelings about Byrnes, who had snubbed him when Truman had first come to the Senate and who now, as secretary of state, occasionally seemed faintly insubordinate, as if it were pushy for a president to interfere in the making of his own foreign policy. But soon after the president's return from his Chesapeake Bay cruise on April 29, the two had talked noncommittally about the Court vacancy. Byrnes had admitted that it was a post he wanted and would accept. But now that the Russians were making trouble in Paris, it had begun to seem foolish to Truman to remove the man who had been meeting with them and who knew the ropes.

At the same time the president was hearing from old friends that Robert Jackson was considered an enemy of organized labor. This was the reiterated message of Philip Murray of the Congress of Industrial Organizations, and of other union spokesmen with a pipeline to Hannegan. Jackson's vote and attitudes in the portal-to-portal pay cases, the last of which had sparked the differences with Black, were recalled without gratitude at CIO headquarters.

Another source of some influence was the president's old friend, the eminent journalist and Court-watcher Irving Brant, who forwarded his advice on the pending appointment through Truman's press secretary, Charles Ross. In a letter of April 29, Brant entered a subdued protest against Jackson, for whom he declared "a very warm feeling" otherwise. Jackson's promotion to the chief justiceship would deal a "demoralizing blow" to the Court, Brant asserted. It would reward the scheming of Frankfurter, whom Brant accused of dangling the post before Jackson as an enticement to him to enlist in some of Frankfurter's pet judicial causes. Brant's analysis mirrored the thinking of the Court liberals: A joint appointment of Jackson (as chief) and Louis Schwellenbach (as associate justice in Jackson's place) would probably put Jackson so often in the minority that he might be tempted to vote with the liberals in close cases in order to keep control of the opinions and dilute their force. If, on the other hand, Truman reinforced Jackson with the appointment of a fellow "conservative" like Robert Patterson, Hugo Black would be isolated, degraded to "such a position of futility that it might drive him off the Court." Brant's analysis, presumably by design, led ineluctably to the conclusion that it would be the path of wisdom to make Black chief justice, although Black claimed privately that he was not a candidate and, in principle, believed that a chief should never be picked from among the incumbent justices.

Just how much attention Truman paid to these intricate arguments (which necessarily rested on extravagant divination about the future votes and attitudes of the justices) or to the blandishments of organized labor, it is hard to say. Truman left no known reaction to either. In their willingness to snarl key industries and the railroads some unions had now forfeited some of Truman's habitual sympathy. But the warnings and pleadings had had some effect, if only to flag the president away from appointing a man who was, after all, far away in Nuremberg and unable to deflect what was being said privately against him.

Meanwhile, Associate Justice William O. Douglas, who had been among Truman's rivals for the vice presidential nomination in 1944 and played the political game with gusto, was eager to block Jackson. He had pressed his friend Father White, dean of the Catholic University law school, to lobby against him. Their collaboration had been noted by Frankfurter. A year later, when the great storm had blown by, Frankfurter recorded in his diary that both Douglas and White had been late returning from lunch while the Court was hearing arguments in the religion cases. It was the sight of Douglas and White in collusion that prompted Murphy to muse, "I wonder if Bob Jackson knows what went on here last spring." Douglas seemed to know a great deal about the fluctuating stock of judicial candidates. "Bill Douglas came to luncheon with me on Thursday," Harold Ickes recorded in his diary on May 19. "He told me that at one time it appeared almost certain that the president would make Bob Jackson Chief Justice."

From the perspective of the Court liberals, however, the prospect—or threat—of a Jackson chief justiceship was already receding. That was the view of John P. Frank, a former clerk and future biographer to Hugo Black, who found it the single compensation of his otherwise "vainglorious" visit to Washington to push his mentor's claims. "At least I think the Jackson menace is pretty well over," he wrote to Black. Frank was right. By mid-May, when Jackson was pondering the Doris Fleeson column in Nuremberg, his foes in Washington had indeed prevailed, to all intents and purposes. Douglas, labor, those who feared that the Court under Jackson might again lapse into what they viewed as illiberal economic policies, had carried the day. For Truman the weightiest argument was that Jackson's appointment would deepen factionalism and further aggravate the strains and divisions on the Court that had become so visible under the five-year tenure of Harlan F. Stone.

With Jackson out of the picture, Truman looked to the loyalists around him. Among those loyalists none was stronger than the man who now held the reins at the Treasury, Fred Vinson. Vinson was a gangling, amiable, poker-playing small-town boy from Kentucky. His friends, including the president, knew that Vinson's relaxed manner and friendliness concealed impressive abilities. He had loomed from the outset as the dark-horse rival to Jackson, spoken of by Krock of the *Times* and others. Vinson had a record of distinction in all three branches of government—as a congressman, as wartime economic stabilizer, and as a judge of the U.S. Court of Appeals. In a Truman cabinet unremarkable for brains, Vinson was considered an exception: bright and competent as well as amiable. With his jowly face and heavily hooded and pouched eyes—someone said that he favored "a hungover sheep"—Fred Vinson had the additional advantage of actually looking as a chief justice should. As June approached, Truman was increasingly sure that Vinson not only had the requisite intellect and judicial experience; he also had the tact to subdue the disturbing factionalism. The president had been encouraged by now to think of the Court's squabbles (not altogether accurately) as the product of petty vanity and personal chemistry. In fact, however, as would emerge, there was a serious struggle over the role of the Court and how it would handle some vital policy questions, whether as a court or super-legislature. But for the moment, it seemed to Truman a job for a diplomat and Vinson had credentials as a diplomat. Mathematical whiz, former semiprofessional baseball player, hail fellow well met, gifted public man, Vinson, then, would get the job. By June 6, possibly earlier, Truman had made up his mind and gained Vinson's assent. If the Senate agreed, he and not Robert Jackson would become thirteenth chief justice. None of the players in Washington—not the president, not his advisers, not the intriguers, not those who had seen forty-four days pass since Stone's death—imagined what was taking shape across the Atlantic, in Jackson's office in Nuremberg. None knew that when Truman announced his decision he would ignite a keg of powder that would jolt the small world of the American judiciary as nothing since the *Dred Scott* decision almost a century earlier.

VI

When Jackson considered Doris Fleeson's *Evening Star* column of May 16, he felt a stiletto at his ribs. There had to be a response, but what kind? Fleeson had been fed a poisonously biased picture of his parting scrap with Hugo Black over the coal wages case, and confidentiality at the Court had been breached in a very self-serving way. Somehow the public must be told the other side of the story, but who else could tell it? There was as yet no word about the succession, though among Jackson's friends in Washington there was a sense that his chances were slipping away. If he responded before the impasse was resolved, it would seem the undignified flailing of a man clinging to a faded ambition. But the time would come; Black could not go unanswered.

When Jackson reflected on what he knew and thought of Hugo L. Black, what was astonishing was how little he really had grasped about Black's methods, his view of the law, before joining the Court. Like everyone else, he had watched Black writhe in the humiliating spotlight played upon him in 1937, when a Pittsburgh newspaper exposed the secret of his former Ku Klux Klan connection. But Black had lived down whatever imputation of bigotry might arise from that episode; and it now seemed to Jackson a secondary and venial matter, symptomatic at worst of larger things.

When Jackson took pen in hand to sort out his impressions of the Alabamian, he had to conclude that Black, more than most jurists, took an overtly, unabashedly political view of the nature of judicial power. Black's philosophy of judging was little removed, save in substantive doctrine, from that of the men—McReynolds, Butler, Sutherland, Van Devanter—who a few years earlier had interposed their economic beliefs to obstruct the Roosevelt program in the name of the Constitution. Black seemed to Jackson to take, otherwise, a similarly unapologetic delight in judicial power.

Black also gave the impression, though he never said so explicitly, that he resented Jackson's independence. When Jackson as a Roosevelt appointee ventured to deviate from some administration line, as he often did, it was taken as a gesture of rebellion against Black. Even though he himself had come to the Court with a strong New Deal commitment, Jackson had been shocked by Black's economic radicalism. It seemed to him further to the "left" than anything he had previously encountered, even in FDR's cabinet. It was a form of "collectivism" in Jackson's view, mistaken for liberalism. One could often predict Black's vote on the Court once the names and positions of the parties to the case were known. The aberrations occurred only when, as in the *Bethlehem Steel* case, Black was following some other agenda. It was not a question of integrity, as the Fleeson column had implied, so much as it was of political will. Jackson did not question Black's honor. He did question, and emphatically, Black's sense of judicial propriety, his judgment and his detachment.

Now, in this press offensive against him, Jackson thought he detected the fine hand of someone—Black, Douglas, or an agent of theirs—who knew the subtleties of Court procedure. The source or sources had told Doris Fleeson how to follow a sophisticated trail of documents back to the conference room clash in June, the day Jackson and Black had exchanged heated words over the *Jewell Ridge*

rehearing petition and Jackson had resolved to isolate
Black's judgment. After all, Jackson thought, Black had
carried his political assertiveness very far. He had not
disqualified himself when Harris appeared for the Mine
Workers. He had probably influenced Stanley Reed to
change his vote, altering the majority in the coal case. Then,
as senior majority justice, he had assigned the writing of the
opinion to the pliable Murphy. Then Black and Douglas had
apparently chivvied Murphy to get the opinion written in a
hurry, so as to help John L. Lewis. This was a stiff bill of
particulars; but Jackson thought it accurate. Yet the Fleeson
column breathed not a word about these very relevant facts.
Instead, Jackson had been sketched as a blackguard, im-
pugning Black's honor as a southern gentleman. And the
crowning touch, the really intolerable insinuation, all but
stared out of the words in which Miss Fleeson described the
use of the quarrel to influence the president:

> . . . This inside story of the clash has been laid before
> President Truman. The harassed President, a southerner
> himself, was quick to perceive the affront which Mr. Black
> feels he suffered. He has confided to a senator: "Black
> says he will resign if I make Jackson Chief Justice and tell
> the reasons why. Jackson says the same about Black."

This was nonsense, of course, from Jackson's point of
view: pure cock and bull. He had said nothing at all to the
president about Black, or about resigning—nothing. And as
for this supposed "affront" to which southerners were so
sensitive, it was no more than a twisted version of Jackson's
insistence that Black openly take responsibility for deciding
an important case argued by his onetime law partner. (And
more than that, the sometime counsel to Black's Senate
investigating committee had assisted Black personally when
Black was sued by William Randolph Hearst.)

That was all. Jackson had filed a decorous concurring opinion making it clear whose responsibility it was, refusing to join in camouflaging Black's judgment as the judgment of the whole Court. If Black saw that as insulting, perhaps the questioning of his judgment was not misplaced. Black had threatened to go to "war," whatever that meant. Jackson had responded that he would not be bullied and left the following day for London to arrange the war crimes trials. The acrimonious exchange had jolted their seniors, Stone and Roberts. Roberts had resigned; Stone was dead.

Fleeson's distorted picture must be corrected, and quite a few material facts added to the record. But not yet—not until President Truman filled the vacancy. Between bouts with the Nazi defendants at the Palace of Justice, Jackson worked on what amounted to a draft brief in the great case of Jackson versus Black—and waited.

The wait was of about three weeks. On June 8, President Truman summoned reporters to the White House and told them that his choice, no longer very surprisingly, was Fred Vinson. The press soon took up the theme that Vinson had been chosen as a healer and peacemaker. He would apply soothing anodynes to the cuts the fractious justices had inflicted upon one another out of their unfathomable petty enmities. This, from Jackson's perspective, was another fairy tale.

From the Fleeson column, it could easily be gathered that a very tendentious view of the argument had been "laid before" Truman. The courteous first step, now that the appointment had been announced, was to warn the chief executive that he, Jackson, planned to go public with his own version of the story. Jackson cabled the warning from the U.S. chief of counsel's office on the afternoon of June 9, eliciting an almost instantaneous, and alarmed, response from the president. He knew nothing, Truman said, of Miss Fleeson's mysterious references. Indeed, he had not read the column. He urged Jackson to contain himself until they could talk directly. But Jackson was resolved to go ahead; it was publish and be damned. To Truman, once again, he wired:

> I have your reassuring telegram and was confident that you had not been a party to creating this situation . . . The participation in a public controversy is most distasteful, but however regrettable publicity may appear at the moment it is far better that this matter be cleaned up now than left to break out in some form after Vinson takes over or to embarrass him by smouldering in the secrecy of the conference room. It ends here if they want it to. If not, I am in the disgraceful brawl to the finish. You have my resignation as chief of counsel in this international trial for acceptance at any moment I become embarrassing to you but I will not run out on it unless you relieve me.

Thus it was that on the fine spring day of June 11 a shocked capital heard, many people for the first time, that an internal "brawl" between two justices of the Supreme Court had erupted into the light of day. If there were a precedent for such a turn of events, no one could recall it. And indeed there was none.

In his lengthy cable, addressed to the chairmen of the two congressional judiciary committees, Jackson related the story as he saw it—or at least as much of it as he thought the rebuttal of Miss Fleeson's misimpressions demanded. The Fleeson column had focused on the disqualification dispute. That aspect of the affair was to dominate the reporting of Jackson's response—it was the point at which an otherwise arcane dispute over points of law and legal procedure could be personalized. Jackson would later conclude that this personalization of his cable around the figure of Colonel

Crampton Harris had so much overshadowed other key facts that the main points had largely been missed. To most of the press and public, except for a few subtle and well-informed interpreters, it all seemed blindingly clear: The two justices were quarreling over judicial honor. But Jackson had carefully, perhaps too carefully, muted the central point he wanted to make. He had meant to show that Black had been directing a sweeping reinterpretation of the Wages and Hours Act, of which he as a U.S. senator had been a major architect; and he was now assigning to the legislation a far less restrictive meaning than he had spoken of on the Senate floor. Case by case, beginning well before the *Jewell Ridge* arguments, he had been laying the groundwork for huge back pay claims for miners. It was judicial legislation of a particularly flagrant sort; and worse, during the drawn-out coal strike of the past spring, the Court had plotted putting the judgment to rank political uses, handy to John L. Lewis's cause. That explained the pressure on Murphy the previous April to get his opinion hurriedly written while the miners and the coal operators were still at odds. It was, Jackson thought, a judicial *coup de main* in the making; but now his reference to it was cushioned in words so careful and neutral that their weight might easily be missed:

> ... While Mr. Justice Murphy was preparing his opinion [in the Jewell Ridge case] a strike of the mine workers and negotiations with the operators were proceeding. It was proposed to hand down the decision in favor of the miners without waiting for the opinion and dissent. The only apparent reason behind this proposal was ... to influence the contract negotiations.

"It was proposed ... " "The only apparent reason ... " For a writer of Jackson's subtlety and skill, these carefully nuanced words hinted at, but at the same time palliated, what he considered a shocking abuse of judicial power—at least if his assumptions were accurate. The Court had been on the verge of violating one of its oldest traditions, that it only decides genuine cases and controversies and leaves advisory opinions or political gestures to the legislative and executive branches.

Murphy had circulated his draft opinion favorable to the Mine Workers—entitling them to be paid retroactively for time spent en route from mine entrances to the coal faces—on April 5, 1945. This was according to custom. After a case had been voted on in Saturday conference, the majority and minority, if the Court was divided, sent these "circulations" to other chambers, permitting the other justices to preview what they proposed to say, to prepare possible dissents or concurrences, to urge amendments to opinions with which they agreed. The process allowed everyone to refine his views on the case in question. Suddenly, however, Murphy had sent a note to Jackson, who was writing a dissent. "Some of the brethren," wrote Murphy, adding that he was not among them, "spoke of offering a motion today to hand down on Monday the judgment in portal to portal. I don't want you rushed . . . but I thought you would want to know how some feel about delaying this case." (Some of the brethren, obviously, meant Black and Douglas—at least).

"What is the rush in their view?" Jackson queried, by return memorandum. (Meanwhile, the weekend passed, the strike was settled, and the urgency subsided.) "Maybe they have changed their minds since negotiations ended," Murphy responded, referring to the strike settlement. "I rushed my opinion to accommodate others." As Jackson would later note in a more explicit and searching discussion of this critical point, Murphy's note had reached him on Friday, April 6, when Lewis's talks with the mine operators were still deadlocked. A Supreme Court decision so favorable to the UMW would presumably have handed the flamboyant Welshman a handy goad in his costly duel with the mine operators. Four days later, however, the government had seized the mines. And on April 11, a day after that, the miners came to terms with the secretary of labor. The judicial prod the Court majority had seemed to be fashioning would no longer be useful.

As Jackson now pondered his differences with Hugo Black, the gravamen of his disapproval shifted increasingly to this furtive plan to use the Supreme Court as a weapon in an economic struggle outside the Court, the merits of which were not before it, and to use it in a highly partial way. Perhaps there had been other equally astonishing bids to wield the judicial power so politically, but not during Jackson's time on the Court. Jackson's riposte—at least its more personalized overtones—had become the radio and newspaper sensation of June 12, 1946, an explosion sure to echo in the halls of Congress, at the White House, and of course at the Court, which was just now reaching the end of its long, trying term without its ninth justice.

VII

Washington buzzed over the blistering cable from Nuremberg. But its target kept a mystifying silence. Secluded at his house in Old Town Alexandria, Virginia, downriver from Washington, Hugo Black had nothing to say to the press or anyone else. The senior associate justice instructed his elder son to ignore the clamor. In a later reminiscence, Hugo Black Jr. would recall:

> At that time . . . Daddy and I were working very hard on improving our tennis game and Daddy had no time for plotting and scheming. He was much more interested in developing more top spin on his forehand.

"Whatever it is, Son, I don't want to make any more of it, it will pass. It's silly, silly stuff. This Court doesn't need any public rows among its judges." He refused to comment to the papers, despite a veritable siege of the house by reporters. "Tell 'em I said 'No comment,' Son," and that is what I did.

For public purposes this would be Black's unbroken refrain. But Black's mailbox at the office soon overflowed with messages from friends and allies. Loyal former clerks like John P. Frank and Charles Luce longed to avenge the slights which in their view Jackson had visited on "the Judge." Frank, the most aggressive partisan, referred unrebuked to Jackson in his letters to Black as "the mountebank of Nuremberg." On hearing the news of the Nuremberg cable, he congratulated Black on "the unmasking of a bad man." Black calmly replied that he was not in the least upset. Misunderstandings among colleagues, he said urbanely, were inevitable and time would correct them. So far as he revealed himself to young disciples like Luce and Frank, that was as far as Black would go. It was "silly, silly stuff."

To his old Senate colleague Sherman Minton, however, Black disclosed more of his inner thoughts. Jackson's outburst had done him no personal injury, Black wrote, but the cable had done "great injury" to the Court as an institution. His personal stake was small; but his sense of history told him that "individuals who from time to time have dared to assert that the status quo might not be perfect" would be attacked. "The only way a public man could escape smears was either to actively espouse or acquiesce in conditions and practices abhorrent to his sense of justice." Black could not; criticism was his inescapable portion. That was the message to Minton, himself a federal judge in Indiana.

As for the merits of the quarrel, what could be said?

Frank, it seemed to Black, had uncannily framed his own thoughts: "You heard a case argued by a man whose association had been terminated because of personal dissatisfaction. Good heavens, so would any judge. You were the author of the Wage-Hour Act. Is the new Chief Justice to participate in no tax cases because he was chairman of the Ways and Means Committee? Please," continued Frank's impassioned letter of June 11, "Please, don't let this fantastic incident spoil your well-earned rest."

Black's surviving public papers reveal no effort on his part to write an answer to Jackson's cable. Black knew, however, that his professional relationship with Crampton Harris had been considerably closer, and more complicated, than Frank now recalled. As a senator, Black had staged a crusading investigation of the lobbying of Western Union and Postal Telegraph against the Holding Company Act. (One columnist savagely commented that Black's inquisitorial methods resembled those of the Russian secret police.) Black had summoned his old associate, Harris, to represent the committee. And Harris had also represented him personally three years later when William Randolph Hearst sued him for slander. But what of it? What did it have to do with wage policy? Black found it "silly." Did anyone really believe that the mere appearance of a certain advocate before the Court, whatever his former connections, would sway his views, views deeply and tenaciously held? Black's convictions needed no defense. No one in the Court's history had so often written or voted so unconventionally as he—dissenting, often alone, from majority views and writing opinions that sometimes struck more conventional jurists as overadventurous.

Indeed, Black's unconventionality had on one occasion moved Harlan Stone himself to gossip to the columnist Marquis Childs. The two often walked into town together, and during those morning walks Stone had told Childs that

Black, then the new boy on the Court, seemed to him naive about judicial strategy. He was, in the analogy that occurred to Childs later when he wrote the story for *Harper's Magazine,* like a novice tennis player, ignorant of the rules, who wanders into a fast game and swats at every passing ball with a board. Childs passed this patronizing view of Black's naiveté into general circulation not much more than a year after the Alabamian had taken his seat. Black had not forgotten it, nor would he.

In the ensuing years, as Black mastered the judicial craft, his unconventionality had not noticeably diminished. It was naive to think that Stone's and Frankfurter's fine-knit folderol about judicial restraint would stay his hand, especially when it came to construing the intentions of Congress in a piece of labor legislation he had helped to write. Black was jumps ahead of jurists who encumbered themselves, as he thought, with excessive deference to the legislative branch—Frankfurter's special hobgoblin. Congressional intentions were sometimes very clear and when they were, they might be deferred to. But the great apostles of judicial restraint had not served in the Senate, as he had. They did not know the chanciness, the caprice, of its processes. A decade in Congress had not inspired in Black a reverence for legislative wisdom, and still less for disguised legislative sovereignty. In their own narrow terms, the apostles of judicial restraint had all the good tunes, like the Devil. What they said about the need for judges to defer to legislative will in a working democracy sounded almost airtight, almost unanswerable. But there were answers; and Black knew them. If the judicial restraint people were also political conservatives, as by temperament they often were, their natural ease with the status quo could be passively served simply by sitting back and pretending that the Court had no constitutional authority or duty to interfere in the great Hobbesian struggle of life. For them, the "political question" doctrine covered a multitude of sins—literally. But for a progressive to abstain from battle, to take so passive a view of judging, was often to endorse by default some social or political outrage that could be fixed. Meanwhile, real people suffered.

The differences between Black's and Jackson's views of the FDR "court-packing" bill of 1937 told a good deal about their respective philosophies. Both had supported the plan, Black enthusiastically, Jackson sedately. But Black had not taken the pains, as Jackson had, to construct an elaborate historical case. For all he cared, Black had told FDR, it might be a good idea to solve the problem by splitting the Court in two. He had supported the legislation to expand the size of the Court without compunction. It was a political cause. Jackson, meanwhile, had worked out an involved and elaborate theory—elegantly written, as usual—and later expanded it into a book which he called, to emphasize the key issue, *The Struggle for Judicial Supremacy.* The theory was that this "struggle for judicial supremacy" had been a great tidal theme of American history. Jackson was as impatient as Black and the other New Dealers with the obstruction of Van Devanter, Butler, McReynolds; yet he had gone so far as to credit them with an elevated motive. Black thought this much too generous. The "four horsemen" had been spokesmen for entrenched interest and greed. When one was moving with the tides of history and progress, pedantic flourishes about restraint served as nothing more than disingenuous camouflage. That was the Black philosophy.

In pursuit of the role that he thought history had summoned him to play, Hugo Black would, then, leave no trail of self-justifying special pleading behind. He would act on his convictions. Frankfurter, Jackson, and others who professed to believe that judges should be political monks could say and do as they liked. But it would matter very little in the long run. Who could predict how the history of their era would be written? Black was sure of only one thing, when it came to that subject. Historians would view matters, would write the story, in the light of their own political biases. Bias was the ultimate controlling influence in history, as indeed in jurisprudence—apart, of course, from who won the struggle. So much seemed obvious to Black from his consideration of even the earliest classical times. Tacitus and Livy, whose Roman history he had perused in his extensive program of self-educational reading, were marvelous storytellers. But you had to watch out. Both of them reflected the outlook and prejudices of their class. It was no different now. Black, he told two visiting historians, thought of Livy as "the David Lawrence of his time." (The reference was to the noted conservative columnist and longtime founder-editor of *U.S. News & World Report.*)

It was a close question whether historians ever surmounted their political bias, or measured motives accurately. If motives would probably be misunderstood, and even misrepresented, what did they matter in the great struggles over principle that were the real stuff of political history? Black had kept a diary for a while in the Senate. But he soon saw that a reader far off in time, perhaps a historian looking for primary sources, might be led by it to think that Hugo Black had been the very center and focus of every event he recorded. So he had abandoned the diary. As with history, so with justice. All one could know with assurance about another judicial opinion, Black believed, was how cleverly it was argued and whether or not one agreed with it. These, finally, were the real touchstones.

As for the *Jewell Ridge* case, over which Jackson, Stone, and Frankfurter had made such heavy weather, Black had given little thought to Crampton Harris. The real irritant, for Black, was that Jackson could not easily resist the temptation to add biting little ad hominem touches to his opinions. The querulous footnote in Jackson's *Jewell Ridge* dissent was typical. Jackson in effect had accused Black of fancy footwork, of playing the artful dodger. He had exhumed the Senate floor debate on the Fair Labor Standards (Wages and Hours) Act. In his May 5, 1945 memorandum to the conference, Black had warned Jackson and his allies that they were off base. Jackson's insulting footnote reflected basic ignorance of parliamentary maneuver. The remarks Jackson quoted from him had been spoken about a draft of the bill quite different from the draft that had ultimately passed into law. There was *suggestio falsi*, then, in quoting them. Black had protested that if the opinion went down as written it would not truly represent the facts. Yet Jackson persisted in publicizing this rebuke. Even duly warned, he had made it his business to cast Black in the turncoat's inconstant role, saying one thing as a senator to get the bill through and then as a justice saying quite another for the benefit of John L. Lewis.

Such little touches tended to trivialize great issues, Black thought. What it came down to, in the last analysis, was that he and Jackson took very different views of labor unions. Jackson was not exactly anti-union, of course. Black knew that unions had been among Jackson's clients in pregovernment days, and no New Dealer could be hostile to so central a progressive cause as the rights of labor. Yet Jackson had come out of the sedate rural conservatism of upstate New York. He valued his horse farm, his amenities, his elegant clothing, his country manor at Hickory Hill. It was natural for Black to wonder what Bob Jackson, the product of that almost bucolic setting, knew of the roughhouse days in Birmingham, the griefs and miseries of coal miners. The only other member of the Court who really understood was Frank Murphy. Black and Murphy had joined hands in behalf of laboring people and their rights at the 1936 Democratic convention, when New Deal policy was still being shaped. Murphy knew. But what could Jackson know of the old practice of cheating unrepresented coal miners by the device known as "short-weighting," deliberately underweighing the coal they dug—a foul practice Black had attacked in Birmingham thirty years earlier? Did Jackson know real ruthlessness when he saw it? Did he understand a man like Richard Hopkins, the Kansas attorney general who once had prosecuted striking miners for *vagrancy?*

Black's early experience with the Alabama steel and coal barons—and, since then, his reading of the writings of the British don and Labor Party theorist G. D. H. Cole—did not dispose him to see labor's struggle for daylight as a tea party. It was a cold, hard fight. The combatants did not observe the Marquis of Queensberry's rules. It was a brutal, sometimes bloody struggle, a class war, and there was in Black's mind no doubt where a radical Jeffersonian democrat should take his stand. Inhibitions arising from the cult of judicial restraint could too easily become an excuse for acquiescence in wrong and oppression. Let Felix Frankfurter (and, by inference, Jackson) see his judicial views as essentially lawless and fanatical. So be it; Black had no apologies to offer.

Black, moreover, had reason to believe that Jackson had really not thought his appointment to the Court lawful. When Roosevelt chose him, there had been a brief but futile effort, even before the Klan embarrassment, to block Black's appointment. An argument had been offered that he was constitutionally ineligible. As a voting member of the Senate, Black had supported the improvement in Supreme Court pension benefits that were to be the carrot, inducing elderly justices to retire before time outran their views. This vote had undoubtedly increased the "emoluments" of the office, and the Constitution unambiguously said that no member of Congress could be appointed to an office whose emoluments had been increased during his term of office. The case had been dismissed for want of the plaintiffs' ability to show direct or personal injury; but the effort had been closely watched by people with niggling views. Black suspected, with reason, that Jackson would have preferred a hearing of the case on its merits.

In any event, Jackson had now exploded from Nuremberg and relations at the Court were certain to be a bit frigid for a while. Given his view of the working of the tides of history, and of judicial politics, Black could see no profit in responding. If he did so, the two of them would only be grappling, to the further injury of the great institution they served, over the elusive and mercurial substance of history—and, of course, the bubble, reputation. However one might contrive to try to shape it, the record would tell its own tale in the end. The Court was in recess; Black would relax on his tennis court on South Lee Street in Alexandria and let the storm rage. Nine years earlier, the Klan story had forced him to give a public accounting for himself on nationwide radio. Having worn the sackcloth once, he would not wear it again—ever.

VIII

"Mr. President," drawled the portly, moon-faced senator, "Mr. President . . . " It was June 18, and by now Jackson's blast at Black had been the political sensation of the season for a week. "Mr. President, the people are sick of the bickering, the internal schism, and the floating of rumors and petty factionalism in their highest judicial tribunal."

The people's tribune, self-styled, was James O. Eastland of Sunflower, Mississippi, a Deep South Democrat of the neanderthal tendency. Eastland and his collaborator for the oratorical exercise, Senator Styles Bridges of New Hampshire, had seized upon the Supreme Court quarrel as a sign of the need for "reform" of the Court itself. Few would heed them; and they probably knew it. But Eastland droned on undaunted, ladling out gobs of statistics, deploring the "confusion, perplexity and bewilderment" into which the strife at the Court had plunged the nation. In his hands he held the remedy, just what the situation needed. It was Joint Resolution 167. If only Congress would pass it, submitting his proposed constitutional amendment to the states, political manipulation on and by the Court would cease—as, incidentally, would its independence of Congress.

Eastland and the other southerners for whom he was known to speak were, in fact, less interested in altering the structure of the Court to prevent further mischief than in assuring themselves a veto over its membership. A developing line of cases seemed to put the Court on a potential collision course with the segregation laws, though Eastland did not speak of that directly. Instead he muffled his oars. Now that Roosevelt had tampered with the Court, he asserted, it was tearing up the settled law of the land by the roots. In a mere seven years, the "Roosevelt Court" had in no fewer than 40 percent of all its decisions overruled lower courts. From January 1942 to the end of the most recent term, it had reversed more lower court decisions (336) than it had affirmed (306), often by 5-4 decisions. (Of course, the Supreme Court tends to grant discretionary appeal mostly to those lower-court decisions that seem troublesome or controversial, making it plausible that it might reverse a high percentage of them; and how one-vote margins of decision would be eliminated by the reforms Eastland and Bridges proposed neither senator explained.)

Not only did this recent history demonstrate the Court's cavalier disregard of settled precedent, Eastland claimed. It disclosed a sinister aim: "To bring about by judicial decision a social and economic revolution to suit the predilections of its members." Had the Court not, in a recent labor union case, held that "the law of robbery and extortion does not apply to a labor organization which interferes with the movement of goods in interstate commerce"? This menacing drift should be stopped by constitutional amendment. Henceforth, presidents—including Roosevelt, retroactively—would be limited to three appointees to the Court. The amendment presumably would bump four FDR appointees, including Jackson, from the Court, although it would spare Hugo Black. They would be replaced by justices specially elected by Congress, with each state casting a single vote.

Among those who sat listening in the nearly empty Senate chamber to Eastland's tirade was the liberal Senator Claude Pepper of Florida, who with others southerners of his liberal racial views would lose his seat in the upheaval of 1950. Pepper rose to ask an obvious question: If the Court were bent on subverting the law in the name of some hidden social or economic agenda, as Eastland charged, how then could one account for the "sharp difference of opinion" among the justices, and the "intensity" of mixed feelings echoed in Jackson's cable from Nuremberg? Surely, the Court was far from being as monolithic as the gentleman from Mississippi was suggesting. And, asked Pepper, if Congress should gain the power to remove justices from the Court and replace them with its own creatures, would it not convict itself of just that "court packing" conservatives had condemned in 1937 when Roosevelt attempted it? Pepper's acute questions revealed the hollowness of Eastland's rhetoric. Everyone knew that it was a political exercise, having little or no direct bearing on the crisis that was troubling the Court. But dialectic of a serious sort was not Eastland's errand, or Bridges's. Both had dropped their fishing lines in ruffled waters, and their draconian "reform" was designed for a day's agitation. It would not be taken seriously in the Senate or elsewhere, except perhaps for a few gullible readers of the *Congressional Record*. It did illustrate the tendency of people to read their own preconceptions into an institutional uproar. In that, Eastland and Bridges were not alone.

The same tendency could be seen in the press. Reporters, editorialists, and radio commentators—then still an influential journalistic breed—tuned up to pronounce upon what was now being called the "feud" between Jackson and Black. There were newspapermen in the capital—notably the shrewd and well informed Arthur Krock of the *New York Times,* and the *Washington Post*'s Merlo Pusey—who grasped the point: The judicial disqualification issue was at least the visible core of the dispute. Many other analysts, however, weighed in with spicy political or ad hominem interpretations, not all of them so flamboyantly as John O'Donnell of *The Washington Times-Herald,* the Washington outpost of the McCormick family newspapers. O'Donnell reported with an air of authority that President Truman, outraged by the quarrel on the Court, had demanded wholesale resignations, specifically those of Black, Murphy, Jackson, and Frankfurter. (The Constitution gives presidents the power to appoint Supreme Court justices "by and with the advice and consent of the Senate," but it confers no power of removal.) O'Donnell was not deflected from his exciting theme by constitutional trifles. Warming to the tale, he told *Times-Herald* readers that "the request that the resignation of the quarreling quartet would be most welcome at the White House has been conveyed to each by word of mouth. Frankfurter [who in fact had not set foot in the White House since Truman's accession] got the bad news directly across the . . . desk from Truman." O'Donnell's screed, which was among the more fanciful of many strange reports, caught the eye of the president's press secretary, Charles Ross. Ross was offended. The report was, he said, "so utterly cockeyed and fantastic that I hate to dignify it by a denial."

Among conservative journalists, there was some wishful thinking of the same stripe, a hope that somehow some of the Roosevelt appointees might be purged. Other columnists simply took sides. Robert Allen, who had been by turns the partner of both Drew Pearson and Joseph Alsop, pictured Hugo Black as the "blameless victim" of his colleagues. One, presumably Frankfurter, was "a scheming, power-hungry manipulator," while the other, presumably Jackson, was "a jealous and disappointed job seeker." The whole affair had been sparked, Allen wrote, by Jackson's frantic effort to hold onto his chances to be appointed chief justice. Just why, in that case, Jackson had held his fire until Vinson's appointment was announced, Allen did not explain.

Among some senior commentators, factionalism and fancy gave way to haughty and censorious judgment. In a *Washington Star* piece of June 14, Raymond Moley, the former Roosevelt adviser and speechwriter, patronized everyone. He traced the quarrel at the Court to FDR's "purely political concept of the Court's function . . . as an adjunct to a temporary political regime." In a Baltimore campaign speech in 1936, Moley recalled, Roosevelt had gone so far as to paste a partisan label on the Court, calling it a tool of the Republicans. It could hardly be surprising, then, that the half dozen justices FDR had himself placed on the Court, or at least a majority of them, reflected the same ultrapolitical notion of the judicial role. John S. Knight took a similar line in the *Detroit Free Press* of June 16. "The present demoralization of the Supreme Court," he intoned, "dates from Mr. Roosevelt's packing the Court with men temperamentally and judicially unfitted for the duties to which they were assigned. In his petulant impatience with decisions of the Supreme Court which he did not consider in keeping with the wishes of the people, Mr. Roosevelt elevated political lawyers and small-town judges of limited experience." (Obviously, the "political lawyer" was Jackson; the "small-town judge," Black.) What the country needed, Knight pontificated, was "a national housecleaning," presumably including the unfit justices.

When they connected the unsettled state of the Court to

the judicial revolution of the preceding decade, the commentators had a point, although most of them drew from it largely irrelevant inferences. Except for a few newspapers with a traditional and serious interest in the Court, notably the *Times* and the *Post,* little solid information and less reflection was evident in the great spate of comment that followed Jackson's cable. The only useful editorial proposal came from the *Post* (it was probably written by Merlo Pusey) and urged the justices to adopt disqualification rules recently adopted by the World Court at The Hague. Otherwise, the uproar of 1946 was no exception to a more or less constant rule of journalism: In the grip of a fascinating and fast-breaking story, involving complex institutions with esoteric working habits, reporters and commentators are often tempted to consult their crystal balls. Predictions abounded, as usual: Jackson or Black or both would resign. Once Congress opened the inevitable "investigation" of the affair, Black and perhaps other justices would be impeached and probably removed. At the very least, a congressional investigation would unearth shocking abuses and make tight new rules of judicial behavior inevitable.

Without exception, all these breathless predictions were wrong. Senator Hatton Sumners, who as chairman of the Senate Judiciary Committee was one of the two addressees of Jackson's cable, had learned of the document in a newspaper report. After a few days of reflection and counsel, Sumners calmly announced that there would be no "investigation," at least by his committee. There was nothing within the Senate's cognizance to investigate, he told reporters. The separation of powers principle seemed to bar Senate dictation of internal rules or procedures to Supreme Court justices. There were no other investigations, either; nor did resignations or impeachments follow.

As for Eastland's speech to the Senate on the proposed Joint Resolution 167, it served only to herald a theme common to conservative critics of the Court. The problem at the Court, whatever it was (and there was one, wasn't there?) flowed directly and inevitably from Roosevelt's tampering. This was in fact a bit of a non sequitur, since one "Roosevelt justice" was assailing another. Whatever political manipulation might be implicit in the subtle and largely technical issue of judicial disqualification went unexplained, perhaps because it was far from obvious.

Press comment largely reflected the usual but unhistorical assumption that any Supreme Court crisis of the day must be an absolute novelty, utterly unheard of before. Those who knew little of the Court's history pictured a long and uninterrupted golden age, now rudely shattered. Until this sad moment, or at least until Roosevelt tossed the apple of discord among the justices, the Court had been a quiet, orderly place where no one ever raised his voice. Its serenity, its gentlemanly observance of the proprieties, had now been carelessly crushed by thoughtless, petty, power-hungry men. The rows between Thomas Jefferson and his cousin John Marshall over the Aaron Burr trial, the Chase impeachment, Andrew Jackson's defiance of the Court over Indian and banking policy, the storm stirred by the *Dred Scott* case, the post-Civil War battles over military tribunals and habeas corpus, the anti-Semitic unpleasantness of Justice McReynolds to Justice Brandeis—all these earlier episodes tended to show that human chemistry did not evaporate at the portals of the Court. But all these things went unmentioned in the threnody of lament.

As for Jackson and his cable, it was widely taken for granted, and not altogether by commentators hostile to him, that Jackson had assumed the prosecutor's job at Nuremberg for political reasons—undoubtedly in the first instance to set himself up to run for governor of New York. It was solemnly reported as fact that the Jacksons, who lived in an ante bellum mansion at Hickory Hill, near McLean, Virginia, had not registered to vote there, so as to keep their New York residence for future political purposes. Mrs. Jackson, in a rare public statement, declared that this had nothing at all to do with New York politics. The justice simply took the view that the Court should not be partisan. From the press and the vocal politicians, in short, there was a great deal of dust but little light on the question of what, exactly, was going on.

IX

On July 29, a Saturday, just before leaving for a Maine vacation, Harold and Jane Ickes gave a small dinner party for the new Chief Justice and Mrs. Vinson, both of whom struck Ickes as "democratic and simple" people. Mrs. Vinson talked freely about her husband's new role. He was much too lacking in guile to take on a peacemaking mission at the Supreme Court, and she had strongly opposed it. "Fred," she declared, "is just like a friendly puppy, he loves everybody and wants to be friends with everybody." What if the celebrated combatants on the Court did not want to be friends with him, or with each other?

But it was too late for second thoughts. Vinson had been sworn in as thirteenth chief justice in an elaborate White House ceremony the Tuesday before, July 25, in a ceremony designed to emphasize that insofar as one man could make a difference, bygones would now be bygones. Peace would settle at the touch of Fred Vinson's healing hand over the warring Court.

Circulating in a large crowd, estimated by the Washington police at more than four thousand, many familiar faces could be seen. One reporter remarked the stooped figure of Homer Cummings, once attorney general, the designer of FDR's "court-packing" strategy, hence the instigator of the last controversy over the Court. Also seen, shaking hands as the Navy band played gay and martial airs from Elgar and Tschaikovsky, was the nation's favorite military hero, General Dwight D. Eisenhower.

Sam Rayburn called the gathering to order. A solemn Vinson stepped before his friend Judge Lawrence Grover of the District of Columbia Court of Appeals to take the constitutional oath. Applause rippled across the lawn, and Vinson bent to kiss the wedding-day Bible he and Mrs. Vinson had been given thirty-two years before. It was inscribed, a reporter discovered, "Chart and Compass for the voyage," but what course Vinson might now chart for the Court, which was imagined to be in a state bordering on anarchy, was a matter of speculation. The president did not dispel the uncertainty when he moved forward after the oath-taking for a few friendly remarks. It was, he said, "a lucky day for the United States and a lucky day for Mr. Vinson." Then Harry Truman paused. "At least I hope it is," he tentatively added, a remark that was greeted by uncomfortable laughter.

Four days later, the *Washington Post* carried the results of the first Gallup Poll on the Jackson-Black controversy. A majority, Dr. Gallup reported, had not altered their view of the Court at all in recent years, and 25 percent of the people polled had no opinion about it at all. Of those who said they had changed their estimate, however, most now declared a "lower regard" for the Court than before. Forty-three percent of all those sampled agreed with the statement that the Court "decides many questions largely on the basis of politics." If the poll accurately reflected popular attitudes— this was two years before the pollsters' predictions of a Dewey victory over Truman in the 1948 presidential election would embarrass most of them, including Gallup—the latter attitude matched that of one eminent insider, Felix Frankfurter. In a casual note to Frank Murphy on the day of Vinson's appointment, Frankfurter said that if he were suddenly transported back to his Harvard Law School classroom and forced to tell his students the truth about the war years on the Court, he would have to say that "never before in the history of the Court were so many of its members influenced in decisions by considerations extraneous to the legal issues."

For all the speculation, however, the Court itself was shrouded in its usual decorous silence—most of the justices were out of Washington for the summer—and there was little solid information to be had about how Fred Vinson and his colleagues would knit up the torn places. On September 10, with summer vacations ending and people beginning to straggle back into town, Drew Pearson had one tidbit for his readers. With the Court's opening day now three weeks off, Pearson said, Vinson had had an "important talk" with Robert Jackson. Jackson—Pearson was presumably relying on first-hand impressions transmitted by Vinson—now "seemed to have regained his perspective and was more rational than at the time he unloosed his blast." Jackson's friends, Pearson continued, were blaming his "erratic" outburst on the depressing effects of the Nuremberg trials. Having to deal day after day with the subhuman crimes of men with the blood of millions on their hands was "enough to get any man down." (The view that Jackson's lucid cable had been an act of uncalculating impulsiveness would emerge as an article of conventional wisdom among Black's partisans.)

Still later in the month, Hugo Black lunched with Harold Ickes. He told Ickes that he had spotted Jackson at a distance around the Court but that the two of them had not had occasion to speak or meet. Black looked very well, Ickes recorded in his diary, but talked mostly about foreign policy issues and not about the Court.

* * *

The first Monday in October is by long tradition the gathering day for new terms of the Supreme Court. On

Monday October 8, the editors of virtually every major newspaper in the country felt obliged to alert readers to the occasion and to remind them that the nation would, at last, view the two antagonists together in public. There was an air of drama and suspense. It was also Vinson's first day to preside over the Court, and a reporter noted that the billowing sleeves of his new robe fell down over his hands as he administered the oath of admission to fifty new members of the Supreme Court bar. But there was nothing in the almost staid scene to indicate what, if anything, Jackson and Black had had to say to one another, or might be doing to hold in check the now celebrated animosities that had been front-page news in June and July. Black, seated to Vinson's right, whispered occasionally to the new chief. Two chairs to the left, Jackson chatted with Douglas and with Harold Burton, who had replaced Owen Roberts in his absence. Burton, in fact, would supply an important bit of behind-the-scenes information. Two days after the term began, Burton scribbled an account of the first conference in the vest-pocket diary in which he meticulously recorded in a tiny script the humdrum details of his daily routine, including his punctual swim in the Senate pool:

> When we came into the conference, Justice Jackson was sitting beside me in his chair when Justice Black came in. Justice Black shook hands with him immediately—and Justice Jackson said, "Good morning, Hugo." Also, during the conference . . . Jackson & Black joined in a brief discussion—all in the best of quiet manners. I mention this because of the popular idea of such feuding between these justices that they would not speak to each other. (These were the first instances of their speaking together that I have seen this fall).

Whatever the private feelings, the custom of shaking

hands established by Chief Justice Melvin Fuller went uninterrupted. Indeed, for all that impartial observers could see, everyone was striving to put a civil and convivial face on things. Vinson, presiding at the weekly conferences, seemed to Frankfurter "all ease and good humor, disposing of each case by choosing . . . to float merely on the surface of the problems." As for Black, however, his sternest critic noted in the same diary entry that the senior associate had seemed all sweetness until a Hatch Act case came up for discussion. He had "let loose," Frankfurter recalled. The Hatch Act's restrictions on the political activities of government employees were all wrong, Black had pronounced in his "irascible and snarling tone of voice." The right to vote carried with it a right to persuade others, and in a democracy that right should not be restricted. "Oh, democracy," Frankfurter exclaimed with disgust, "what flapdoodle is delivered in thy name." Frankfurter found himself equally annoyed, a few days later, at the spectacle of Black's pretensions to almost virginal indifference to what was happening in the mid-term elections. It was widely forecast, accurately as it developed, that the Democrats would loose control of Congress for the first time since 1932. After leaving the lunch table, Frankfurter and Reed compared notes. They agreed that Black's feigned political neutrality was staged for the benefit of Vinson, who was being courted "like a new girl at school."

In Frankfurter's skeptical view, Fred Vinson deluded himself if he really supposed that the brotherly suavity of his honeymoon period ran deep, or would last. It was mere blind luck that Black and Jackson had happened to agree on most of the first list of cases. But the clemency of the weather in the conference was deceptive, Frankfurter told Dean Acheson as the two strolled to work. As to the new chief justice, Acheson exclaimed: "Old boy, you don't know nothin'." Meanwhile, Stanley Reed found the atmosphere at the Court "sultry," thick with storm clouds ready to burst.

In early December, Raymond Ickes was to be admitted to the Supreme Court bar and his father went up to Capitol Hill to watch. It was the first time he had seen Jackson since the latter had left for Nuremberg a year and a half earlier, and as he later noted in his diary, he was shocked at the change. "He had aged decidedly, in addition to which his face seemed to be full of lines and unhappy in expression." Ickes tried to catch Jackson's eye in the courtroom but failed. He was, he concluded, probably "persona non grata" because of what he had written about the controversy in his syndicated newspaper column.

In fact, the calm exterior at the Court reflected the resolve of both Jackson and Black to quiet things down, perhaps to the disappointment of those who expected, even hoped, that the fight would continue. Privately, the two antagonists were determined not to let the quarrel mar their professional relationship. Jackson for his part was already beginning to wonder if he had not committed "a capital blunder." Not that his feelings had subsided about the issues. The problem was that the real issues had been so obscured, or skewed, by the way the story had played and had been interpreted in the press that the conduct of Black and his judicial allies had escaped serious scrutiny. Black's supporters in the press, including Ickes and Pearson, had seen to it that the key points had been clouded by personalities. Among his friends, Black continued to protest that the uproar had been inconsequential. He had no "feud" with Jackson, and no intention of responding to his charges.

Was the whole thing a mirage, then, or a tempest in a teapot? It might seem so to those who watched as the Court resumed its work without further public buffeting, and Black and Jackson took their accustomed places as if nothing had happened. But the placidity on the surface was deceptive, and gave no hint of what was stirring under it. It would be many years, and both the antagonists dead, before the full story could be pieced together.

X

Robert Jackson had been dead for fourteen years and his old antagonist, Hugo Black, was no longer the grim, chain-smoking, "rarely smiling" figure he had seemed at the time of the great uproar of 1946. By 1968 Black had seen a new Court, under Earl Warren, write many of his ideas into law. He had become a judicial patriarch, the grand old man of the Court, a legend, avuncular and benevolent. On December 3 of the nation's most turbulent year in a generation, CBS televised an interview with the elderly justice, conducted by Martin Agronsky and Eric Sevareid. In an enthralling voice and manner, Black reminisced about his years on the Court and mused incisively about the Constitution. The millions who watched were charmed. But few in that large audience (which, though responsive, was dwarfed in number by the crowd NBC drew by showing an old Brigitte Bardot movie) recalled the Jackson controversy, now twenty-two years in the past, or the humiliating revelations about Black's one-time membership in the Klan. That was all ancient history, or almost so.

For the most part, the Court's elder statesman spoke quietly and persuasively of the growing passion of his later years, his theory that the Bill of Rights contained "absolutes," barriers against government infringement of personal liberties which could not be compromised by so much as a trifle. He brandished a Government Printing Office copy of the Constitution which he carried in his pocket. Only occasionally, as if in a code that only initiates might decipher, did Black deftly allude to the conference-room battles of the past. Did justices ever "lose their tempers" with one another, Agronsky asked at one point.

"Well," Black responded. "I guess you could never get nine men together where the justices wouldn't sometimes lose their tempers." But neither interviewer pursued the opening, and no example of lost tempers was asked for or volunteered. Later, however, describing the great advocates who had argued before the Court in his time, Black added a grace note whose meaning was clear to at least a few viewers with long and specific memories. To his select list he added the name of "Bob Jackson, who argued cases before us as Solicitor General. He was always magnificent. His language was fluent. His knowledge of the law was good, and he never objected to your asking him a question which most people would think too hard to answer." When a private correspondent later commended him for this quiet but handsome tribute to his old rival, Black responded that he did indeed "recall . . . what happened when [Jackson] was coming back from Europe but that episode, I hope, was completely forgotten by him before his death. At any rate, we never discussed it after he returned."

* * *

There had been one last, brief round in the saga of Robert Jackson's ambition for higher judicial office. When Fred Vinson died suddenly in 1953, the first year of the Eisenhower presidency, Jackson's friends rallied once more, though this time more quietly and in smaller force than at the time of Stone's death. (No one, unless it was Jackson himself, suspected that he had only a year to live.)

Learning of Vinson's death, Jackson's old Nuremberg associate, Robert Storey of Dallas, now president of the American Bar Association, went into action. From Quebec, where he was meeting with the Canadian Bar Association, he wrote to Attorney General Herbert Brownell to urge Jackson's appointment. In his *Newsweek* column for September 21, Ernest K. Lindley, a Washington newsman whose memory of New York politics was long and detailed, made a strong pitch for Jackson as well, "the man most conspicuously qualified by age, intellect, learning, character and command of the language," to be chief justice. Jackson had been a Democrat, Lindley conceded, but he cited the recent historical precedents: Taft had appointed the Louisiana Democrat (and Confederate veteran) Edward D. White, and of course, Roosevelt had chosen Stone, a former Republican, in 1941. Lindley sent Jackson an early copy of the piece, but Jackson was skeptical. "Knowing something of the pressures that the President is under," he wrote to Lindley, "I cannot imagine that he will concur in your solution." Jackson was right, of course; and there is no evidence that he was ever seriously considered. The optimists among his friends were less realistic and managed to persuade themselves that his chances to follow Vinson were strong. In Jamestown, New York, the local newspaper even predicted his appointment. When their hopes were dashed, Jackson's supporters decided that he had been high on Eisenhower's list until someone recalled Jackson's support for the 1937 court-packing plan, an item of history that did not jibe with the new administration's proclamation of deference to the other branches of government.

Hugo Black was wrong in "hoping," in the Agronsky interview of 1968, that Jackson had forgotten their feud before his death. It was true that no symptoms of personal animosity had reappeared during the Court term that began in the autumn of 1946—or later. The "feud," the newspaper and radio news sensation of the summer, had subsided as mysteriously as it had boiled up. No incivilities marred the decorum of the courtroom; the Court had resumed its usual sphinx-like composure. Indeed, urbanity had won out since at the level of personal chemistry there was no such animosity as had been imagined; and in any event the press of day-to-day judicial business made it difficult to nurse old arguments. But behind the scenes, the process of elaboration and rationalization continued in both chambers.

Black, for his part, appeared to take an almost passive view of the supposed feud. If he wished vindication, he was content to leave the task to devoted ex-clerks, led by John P. Frank, now a young law professor. Frank would devote several pages to the quarrel in his 1949 biography, *Mr. Justice Black*. As Frank was writing, Black told him that, in his own view, no incumbent justice should ever be a candidate for chief justice, though had it come to that after Stone's death he would have found either Douglas or Reed "perfectly satisfactory." For the rest, he assured Frank in a letter of May 11, 1948, the controversy aroused by the Jackson cable had been "a very small event in my life. . . . I have never had anything whatever to do with carrying on a 'feud' and I do not intend to do so."

Real or feigned, Black's equanimity contradicted Fleeson's colorful ascription of anger and "fiery scorn" to him. The discrepancy remains a minor puzzle. Black's correspondence shows that the justice countenanced, if he did not actually encourage, characterizations of Jackson by his young protegés that were hardly flattering: "a bad man," "the mountebank of Nuremberg," etc. But it was not in Black's nature to nurse enmities, especially those that were not rooted in substantial issues. He seems to have had a personal toughness and resiliency that were quite beyond Jackson's capacity. Historian Arthur Schlesinger Jr., who interviewed all the justices for a *Fortune* magazine article soon after the "feud," described Black, at sixty, as "intense, stubborn, suspicious. . . . [tending] to distrust the motives of those who oppose him; and people who remember his cold, bitter manner in the Senate sympathize with Jackson's remark, 'I would not stand for any more of his bullying.' But his emotions center around ideas, not personalities. . . . He is an honorable person, not given to petty politicking."

If, indeed, Black's heart lay in his causes, that of organized labor was paramount in his affections. The pursuit of these causes left little surplus energy for public wrangling, or the perpetuation of quarrels. What Frank and others did in his behalf, and often with his cooperation, was another matter.

*   *   *

Jackson's attitude was clearly very different. He continued to be haunted by the episode, not, perhaps, by any lingering dislike of Black but by the gnawing sense that he had taken on a risky duty and failed at it. He had exposed judicial misconduct of which he took the gravest view, and yet the exposé had misfired. It had produced great noise and controversy, but neither understanding nor censure of the judicial sins he had thought he was attacking.

No one who has studied Jackson's systematic and articulate consideration of the responsibility of judges in the American system of government can doubt the gravity with which he viewed Black's stratagems, as they appeared to him. Black might be amiable enough, he might even be a gentleman. But the official Black was so relentlessly political, so heedless of the appropriate limits of judicial competence, as to border—as Jackson saw it—on being a fanatic. When he returned to Washington from Nuremberg in the summer of 1946, Jackson went on wrestling privately with the implications of his public dispute with Black. Between the time of his return and the year of his early death, 1954, Jackson composed or dictated four narrative accounts of the origin and issues of the dispute. These narratives vary in tone, candor, detail and length, and they all overlap at certain points. But taken together, the tale they tell is that of a disputant unwilling to let the matter rest until he is sure posterity will understand his view.

It was a commonly heard suggestion at the time—and not only among Jackson's detractors—that the cable from

Nuremberg had sprung from a temporary lapse of self-control, brought on by strain and fatigue. Arthur Schlesinger, for instance, had written that it "was the act of a weary and sorely beset man, committed to a harassing task in a remote land, tormented by the certainty that the chief justiceship had now passed forever out of his reach." Jackson, suggested Schlesinger, had reacted to Doris Fleeson's column and the complex of rumors it represented "as a GI would to rumors of his wife's infidelity."

Was there something "irrational" in the act? A time would come, as Jackson reminisced with Professor Harlan Phillips for the Columbia Oral History Project, when he himself would muse, half-humorously, that perhaps he had been a bit overwrought. The stress theory put out at the time by Drew Pearson and later echoed by John Frank's biography of Black was, he said, "that I was under the enormous strain of the Nuremberg trial, which resulted in an irresponsible act for which there is not rational explanation." Pausing, Jackson added, "Well, I may have been mentally irresponsible. That, someone else will have to judge." But when he edited the taped transcript Jackson crossed out in pencil the concession that he might have been "mentally irresponsible." He knew it was not true, that this was a canard. No doubt the frustrations of Nuremberg had been real enough, as he knew only too well, but there had been nothing at all "irresponsible" in his reaction to the situation in Washington.

What then explained it? A certain lingering disapproval of Black was clearly part of the explanation, as Jackson's personal narratives show. Black had seemed to Jackson not only a "government judge" but also "one of those liberals with no background in liberalism, as one would know from his KKK associations . . . and he embraced that form of collectivism which is so often confused with liberalism." Even when Black seemed temporarily to jump the traces of this "collectivism," as he did in the *Bethlehem Steel* case, it was usually for some ulterior purpose. Jackson also despised what he took to be Black's cavalier mixing of judicial and political duty, and his scornful attitude toward the organized bar. Had he not consented to attend a great testimonial dinner arranged by all the liberal special interests, at which silly and undignified things had been said of the justices who stayed away? And hadn't Black boasted to people like Fred Rodell that the only organization he regretted joining was not the KKK but the American Bar Association?

Yet these were peripheral matters by comparison with Black's tendency to use judicial power in pursuit of his personal political agenda, whatever the institutional cost. That was the heart of Jackson's complaint, and it had been the gravamen of the cable from Nuremberg, lost in the ensuing confusion. Now, in the quiet of his chambers, Jackson tried to distill the essence of the feud—more than once.

When he thought about it, the dispute could not be separated from the paramount economic peril facing the nation, now that the war was ending—the power of unions to disrupt the economy, to gouge business and the public with ever-higher wage settlements. In the parlous climate of 1945-46, no one could yet foresee the stable, prosperous future that stretched indefinitely ahead. The prospect looked darker and, if the times were a harbinger, likely to be full of economic strife and uncertainty. No one could foresee that the Republican-controlled Eightieth Congress, elected in the fall of 1946, would act to restore the balance. It would be remembered as the Congress whose name Harry Truman would turn into a famous political epithet, the "do-nothing 80th Congress." It would also be the Congress that passed, over Truman's veto, the Taft-Hartley Act, the first major reversal the unions had sustained since the advent of Roosevelt and the New Deal. The hated antistrike injunction of earlier days was not restored. In its place came the sixty-day "cooling-off period" and the temporary judicial restraining order, a substantial check to the threat of mass walkouts. But when the Court was wrestling over the interpretation of the Fair Labor Standards Act and the extension of portal-to-portal pay to the nation's coal miners, the Taft-Hartley Act still lay in the future. In that uncertain climate it had been possible for justices like Black and Murphy, passionate in their prolabor views, to bend the Court to open partisanship on the side of the unions. That, at least, was how Jackson saw it.

The man at the center of the quarrel, really, was not a justice of the Supreme Court; he was the flamboyant beetle-browed Welshman, John L. Lewis. Lewis's United Mine Workers had pursued a course of arrogant defiance. Even in the midst of the war, in May 1943, Lewis and the coal miners had defied the War Labor Board. Lewis had called a general coal strike. Only a threat to draft the miners into the Army, the standard government response in those post-injunction but pre-Taft-Hartley days, brought them back to work. And no sooner had the war ended in Europe (though not yet in the Pacific) than the coal miners had joined millions of others in walkouts. With more than two million laborers in the streets and picket lines, it looked as if an unmanageable industrial crisis, the worst since the Depression, might be upon the country. Lewis, for his part, delighted in the maverick's role. He called himself a Hoover Republican, but he certainly did not act like one. A Bible- and Shakespeare-quoting figure of Celtic theatricality, he was— some of the Washington gossip columnists noted with a sneer—the darling of fashionable liberal salons in the capital, half bard and half revolutionary.

It was difficult to exaggerate the potential power of Lewis and the mine workers. They held a whip hand over the American economy, the equivalent of that life-threatening power of economic blackmail that would, many years later, accrue for a time in the 1970s to the oil baronies of OPEC. The American economy in 1946 depended on coal for 62 percent of its electricity, and 55 percent of its industrial power. Most railway locomotives still ran on coal; the conversion to diesel fuel was barely underway. In this setting, the prolabor cabal on the Court had in Jackson's view acted slyly, even conspiratorially, to extend the wage base of the miners, then had tried their best to rush forward the decision in the portal-to-portal case to reinforce Lewis's already excessive power.

By a historical irony, Frank Murphy was cast as the author of the pivotal *Jewell Ridge* opinion. Ten years earlier, in 1937, Murphy had been governor of Michigan when John L. Lewis joined the famous "sit-down" strike of General Motors auto workers in Detroit. The men on the assembly lines had refused to work and also refused to leave the plant. A federal judge ordered the workers to vacate the building, and Murphy dutifully mobilized the Michigan National Guard at the Chevrolet plant in Flint to enforce the court's order. Then Murphy's resolve flagged. He consulted Lewis. Lewis roared at him over the telephone. "I shall personally enter General Motors Chevrolet Plant Number Four," he shouted dramatically, "I shall order the men to disregard your order, to stand fast . . .

> I shall walk up to the largest window in the plant, open it, divest myself of my outer raiment, remove my shirt and bare my bosom. Then, when you order your troops to fire, mine will be the first breast that those bullets will strike. And as my body falls from the window to the ground, you will listen to the voice of your grandfather [who had been hanged for treason in Ireland] as he whispers in your ear, "Frank, are you sure you are doing the right thing?"

Perhaps intimidated by Lewis's histrionics, and unsure

that he was right, Murphy had all but enlisted in the sit-down strike himself. His colleagues on the Court probably had not forgotten that colorful and well-publicized episode. It is not far-fetched to suppose, in fact, that Frankfurter and Jackson gathered from it that Murphy was still unwilling to stand up to Lewis—or, for that matter, to Hugo L. Black.

XI

Everyone who read the famous cable from Nuremberg in June 1946—and it was widely reprinted—thought it was clear enough what Jackson was saying. But was it? Jackson had, in fact, muted his most serious charge against Black, and so successfully that it passed nearly unnoticed. This was the charge that Black and others among the justices forming the majority in the *Jewell Ridge* decision had for a time planned to throw the Court's weight and prestige into an active labor dispute. In the Nuremberg version, Jackson confined himself to careful understatement:

> While Mr. Justice Murphy was preparing his opinion a strike of the mine workers and negotiations with the operators were proceeding. It was proposed to hand down the decision in favor of the miners without waiting for the opinion and dissent. . . . Chief Justice Stone protested such proposed irregular treatment vigorously. I do not believe Mr. Justice Murphy favored it. In all events it was abandoned, but the conduct of this case following the Tennessee case [*Tennessee Iron & Coal Company v. Muscoda Local*] created uneasiness in my mind.

"Uneasiness," as Jackson's later reminiscences show, was stark understatement. The extent of the uneasiness emerges with great emphasis in what he wrote later. He had believed, or came to believe, that a shocking judicial impropriety had been in the wind for a time, bruited among some justices: that the Court might accelerate the announcement of its as yet unwritten 5-4 ruling in the pivotal coal cases for the sole purpose, it appeared, of tipping the deadlocked strike negotiations in the United Mine Workers' favor.

Beyond that, Jackson believed that when Black and others undertook to inject the portal-to-portal pay doctrine into the coal mines, this was not by chance. It was rather the culmination of a calculated strategic design to revise the Wages and Hours Act, step by step. And of that plot he believed Black to be the architect and impresario. Yet Jackson remained reluctant to make these dire conclusions public, in every damning detail. That is clear from a curious incident. Jackson sent the lengthiest and most detailed of the four narratives of what he called "The Black Controversy" to his biographer, Eugene Gerhart. It was to help Gerhart to reconstruct the story, from Jackson's perspective, and the discretion with which he wrote the narrative is evident in his use of the third person—as if some neutral observer had been looking at the quarrel from the sidelines. But when he sent the document to Gerhart, Jackson withheld three crucial pages (35-37). At the time he was still serving as Black's colleague, after all, and their relationship was by all accounts cordial and correct. He had to be careful. Shortly after Jackson's untimely death in 1954, the three missing pages became the object of an anxious quest by Gerhart, as we know from the transcript of an October 29 telephone conversation between the biographer and Professor Harlan Phillips of Columbia, who had conducted the oral history interviews with Jackson. Gerhart was eager to persuade Phillips, who was then acting as a sort of temporary caretaker of the Jackson files, that the justice had promised that he might see the three missing pages if anything "happened."

In those three pages Jackson related at length, and far more explicitly than before, what had happened behind the scenes at the Court during those tense spring days of 1945 when the European war was drawing to a close and the coal miners were on strike—and the great "feud" was germinating. The *Jewell Ridge* case had been argued before the Court on March 9. On the following Saturday, the justices met in their weekly conference to discuss and vote on the case. The vote went 5 to 4 against the extension of portal-to-portal pay for the coal miners, reversing what Jackson and Stone considered a misreading of the *Muscoda* precedent by the Fourth Circuit. As the conference was breaking up, Stone assigned the majority opinion (or what would have been the majority opinion, had the vote stayed the same) to Jackson. Before the weekend was out, however, Stanley Reed had second thoughts. On Monday morning, Reed informed Jackson that he now planned to vote the other way, which meant that the majority had swung 180 degrees in the other direction, giving Black, as senior associate in the new majority, the privilege of assigning the opinion. Thus Black had not only not recused himself despite the role of his former law partner; he had now "got the privilege," Jackson wrote, "of privately managing the assignment of the case and greatly influencing its handling behind the bench while Harris was handling it at the bar. Black assigned the writing to Murphy, as he had, a year earlier, in the Tennessee Iron and Coal Company Case, which despite the impression given at the time would figure importantly in the decision. The really sinister thing," Jackson continued, was the pressure on Murphy to hurry the draft of his opinion. Jackson cites the short note Murphy wrote to him (see above, p.48) just before the conference at which Murphy's draft was to be considered. The essence was that "some of the brethren" wanted the decision immediately announced.

Jackson had mildly asked Murphy then, "What is the rush in their view?" Whether he then suspected that the rush was to help John L. Lewis win a major concession, the documents do not indicate; nor, for that matter, do they suggest whether the idea of hurrying the decision out was a serious and urgent project or a passing whim, casually mentioned off the cuff. But by the time he came to reflect on the feud, Jackson had satisfied himself that the importuning of Murphy by Black and others was far from innocent and implied the gravest political purposes. If his allusion to the incident in the Nuremberg cable had been muffled, it was muffled no longer:

> What had happened was that the Murphy opinion was circulated Thursday, April 5th, at a time when the private owners were negotiating with Mr. Lewis. The [Murphy] note was written on Friday, the 6th, on which day these negotiations ended in deadlock. The mines were seized by the government on April 10th and an agreement was signed on April 11th by the Secretary of the Interior with the mine workers. Hence, the decision of the Court could no longer be of help to Mr. Lewis in negotiating it and, aside from Chief Justice Stone's vigorous opposition . . . the plan . . . seems to have been given up on this account.

Jackson carefully absolved Murphy of connivance in the plot to bolster John L. Lewis with a thunderbolt from the Court. He may have shared Felix Frankfurter's waspish view that Murphy functioned, rather unwarily, as Black's dupe. That Frankfurter believed this is clear from an amusing comment he wrote when Jackson later showed him, in confidence, a draft of the "coal cases" narrative. Jackson described the portal-to-portal pay doctrine in his account as a gratuitous "injection" into the *Jewell Ridge* opinion. Seizing on the word, Frankfurter wrote in his flamboyant scrawl:

> You don't know how it was injected! The saint's [presumably Murphy's] first circulation was very different

from what you now read in the Report!! Even the saint couldn't at first stomach what he did later, and wrote in a way that except for piddlin' stuff denied recovery in Mt. Clemens [a subsequent portal-to-portal claims case, decided while Jackson was in Nuremberg]. Then his leader [presumably Black] got hold of—not the Brother but his "ghost" [presumably Murphy's law clerk] & worked over & out what you now read.

The *Mount Clemens* case proved to be the end of the line in the portal-to-portal pay series. It had so shocked the lower court federal judge who had tried the case that he spoke out about it. It also prompted prolonged congressional hearings and a bill reversing the decision. The core of the dispute, as Jackson saw it, was simple but fundamental. All along, the string of portal-to-portal decisions constituted judicial legislation of a flagrant variety, a variety he had so roundly condemned in *The Struggle for Judicial Supremacy* five years earlier. If the primary aim of the Wages and Hours Act of 1937 was to aid nonunion labor, powerless to bargain collectively, how could it also apply, as the Supreme Court now had held, to industries where there had been a strong union and collective bargaining tradition? And where its help was unneeded, and judicial intervention essentially legislative in nature?

Jackson's answer was that the Court was deliberately, one might even say cynically, misreading and twisting the statute. Its interpretation of legislative history, and even of remarks Hugo Black himself had made on the Senate floor, was far off the mark. And to compound the duplicity, Harris had offered the Court a misleading argument, a poisoned pawn, in the Tennessee Coal and Iron case: The justices, he said, shouldn't hesitate to rule in favor of the iron-ore miners, whose unions were weak or nonexistent, for it would imply no future obligation to rule in favor of the coal miners.

Yet the one ruling had been adopted as a "precedent" for the other.

All this—the twisting of the intent of the statute and the furtiveness with which the precedent had been established and extended—had prompted Jackson to dissent sharply. "We doubt," his dissent said, "if one can find in the long line of criticized cases one in which the Court has made a more extreme exertion of power or one so little supported or explained by either the statute or the record in the case. Power should answer to reason none the less because its fiat is beyond appeal."

As for the economic cost of expanding portal-to-portal pay throughout the mining industry—and retroactively, at that—it could not immediately be calculated. But it would run into millions of dollars, with back pay and interest. This tide of unanticipated mining costs would then work its way into the cost structure of every energy-using industry, possibly with severe inflationary consequences. Such, in Jackson's view, was the result of this unapologetic use of judicial *force majeure* to override both custom and the intent of Congress.

Was Jackson right? Was it, as he would steadfastly maintain, so shameless an exercise in judicial legislation as it seemed? While his draft opinion in *Jewell Ridge* was circulating, Murphy had sent Black a revealing memo:

> Hugo:
> I now have a majority of the Court in the portal-to-portal case. This morning Wiley [Rutledge] sent me a note saying he did not disapprove a word in it. Felix is upset about my dramatic recital of the facts. Bob [Jackson] told me today he was fearful of this recital of irrelevant facts on other cases.
>
> I am willing to sharpen up the opinion on the issues of control, supervision and the two-court rule. But I am not willing or disposed at all to strip this case of the true

facts because two of our colleagues are of the view that it might effect [sic] other cases to leave the facts as I have outlined them. Since when did a realistic view of the facts cease to be an appropriate setting for legal conclusions? FM

Considered in its setting, the Murphy note is a mixed comment on the Frankfurter-Jackson theory that Black (and Murphy's clerk) were calling every shot in the case, with poor Murphy acting as a sort of puppet. Indeed, it comes near refuting it. Here Murphy seems to be reporting, as if to a superior; yet he is also boasting of his own ingenuity in laying down a rationale for the decision the Court had agreed to render. The note also shows, of course, that Murphy had persuaded himself that "a dramatic recital of the facts" as he saw them would suffice to explain his case in a legal sense. Murphy, the old-fashioned sympathizer with labor who had once yielded to Lewis's dramatic bluster about his grand-father, was clearly with the miners in spirit. Whatever the words or legislative history of the Wages and Hours Act might suggest, they deserved to have better pay; and that was that. The "facts" he had in mind were rhetorically powerful, if judicially immaterial:

> [Coal miners] must journey beneath the crust of the earth, far removed from the fresh and open air and from the beneficial rays of the sun. A heavy toll is exacted from those whose lot it is to ride and work and mine beneath the surface. From the moment they enter the portal until they leave, they are subjected to constant hazards and dangers; they are left begrimed and exhausted by their continuous physical and mental exertion.

Further, added Murphy in a footnote of rather adven-turous syntax, it was "widespread practice in other coal-producing nations of including travel time or portions thereof in the workday." This common custom, he declared, "bears out the conclusion that underground travel is work." These views about the practice in other nations might be indisputable as far as they went. But like the hardship of long travel beneath the crust of the earth, they were of questionable relevance to the question before the Court. Sympathize as they might with the grim lot of miners in their dark underground world, the justices were not commissioners charged to dictate pay practices to the coal industry; and the trial record in the case made it clear, in fact, that the negotiated wage scales already made allowance for underground travel time.

To Murphy's argument, Jackson in his dissent offered two powerful rebuttals. The Wages and Hours Act was not, by the unambiguous declaration of its congressional sponsors, including Senator Hugo L. Black, intended to override settlements reached through vigorous collective bargaining. Moreover, to establish the coal operators' liability to pay for travel time as well as work time at the coal faces would introduce great uncertainty into the industry. The "face to face" theory of compensation might have its defects. But it at least had the virtue—which the Court was now dismissing— of bringing order and predictability to the calculation of labor costs. The operators could set wages in the belief that they knew with reasonable certainty what competitors would be paying, in what was at best a business known for cut-throat competition. But what would happen if miners working at the same coal face had entered the mine at different portals? What about older, marginally productive mines "which have burrowed far from their portals"? Would liability for travel time so inflate labor costs per ton of coal as to make the older mines inoperable? Would they close, producing unemployment? The questions were endless; and lawyers of far less formidable intellect than Robert Jackson or Harlan Stone could have raised them by the dozens.

*   *   *

In the perspective of years, it might seem that the *Jewell Ridge* case, the spark for the great feud of 1946, was a cause as disproportionately small as, by fanciful legend, the publication of *Uncle Tom's Cabin* was in precipitating the Civil War. Not that the wages and hours case was a trifle. But now that the nation's industrial machine has so largely shifted its dependency toward oil, the economic stakes in coal mining, as the antagonists of 1945 viewed them, can be appreciated only with some effort of imagination. Yet from the perspective of the players of the day they were enormous. For Robert Jackson, the *Jewell Ridge* decision was the pivot upon which momentous issues of economic and judicial policy might turn. Doris Fleeson's provocative column had given only the faintest inkling of its real significance, in either respect. It had largely personalized the case. And likewise—perhaps a bit artlessly, as Jackson came to believe later on—his cable from Nuremberg had pointed to the Crampton Harris and disqualification issue as the centerpiece of the dispute. The conspiracy to rush to judgment in behalf of Lewis and the mine workers, "truly sinister" as Jackson thought it was, went almost unnoticed. Jackson's realization that his effort to explain his side of the quarrel had misfired prompted him to continue to worry the episode, long after Hugo Black had serenely gone on to larger adventures in what his critics would persist in calling judicial activism. For years, little noticed by those who have continued to take an interest in this intriguing episode, Jackson's effort at articulation has rested in his files. Now we know clearly just what he thought he meant to convey in the cable whose repercussions, that June day in 1946, were felt around the world.

Epilogue

Since the events recited above, the Supreme Court has passed through at least two historical cycles. The stimulating era of the Warren Court was on the horizon, or just crossing it, at the time of Jackson's death in 1954. Indeed, its initiating event was perhaps the May 17, 1954, decision in *Brown v. Board of Education of Topeka,* declaring an end to constitutionally sanctioned racial segregation in the public schools: the last great case on which Jackson deliberated. The Warren Court did not spend all its innovative energy, which derived no little from Hugo Black's past dissents, until the great political debacle of 1968. Lyndon Johnson was forced in that harried election year to withdraw his nomination of Justice Abe Fortas as Warren's successor. On a Court headed by Warren E. Burger and then by William Rehnquist, retrenchment in some areas has followed, and a period of diminishing political visibility for the Court. The second cycle since the days of the "nine young men" is well along, but has not yet played itself out.

Earl Warren was just beginning to assert his leadership when Jackson died. Warren gradually led the Court to a controversial eminence in the nation's political consciousness whose only modern parallel was the negative publicity that came to the Hughes Court when FDR taxed it as a relic of the horse-and-buggy age. Under Warren's stewardship the embers of judicial activism glowed again.

Justices, no matter what the era or the issue, will differ over the prudential and constitutional limits of judicial politics. This perduring tension lay at the heart of the 1946 feud. And while some, then and since, sought to reduce the quarrel to personal terms, it was genuine, involving genuine issues: judicial, political, and philosophical. One cannot discount the quirks of personal chemistry in such a clash. But the record, now as complete as it is ever likely to be, flies in the face of interpretations that overpersonalize or psychologize it. The Black-Jackson argument turned essentially on a profound difference over the standards of seemliness that justices must set for themselves and, above all, on a difference over the use of judicial power. That is the bedrock of the tale.

On the question of judicial activism, Robert Jackson had a carefully considered view, as well articulated as any philosophy of judging perhaps can be. It was born initially of Jackson's need to justify the Roosevelt court-packing plan—to the American public, to Congress, but beyond that to himself. A loyal and active American Bar Association member, Jackson took very seriously the proprieties and standards of the profession. An establishmentarian in this if not other respects, Jackson was shocked by some of Black's political associations, and by certain attitudes of Black's that seemed to him almost cavalier. Altogether they amounted to a substantially more political conception of the role of judges than Jackson could comfortably countenance—not that he himself took a simple-mindedly fundamentalist view of the issue.

Hugo Black, conversely, was by no means so keen as Jackson to justify his judicial style or attitudes before the bar of public opinion or history, supposing as he did that men are primarily governed by their personal biases and social prejudices and that even the light of history will be fitfully filtered and refracted by the favoritism of historians. There was in Black's approach to judging a certain serenity, almost a hauteur, derived in part from his historical views but also in part from the bitter scorn his onetime association with the Klan had brought him in the climate of 1937-38. Such detachment was as temperamentally foreign to Jackson as could be. He believed in explanation.

Indeed, the footsoldier for Franklin D. Roosevelt who had written *The Struggle for Judicial Supremacy* was still recognizable in the grizzled veteran who a few years later wrote long private memoranda on the Black controversy. One senses that Jackson was still striving to explain himself not only to others but to himself. If there was something of the eternal gamin in Black, there was something of the model student in Jackson.

This difference, I believe, largely accounts for the curious and unfortunate one-sidedness of the record on the celebrated "feud." With the largely inferential exceptions noted earlier, Hugo Black is not known to have bothered himself over Jackson's cannonade from Nuremberg. He could hardly help noticing; but he affected, at least, not to care very much, although someone in his chambers filled a large and imposing scrapbook with hundreds of press clippings on the controversy. If Black at any time had felt the "fiery scorn" Doris Fleeson reported, he masked it very well, or had banked the fires quickly. The dispute has been conventionally designated a "feud"; and the label stuck. But properly speaking, there must be at least two parties to a feud; and it was as if, in the great American prototype of the form, the Hatfields had blazed away while the McCoys sat silently in their redoubts.

As all his utterances show, even his prosecutorial addresses to the court at Nuremberg, Jackson was bemused by the issue of lawful accountability—and especially by the paradox of the judge's strong and in some ways unaccountable role in American democracy. An unelected institution in an essentially egalitarian nation, the Supreme Court exercises occasional but decisive vetos, even over decisions made under the best of democratic auspices and procedures. In one of his earliest Supreme Court opinions, his eloquent majority opinion in the second *Flag Salute* case, Jackson spoke pithily of this paradox: " . . . But we [the judges] act in these matters not by the authority of our competence but by the force of our commissions." Jackson was responding to Felix Frankfurter's powerful plea for judicial restraint, even in the face of a state law that seemed to him deeply pernicious. Jackson would play variations on this theme to the very end of his judicial career, whether reviewing Merlo Pusey's biography of Chief Justice Hughes for the *Washington Post* or writing his Godkin Lectures for the Harvard Graduate School of Public Administration on the very eve of his death. In these lectures, Jackson scorned the "vicious teaching" that the Court alone must be the bulwark of personal liberty in a coordinate system whose other branches, as well, must be presumed conscious of, competent to act upon, the issues of freedom.

Jackson's ideas on the accountability of power were undoubtedly enriched, and perhaps deepened, by what he saw and experienced at Nuremberg—not only the novel extension of international law attempted there but also the sordid postmortem on a civilized society in which criminals, thugs, and maniacs had gained the upper hand. Frankfurter, who often constituted himself an interpreter of Jackson to mutual friends, considered that this was so. "I so completely understand what made him do it," Frankfurter wrote of the cable from Nuremberg on June 27, 1946. "His year's experience," Frankfurter confided to Judge Learned Hand, "made him a deeper nature & more sensitive to the evil that acquiescence in skulduggery & bias & brutality brings upon the world." This was, of course, dramatic exaggeration.

Nastiness, some furtiveness, there was in the battle over labor policy and its repercussions on Jackson's fortunes. But they were a far cry from the brutality and evil limned and tried at Nuremberg.

*   *   *

The fierce debate over Lyndon Johnson's attempt, in 1968, to promote his friend Abe Fortas from associate to chief justice (and the later travails of William Rehnquist when his turn came to be promoted from within the Court) invite speculation about what might have happened if Truman, as he had first intended, had nominated Jackson as Stone's successor. In 1946, as has been said, there were those who considered that Jackson had overstepped the separation of powers by consenting to take on the job at Nuremberg, by any definition an executive post. Similarly, Fortas fell afoul of the same issue; and for a reason not without its amusing side. It was no secret in Washington that Fortas had often counseled Johnson unofficially about the war in Vietnam, as well as other issues. In fact, there was some jocular—and, it proved, ill-conceived—boasting about Fortas's two hats. In a *Who's Who* entry of the time, Fortas had flippantly listed as his business address 1600 Pennsylvania Avenue.

The joke lost its savor when the Senate hearings began. Fortas gravely pleaded, with reason, that it would abuse the separation of powers principle if the Senate examined not only his personal fitness, but also the whole fabric of Warren Court jurisprudence, in whose shaping Fortas had played a lively hand. From a strictly neutral perspective, the agenda of Fortas's conservative critics was to scrutinize and protest the work of the Warren Court, as well as incidentally to test Fortas's fitness. It was embarrassing. Fortas, having played Johnson's private counselor, could not easily draw his judicial robes about him and affect a new punctiliousness about the separation of powers.

It is unusual in the Court's history for a chief justice to be drawn from among the sitting associates; and there are those who think it should never be done. If Truman had appointed Jackson in 1946, it is all but certain that his mission to Nuremberg would have been held against him, as would have been his lawyering for Roosevelt in justification of the destroyers-for-bases deal with Britain in 1941. And as the Eastland-Bridges duet indicates, some senators would have been delighted to do a bit of general smashing up of the Court's innovative record. It is conceivable that Jackson was spared a nasty going-over when Truman passed him by.

Otherwise, Jackson's controversial adventure in Nuremberg was the last major extracurricular undertaking for a Supreme Court justice before Earl Warren, in 1963, assumed the chairmanship of the commission to investigate the John F. Kennedy assassination. That was a task into which by all accounts Johnson dragooned the reluctant chief justice. And there has been another substantial change. Supreme Court justices today are rarely if ever "mentioned" for elective office, as it was fairly common for them to be in Jackson's time.

As in 1945-46, however, judicial propriety continues today to be a lively issue. One discovery that helped to kill Fortas's nomination was that he had agreed to deliver four lucrative summertime law lectures at American University in Washington. The generous fee of ten thousand dollars for these lectures had been subscribed by wealthy friends and admirers of the justice who might at some time have business before the Court, and some of whom were clients of his former law firm. No corruption was insinuated. But as in the appearance of Crampton Harris before his old law partner Hugo Black, the appearances weren't quite as they should be.

A 1978 statute, the Ethics in Government Act, now requires for the first time that justices, with other high officials, disclose their financial assets. Early compliance forms showed that at least two justices, the late Potter Stewart and Lewis Powell (who later retired in 1987) had substantial stock and bond holdings. It was soon argued, as a result of these disclosures, that a more complete system of disclosure and recusal was needed to assure that hidden financial interests did not affect, and were not seen to affect, judicial decisions. In response, the Court adopted a new rule (28.1) which requires that petitions and briefs submitted by corporations reveal all parents, affiliates and subsidiaries, so that justices and their law clerks may be aware of potential conflicts of interest.

* * *

That leaves, finally, the ever-fresh issue of judicial activism. The issue—and the vice, if it be a vice—seems inescapable, so long as justices must exercise personal judgment in choices that elude absolute deductive certainty. (There was once a "yardstick" theory of judging, when the words of the Constitution or statutes were thought to yield one and only one permissible meaning; but it vanished long ago.)

As Judge Robert Bork has well said in his distinguished and amusing Francis Boyer Lecture, an appellate judge in the American system must use the elite power conferred on him ("by the force of our commissions") discreetly, if only out of prudent concern to preserve judicial authority for the important challenges. Yet once one leaves constitutional issues and enters the shadowy arena of statutory interpretation or administrative policy (often the most heated and contentious of all), the footing can be very tricky. Judges will often discover ways, consciously or not, to intrude their preferences into policy, although they usually will take care to dress that intrusion in the respectable garb of jurisprudential theory, sometimes not without self-deception.

Among the many distinguishing marks that made Hugo Black an extraordinary judge, a considerable place would have to be given to his open disdain for the game of jurisprudential theorizing—whether of the natural law variety or of the crafting of fine-spun rationales that tend to dominate law review articles. In trying to thrust oneself into Black's frame of mind, even a skeptic of judicial activism may find himself beguiled by the sweep of Black's view, and half persuaded (at least).

The Black-Jackson clash was an instance of the unending debate over activism, by all odds the noisiest and most spectacular, engaging the most interesting minds and pens, in the history of the Court. There have been canings on the floor of the Senate, and equivalent indignities at the White House. There are no other such episodes in the annals of the Court. The debate over the business of judges in the thickets of politics is a struggle that continues in many forms, though less visibly and with less intensity, every day in every era. And it continues, one may suppose, because it reflects a permanent tension not only in great appellate courts but in the minds of men. One may view oneself, as Hugo Black did, as a messenger of historical change or as a patron of the underdog, drawing boldness from the thought that without vigorous and directed change no society can stand or preserve its institutions. Or one may take it as a nearly sacred duty, as Jackson did, to protect the Court's and the law's institutional claims against the buffeting of raw political energies, drawing confidence from the thought that without institutional self-discipline those energies can level in a minute what it took years to build. The argument, the tension, is ever old and ever new, and ever unsettled. It may also be inescapable in a working judiciary that matters as much as the U.S. Supreme Court.

Notes

BLACK V. JACKSON: A STUDY IN JUDICIAL ENMITY. Based on documents (see below) available at the Library of Congress, Washington, D. C. The author wishes to thank the following persons: The family of Robert Jackson and the late Elizabeth D. Black for permission to consult the respective papers of the two justices; David Wigdor and the staff of the Manuscript Division of the Library of Congress, and Penny Hazleton, Anne Ashmore and others of the staff of the Supreme Court Library, Washington, D. C.; The Hon. William Rehnquist, chief justice of the United States and The Hon. Lewis F. Powell, associate justice (retired), the U.S. Supreme Court; and many others for sharing their impressions with me, including: Prof. A. E. Dick Howard, The Hon. J. Harvie Wilkinson III, Prof. Walter Dellinger, Robert W. Spearman, William Joslin, Prof. Eugene Gressman, Dan Boorstin, Barrett Prettyman, Jr., David McKenzie Clark, John Kester. I am alone responsible for the views and judgments expressed in the study.

Page 3: The collapse of Chief Justice Stone is described in detail in Lewis Wood's dispatch, *New York Herald Tribune*, April 24.

Page 4: " . . . a cheerful man . . . " Vivid personal impressions of Jackson are rare, but he was well liked. See Jonathan Daniels, "The Battle of the Bench," *Collier*'s magazine, August 17, 1946: "Off the bench Jackson has a bright eye and a gay manner." Arthur Schlesinger, Jr., "The Supreme Court: 1947," *Fortune*, 35, 1: " . . . 54 years old, [Jackson] is another complex character, winning in manner, intellectually vivacious and even cocky . . . the best writer on the Court but given to playing with ideas rather than possessing them." The latter eccentric judgment was not widely shared.

Page 4: " . . . the primary suspect . . . " Daniels, loc. cit.: "Black is lean

97

and grim and his rare smile comes slowly, like the rising smoke of his incessant cigarettes. . . . He looks like a determined zealot." In the same article, Daniels, who served as White House press secretary to both Roosevelt and Truman, recalls Gen. Hugh Johnson's comment when Black's former Ku Klux Klan membership was revealed: that Black was "a born witch-burner—narrow, prejudiced and class-conscious." But "Ironpants" Johnson was not widely noted for discernment.

Page 5: " . . . a seat that Robert Jackson had long had his eye on . . . " In the Columbia Oral History Interviews, Jackson recalled several cursory conversations with FDR about Supreme Court vacancies. Soon after the retirement of Chief Justice Hughes, Roosevelt told Jackson that he was inclined to appoint Stone. Jackson recalled responding: "Mr. President, if you feel disposed to appoint Stone . . . that's perfectly satisfactory. If you were going to appoint a New Dealer . . . anyone other than Stone—then I think my claims would be entitled to consideration." Roosevelt, according to Jackson, responded: "So do I. I think they'd be unanswerable."

Page 5: " . . . arguments about taxes on golf green fees . . . " Philip Kurland, "Robert Jackson," in *Justices of the United States Supreme Court*, p. 2564.

Page 10: " . . . took delight in being known . . . as a maverick . . . " Jackson had opposed U.S. involvement in World War I as a "conscientious objector."

Page 11: " . . . pretended to believe that Jackson had the job in his pocket . . . " See personal narrative, Jackson Papers, Library of Congress, p. 6: "It was Jackson's misfortune to go upon the Court with its members believing that President Roosevelt had promised him the Chief Justiceship upon the retirement of Stone. . . . What matters at this point is that it was accepted as fact by his colleagues. . . . "

Page 11: " . . . stories whispered to his discredit . . . " Jackson was especially annoyed by the false tale that he had threatened to resign from the Court if someone else were appointed chief justice—possibly a confusion with his offer to resign when the prosecutor's job at Nuremberg detained him abroad.

Page 12: "Douglas had complained . . . " See William O. Douglas, *The Court Years*, pp. 28 ff.: "I thought at the time [Jackson] accepted the job that it was a gross violation of separation of powers to put a justice in charge of an executive function. . . . If Bob did that, he should resign."

Page 12: " . . . But he was talking . . . " Douglas denies (ibid., p. 29) that he worked against Jackson's appointment as chief justice, which he declares, in the face of considerable evidence, Truman had never seriously considered. His denial is evasive: " . . . Truman never broached this matter to either of us [that is,himself or Black] and neither of us sent any message to Truman." Others, including both Felix Frankfurter and Harold Ickes in their diaries, identify Douglas as pursuing the fight against Jackson's appointment through other channels, even if he did not speak directly to Truman.

Page 14: " . . . the real leader of the Court's judicial activists . . . " See Jackson, Personal Narrative, Jackson Papers, Library of Congress, pp. 2 ff.: "Soon after I went on the Court I discovered that I was in the midst of a struggle for power and a political atmosphere the like of which I had never experienced even in the President's cabinet. . . . [Black] regarded himself as the senior Roosevelt appointee, and in a Court where seniority is accorded considerable weight he expected to be the leader of the Roosevelt appointees."

Page 14: " . . . the political convictions of Black . . . " Ibid., pp. 3 ff.: "I had come to the Court from a New Deal atmosphere, but I was shocked to find that Black was far to the left of anything that I had associated with the New Deal. He was one of those liberals with no background in liberalism. . . . " There is textual evidence that this first person narrative of the "feud," written in 1947 or 1948, was more spontaneous in its judgments, as it was more direct and outspoken, than the later more refined versions.

Page 14: " . . . whatever dues were asked . . . " Jackson, op. cit. (III), p. 4: "Membership in the Democratic Party in Alabama was a stepping stone to office and favor; in upstate New York it was a stone tied around the neck, a disqualification for office or power. The Democratic Party was useful to Black, as was the Ku Klux Klan; but to Jackson it held out no promise and his friends and clients regarded his stubborn adherence to it as an eccentricity . . . Herein is a key to a striking contrast in the two men." (Though cast in the third person, the account was undoubtedly written by Jackson.)

Page 15: " . . . He liked to tell friends . . . " In the Jackson Papers, there is a copy, scored in pencil, of a Fred Rodell article in which Rodell reported Black's boasting to friends that the ABA was the only organization he regretted joining. Jackson, mildly scandalized, makes a point of the story elsewhere in his personal recollections of differences with Black.

Page 16: " . . . Black had stiffly protested . . . " See Memo from Black, May 5, 1945, Jackson Papers, Library of Congress: " . . . My remarks were made with reference to a Bill which was entirely different to the Bill finally adopted. . . . If the dissent goes down as now printed, it will not be a fair representation of the true facts."

Page 20: " . . . The difficulty and complexity of the task" "Confusion, erratic leadership and inefficiency plagued the chief of counsel's office from first day to last . . . " Bradley Smith, *The Road to Nuremberg*, New York, 1981.

Page 21: "The Jackson convoy twisted . . . " Robert E. Conot, *Justice at Nuremberg*, New York, 1983, p. 20.

Page 21: " . . . in a roomy house . . . ": William E. Jackson to his mother, September 21, 1945. Family Correspondence, Robert H. Jackson Papers, Library of Congress.

Page 22: " . . . a different difficulty with Dr. Schacht" Conot, op. cit., pp. 400 ff.

Page 23: " . . . a watching brief" Francis M. Shea to Jackson, May 17, 1946, Jackson Papers, Library of Congress.

Page 23: "Shea's appraisal tallied . . . " Joseph and Stewart Alsop, "Truman in Dilemma Choosing Chief Justice," *New York Herald Tribune,* May 18, 1946.

Page 24: " . . . one explosive dose . . . " Doris Fleeson, "Supreme Court Feud," *Washington Evening Star,* May 16, 1946.

Page 28: On the labor-management strife, see Robert J. Donovan, *Conflict and Crisis: The Presidency of Harry S Truman, 1945-48*, New York, 1977, p. 163.

Page 29: " . . . divisions within organized labor . . . " Jackson's Columbia Oral History Interview, 1952-53, Marked Jackson 1412, Jackson Papers, Library of Congress. According to Jackson, Postmaster General Robert Hannegan had tried to persuade him to appoint "a man of his choice as my top assistant at Nuremberg" and Jackson had declined. Hannegan was an influential opponent of the Jackson promotion to chief justice. See Edwin A. Lahey, Chicago Daily News Service dispatch in *Washington Evening Star* (undated): "The opposition to the promotion . . . was shared by Postmaster General Hannegan and his labor friends, particularly Philip Murray. . . . Mr. Hannegan did oppose Justice Jackson in talks with President Truman."

Page 30: Hughes at the White House: *New York Times*, April 30th.

Page 31: According to the Alsops, op. cit., Schwellenbach had "all but fallen sick of desire" when he heard of the Court vacancy.

Page 31: Krock prediction: Arthur Krock, *New York Times*, April 25: "The president admires [Vinson] unreservedly; Mr. Vinson is popular in Congress; he is only 62 years old and other judges have a high regard for his record as a member of the Federal Court of Appeals . . . "

Page 32: " . . . three historians of the Court . . . " Transcript, University of Chicago Round Table, 578th broadcast, March 25, 1945.

Page 35: Minton to Black, June 12, 1946. Hugo L. Black Papers, Library of Congress.

Page 36: Stone's administration of the Court: John P. Frank, "Harlan F. Stone: An Estimate" (reviewing and quoting Alpheus T. Mason's biography of Stone), *Stanford Law Review*, 9, (May 1957).

Page 38: " . . . dirty business . . . ": Frankfurter to Charles C. Burlingham, May 16, Felix Frankfurter Papers, Library of Congress, Box 35.

Page 40: Frank to Black, April 30, 1946. Hugo L. Black Papers, Library of Congress, Box 460.

Page 41: The vivid personal details on Vinson are in Fred Rodell, "The Chief Justice," *Life* magazine 20.25 (June 24, 1947).

Page 49: Hugo Black Jr.'s recollection, Hugo Black Jr.: *My Father: A Reminiscence*, New York, 1975, p. 191. Felix Frankfurter—admittedly a hostile witness—records in his diary (Box 2, Library of Congress, October 20, 1946) a conversation with the historian Arthur Schlesinger, Jr., who was writing his article on the Court for *Fortune* magazine. Schlesinger reported that Black had said he made it a practice never to talk to anyone about the Court. "I did not tell Arthur Schlesinger that that of course is not true, that in the company . . . of partisans of his he talked with considerable freedom to get his self-righteous interpretation of his actions into circulation."

Page 50: " . . . the unmasking of a bad man": Black to Charles Luce, June 15, 1946. Black to Frank, June 19. Hugo Black Papers, Library of Congress, Box 61.

Page 50: Black to Minton, June 15, 1946.

Page 52: Marquis Childs, "The Supreme Court Today," *Harper's* magazine, May 1938: "It is as though, a comparatively inexperienced player, he had stepped into a fast game . . . and, ignoring the rules, made vigorous passes at every ball with a piece of board." Childs recalled the incident, and Black's displeasure, in his column "The State of the Nation" at the time of the feud. One of Justice Black's former law clerks recalls that Black often mentioned the *Harper's* article, even years later.

Page 53: " . . . splitting the Court in two . . . " Virginia Van Der Veer Hamilton, *Hugo Black: The Alabama Years* (Baton Rouge, 1972), p. 262 (citing Black to Roosevelt, January 28, 1937): " . . . [Black] also suggested to Roosevelt that, except on constitutional matters, the high court be separated into two divisions to decide cases, with the chief justice sitting on each. Two more justices might be added . . . he proposed, because nine men made a 'wholly inadequate number' . . . " The intent and possible impact of such a division of the Court is unclear, unless the aim was to segregate constitutional from statutory interpretation.

Page 54: Black's view on the inveterate bias of historians: I am deeply indebted to the Hon. Robert M. Warner, former archivist of the United States, for passing to me a copy of a memorandum of his and Sidney Fine's interview with Black on October 21-22, 1964 ("A Report, Michigan Historical Collections, The University of Michigan," mimeographed typescript): "Black . . . soon launched into a discussion of his views on the writing of history—historians in general—the use of personal papers, in this particular case, Supreme Court justices' papers. Historians are always biased, he felt, and write from the perspective of their own environment. He cited, for example, two ancient historians, Tacitus and Livy, whom he admired as great historians, but felt presented the bias of the class from which they came. He referred to Livy as being the David Lawrence of his time in writing the point of view of the Aristocracy. Although he claimed to enjoy history and to read history widely, he took a dim view of the historian and many of his practices. He objected, for example, to the historian's attempt to determine motivation of an individual, saying that this was virtually impossible and perhaps of no great consequence . . . He conveyed the idea that there were areas about public figures—historical figures—that shouldn't be explored historically. . . . He said jokingly, but with great sincerity, that his criterion for judging whether an opinion of a fellow justice was good or bad, was whether it agreed with his own . . . "

Page 55: "Black had warned . . . ": Memo "to the members of the conference," May 5, 1945, Black Papers, Library of Congress.

Page 56: Hamilton, op. cit., p. 169, notes Black's unsuccessful opposition to Hopkins' confirmation as a federal judge. As attorney general of Kansas he had fired district attorneys who refused to prosecute striking miners for vagrancy.

Page 57: The Eastland-Bridges proposals and arguments are reported in *The Congressional Record*, vol. 92, 79th Congress, Second Session, pp. 6771-8090.

Page 60: " . . . not all so flamboyantly as John O'Donnell": O'Donnell, *Washington Times-Herald*, July 3.

Page 64: " . . . a rare public statement": *Baltimore Sun*, June 13, Hugo Black Papers, 531.

Page 64: " . . . a small dinner party": Harold L. Ickes Diary, Library of Congress, entry of Saturday August 3, p. 12.

Page 64: "Vinson had been sworn in . . . " See Edward Folliard report, *Washington Post*, June 25; also Felix Belair, *New York Times*, same date.

Page 66: "an important talk": Drew Pearson, "Jackson Back to Normal," *Philadelphia Public Record*, September 10, 1946.

Page 67: Harold Burton Diary, Library of Congress, entry for October 10, 1946.

Page 68: "all ease and good humor": Felix Frankfurter Diaries, entry of October 27, 1946. "Like a new girl . . . "; ibid., November 4; "Old boy, you don't know . . . " November 22.

Page 69: Ickes shocked: Ickes Diary, Library of Congress, Reel 7.

Page 69: "a capital blunder": See typed narrative dated January 7, 1947 in "Coal Cases" file, Jackson Papers, Library of Congress, page 6: "The Jackson cable badly missed its mark. The public then saw nothing of what it now sees as to the nation-wide gravity of the real issues between the men . . . The vital thing in this cable was almost completely overlooked." The narrative, one of several Jackson prepared on the controversy with Black, is in the third person and was confidentially sent for comment to Felix Frankfurter. Jackson's narratives are an indispensable source for his attitudes toward Black and the roots of the quarrel. I have drawn on them heavily in characterizing Jackson's view of the dispute.

Page 70: An engaging account of the Agronsky-Sevareid interview is given in Elizabeth Black, "Hugo Black: A Memorial Portrait," in the 1982 yearbook of the Supreme Court Historical Society, pp. 72-94.

Page 71: " . . . When a private correspondent . . . ": Black to Max Goldstein, December 11, 1968, Black Papers, Library of Congress, Box 491.

Page 73: " . . . either Douglas or Reed . . . ": Black to Frank, December 4, 1948: Black Papers, Library of Congress, Box 460.

Page 75: Arthur Schlesinger, Jr., "Supreme Court," *Fortune,* January 1947.

Page 78: Murphy and the General Motors Strike: William Manchester: *The Glory and the Dream: A Narrative History of America, 1932-72* (New York 1974).

Page 80: " . . . a curious incident": Typed transcript of telephone conversation between Eugene Gerhardt and Harlan Phillips, Friday October 29, 1954. Jackson Papers, Library of Congress.

Page 82: " . . . You don't know how it was injected . . . " Frankfurter to Jackson, undated, responding to Jackson's "Coal Cases" narrative. Jackson Papers, Library of Congress.

Page 84: " . . . I now have a majority . . . " Memo, Frank Murphy to Black: Black Papers, Library of Congress, Box 278 "Correspondence with Other Justices" Folder, October Term 1945.

Page 85: " . . . beneath the crust of the earth." Majority opinion of Mr. Justice Murphy, Jewell Ridge Coal Corp. v. Local #6167 United Mine Workers of America, et al. 325 U.S. 161.

Page 90: " . . . a substantially more political conception of the role of judges . . . " Frankfurter's view of Black paralleled Jackson's. In a letter to Judge Learned Hand, he calls Black "a self-righteous, self-deluded, part-fanatic, part demagogue, who really disbelieves in law, thinks it is essentially manipulation of language." His "best brain of the lot," Frankfurter continued, was "an instrument for supporting a predetermined result." H. N. Hirsch, *The Enigma of Felix Frankfurter*, p. 182.

Page 92: " . . . reviewing Merlo Pusey's biography . . . " In a preliminary draft of the review, which eventually appeared in the *Post* on November 18, Jackson writes: " . . . But the attitude which Hughes consistently exhibited toward the judicial office was perhaps more significant than any decision he wrote . . . As Chief Justice he forsook all else for the labors of the Court. He ceased every association, appearance or actuality that might suggest political interests or unsatisfied ambitions. He rebuffed . . . advances designed to draw him into consultations . . . " Hughes, he continues, was a stickler for judicial formalities "not because of any exaggerated valuation of what intrinsically were trifles but because . . . a lifetime in and before courts had taught him that the public can judge the inward and undisclosed qualities of the judicial process only from outward and visible signs." Jackson's characterization of Hughes' attitudes seems in large part to reflect his own.

Page 92: " . . . I so completely understand . . . " Frankfurter to Hand, June 27, 1946.

II

The Unmaking of a Whig

1. The Unmaking of a Whig

In the summer of 1956 I was preparing to go off to read history at Oxford. One day there came a note in the mail from my prospective tutor, the distinguished Renaissance historian John Hale, with a list of recommended preliminary reading. One of the books was Herbert Butterfield's *The Whig Interpretation of History,* a title unfamiliar to me. I borrowed it from the university library at Chapel Hill and devoured it at a gulp. Since that day it has been a defining influence in my life and work.

I want to convey a sense of why that book was, and remains, so very important for me, and then say something about the text and why I believe it might serve as a guide for us all.

But a prefatory word or two about that key word, "Whig." Most of us remember it from English history. The Whigs made and supported the Glorious Revolution of 1688 in England—the ouster of the last Stuart king, James II, and his replacement by William of Orange and his consort Mary. In the history of the English-speaking peoples, this was perhaps the decisive transition from arbitrary to limited government and from oppression to liberty—at least as "Whig" historians depict it. Supposedly—the real story was undoubtedly more complicated—this revolution ushered in an era of unfolding individual freedom, the development of parliamentary and democratic institutions, and the end of the divine-right government which the less prudent of the Stuarts had claimed as the foundation of monarchy. By extension, Whigs were the great progressives who viewed history as a story of developing tolerance, progress, and personal liberty. By further extension, those historians who defended the 1688 revolution and its sequel—including some of the great names in English historical writing, from Lord Macaulay to Hugh Trevor-Roper—came to be known as "Whig historians"; and the term, as we shall see, gradually acquired a far larger meaning than it began with. But with that reminder, on to Herbert Butterfield's text and what it teaches.

*   *   *

The fact of my being an American, growing up at a particular time and place, surely had much to do with the impact of Butterfield's little book on me. By the time I was beginning to reach adulthood—I turned eighteen in 1952— this really had begun to look a bit like what the Luce magazines liked to call it: "The American Century." We had won a great world war on two fronts and designed a generous if troubled peace. Our wealth, power, and influence were unrivaled. And while the times were hardly tranquil—this was the era of the domestic political nastiness called McCarthyism—a young American had every inducement to view the great past as a prolonged overture to this happy hour of American power and benevolence.

The history textbooks we read and studied did little to counter that assumption. In recent years a school of skeptical, even querulous, historians have scorned the history we read back then as "consensus history": history too deeply colored by a complacent faith that the main themes of our past had been unity and harmony. Indeed, the historical process looked very much like a steady upward march with the United States in the forefront, over which unseen forces of justice and rectitude presided. "Progress" was the natural, nearly automatic, product of all contention and strife. Americans, it is fair to say, are natural Whigs. I suggest nothing metahistorical—no mysterious Hegelian rhythms, merely an expansive confidence that the accumulating forces of modernity—science and government by consent and tolerance—had vanquished superstition, tyranny, and bigotry. A broadening enlightenment, rooted in the Renaissance, energized by the Protestant Reformation, confirmed by the Age of Reason, was ascendant. All the earlier revolutions—our own in 1776 and the English revolution of 1688 before it, and even the early and moderate stages of the French Revolution—not only represented success of a sort; they had been vindicated by what followed. History as we knew it seemed a great bank account of justification on which the present might continue to draw. The result was a tremendous belief in our own benevolence and example. The prospect we held up to the world was memorably expressed by a Midwestern senator who proclaimed: "We will lift Shanghai up and up, ever up, until it is just like Kansas City!"

To be sure, this sense of things had been reinforced by the outcome of World War II, in which something like eternal justice was seen to have prevailed. Hitler and Nazism had come as close to absolute evil as history might offer. They had been gloriously vanquished. The side-effects—the growth of a new Soviet empire in Eastern Europe, for instance—might seem to dampen the sense of achievement. But history of the kind we read and studied seldom seemed to weigh up balances of gains and losses; history was essentially a no-lose game.

Imagine, then, that into this Eden of complacency

someone powerfully insinuates the notion that history has offices and duties other than the mindless ratification of outcomes—the proclamation, as in that wonderful book of historical parody, *1066 And All That,* that most things that happen are "good things" merely because they happened. Imagine a compelling assertion that it is our duty to look with sympathy and detachment and even understanding on the losers and even the great villains of the past, even when they seem by our lights benighted and wicked; that a more careful scrutiny of lost causes might be more than an exercise in sentimentality; that getting inside the minds and hearts of those who had obstructed or resisted the coming of the virtuous present might enrich both our understanding of history and our understanding of ourselves.

This was the immediate message of *The Whig Interpretation of History* as I remember experiencing it then; and it came with the force of revelation. It may seem surprising that something so obvious should strike as a thunderbolt. What I am talking about here, however, is not knowledge of the cognitive sort but knowledge of the heart, the kind that penetrates to the intuitive level and alters our temperaments. It was certainly a truism of every elementary class in intellectual history—already familiar to me—that our Western, postclassical idea of time—linear time—represented a revolution in the apprehension of now and then, past and future. There had been much longer epochs—the era in which the biblical Book of Ecclesiastes was written obviously was one—when the idea of cumulative progress so central to the "Whig" view of history would have seemed an absurdity, if indeed it could have been grasped at all. For far longer than we had thought of events as moving ever forward and upward, or building upon one another, men had believed in cycles of revolving time and ever-returning epochs. But reading Butterfield, with his rich warnings against the treacherously narrow perspective of the moment, gave new intuitive life to one's grasp of all this.

Moreover—and this is a bit more personal—the effect on a southerner was in due course peculiarly intense. However valid it might be for America generally, the doctrine of steady and inevitable progress obviously did not fit the facts of the southern past; quite the contrary. C. Vann Woodward, even as I was first reading Butterfield, was explaining with matchless point and eloquence the essential difference:

> An age-long experience with human bondage and its evils and later with emancipation and its shortcomings did not dispose the South very favorably toward such popular American ideas as the doctrine of human perfectibility, the belief that every evil has a cure, and the notion that every human problem has a solution. . . . In that most optimistic of centuries in the most optimistic part of the world, the South remained basically pessimistic in its social outlook and its moral philosophy. The experience of evil and the experience of tragedy are parts of the Southern heritage that are as difficult to reconcile with the American legend of innocence and social felicity as the experience of poverty and defeat are to reconcile with the legends of abundance and success.

Did southerners need to learn these things out of a book? To some degree we did; for we were not immune, even in the South, even with its tragic sense, to the boosterish spirit of modern America. Notwithstanding the impressions one might gather from Tennessee Williams plays or Faulkner novels, these undoubted distinctions of regional tempera-ment are not implanted—or at least brought to a level of self-consciousness—by the experience of growing up south-ern. It isn't until someone like Vann Woodward holds up the magic mirror that, gazing into it, we suddenly understand our heritage and see it in some superior and, I must admit pleasing, sense as literally un-American.

* * *

Here, in any case, was material for a view of the past and present that soon came to seem to me immeasurably deeper and truer to human experience than the giddy progressivist myth of American or world history that we were too often fed in the sunny world of my boyhood. Here was a view that daubed shadows into the landscape, that chimed with the warnings of Reinhold Niebuhr about the ironies of history. Here, commended to our reflection, was a sense of the universal communion of struggle, loss, and despair, and its own unesteemed honors and laurels, as well as victory, gain, and the pursuit of happiness. So it was that this little essay, a mere 132 pages in the standard edition, easily read in a couple of hours, became a sort of initiation for me.

II

I deliberately wrote the foregoing words—a groping for lost time and lost impressions—before rereading the text. I wanted to see how closely my lingering impressions, my estimate of the book's initial force, tallied with what it actually said. Inevitably, as with all powerful influences, the memory of the text—the ghostly grin of the Cheshire cat—differs from the animal itself. So now, in this second of three steps, I move to confront the text itself.

What strikes me today is that *The Whig Interpretation of History* is in the first place much more distinctly a historian's book than it had seemed to me at first reading. It deals extensively with issues of historical interpretation that have intrigued and divided historians since Ranke's day. Among them, the first and greatest is the issue of moral judgment upon the scenes and actors of the past, which is of course inseparably linked to moral judgment about the present and about ourselves. And we are ourselves involved. My close friend and mentor, John M. Evans, has offered this brilliant observation about the "Whig" problem in history:

> . . . The simplest version of Butterfield's argument drifts toward *tout comprendre, c'est tout pardonner.* . . . And to some extent the Rochefoucauld maxim is true. But the main point, surely, is that in looking at the past— history—we can't arrive at the real past (whatever that would mean), but are organizing and systematizing our sense of the present. . . . We are selecting or focusing on those elements of the "past" which we are willing to face in our own times; hence, the selectivity of the Marxist or whatever. The trouble with "Whig" historicism is that it suppresses any honest acknowledgment that we make of the past what we will to see it as; consequently we are left free to thrust upon the past, really project or displace upon it, what we wish to disown.

This persistent issue had had a classic formulation in Lord Acton's famous "Inaugural Lecture on the Study of History," delivered at Cambridge (Herbert Butterfield's university) on June 11, 1895, thirty-six years before Butterfield wrote. Reading Acton's lecture today, we are acutely conscious that Lord Acton was above all a great Gladstonian liberal, one of those whom the Grand Old Man could rouse and rally with thunderous orations upon the iniquities of the Turks and others; and that much of this passion was carried over into his view of the function of historical training and, consequently, his advice to young historians. There was, for instance, his memorable exhortation " . . . never to debase the moral currency or . . . lower the standards of rectitude; but to try others by the final maxim that governs your own lives, and to suffer no man and no cause to escape the undying penalty which history has the power to inflict on wrong." There was the passionate assault on those "who set up the principle that only a foolish conservative judges the present time with the ideas of the past; that only a foolish liberal judges the past with the ideas of the present."

When Acton was inaugurated regius professor of history, the profession was still very young. Most of its development, including the founding of the major journals and associations, was very recent—mid- to late nineteenth century. Before that, in England and America certainly, and to some degree on the continent, history had been principally the calling of gentleman amateurs viewing their craft as a branch of narrative literature—more closely allied to the novel and the personal memoir than to "scientific" examination of the past. Their judgments, to the extent that they were in the least calculated or self-conscious, might be right or wrong, documented or undocumented, magisterial or partisan, liberal or conservative; but they were neither systematic nor "scientific." It was the Germans, led by Ranke, who set out to equip historical study with techniques for the close study of documents, to strip the craft of glibness and partisanship and historians of their common propensity to play moralists and hanging judges. For Acton, the state to which historians of the Ranke school had brought history was deeply unsatisfactory and even dangerous. The duty of judgment needed restoring. Otherwise, who would keep straight the moral accounts of the past? After all, as Acton himself memorably said, not only does power tend to corrupt; "all great men are bad men."

In many ways Butterfield's book must now be seen—as it was perhaps intended to be seen—as a direct if delayed response to the admonitions of his distinguished predecessor, one of two "Whig historians" actually mentioned by name. It is usually agreed (not that it was ever much of a secret) that the "Whig historian" pilloried by Butterfield is the moralistic and judgmental historian Acton called for—if not Lord Acton himself.

By Butterfield's account—and we must bear in mind that in the inexact sciences labels can be as treacherous as they are useful—the Whig historian is one who never shrinks from applying the standards of the present to the past; whose consideration of the great dilemmas and struggles of the past is deeply colored by present-mindedness and the blind spots and filters it imposes. The Whig historian sees the past not as a province having its own integrity and otherness, but as a source of the "origins" of enlightened or praiseworthy features of the present day.

Butterfield has been described by a not entirely admiring colleague as a "tough and highly serious Yorkshire Methodist" with a "well-cultivated moral tone (which had) grown more righteous with the years." It may be thought odd, perhaps, that a high-minded Yorkshire Methodist would inveigh so memorably against moralizing judgments in history. It is in fact conceivable that *The Whig Interpretation of History* began as an essay in self-correction. In any event, Butterfield was then and later deeply concerned with religion and morals; and it is surely more than coincidence that he draws most of his examples of Whiggish fallacies from the historical writing about that great watershed, the Reformation, and its greatest instigator, Martin Luther.

Butterfield suggests that the Whig historian commits the great fallacy of viewing religious toleration—which we see as a great stride forward in history—as the "product" of the Reformation. In fact, Butterfield argues, it is easier to imagine that a more generous religious toleration might have emerged in the course of things from Renaissance humanism than from the revivalist zeal that followed the Lutheran purification of the church. It is, he believes, a safer speculation that toleration really sprang from the realization that a state could find itself harboring two or more irreconcilable versions of the same religion, each of which views the other as a hellish heresy, but neither of which has the power to extirpate the other without incurring costs so cruel, bloody, and extravagant as to mock and discredit both. But this is a proximate point; the ultimate point, directed again to the correction of Whiggish interpretations of history, is that history is more often the study of "mediations" (how things happen) than of "origins" (what *causes* them to happen).

Butterfield's second major point is that the Whig historian too slavishly follows Lord Acton's advice. He makes facile moral judgments as to who was right and who was wrong, who was good and who was evil; and these judgments are apt to skew or hide historical truth. In his zeal to have the last word, to proclaim the argument-settling "lessons" of history, the Whig historian denies sympathy to those who need it most: the losers, the reactionaries who resisted changes that time has ratified. "Behind all the fallacies of the Whig historian," he writes, "there lies the passionate desire to come to a judgment of values, to make history answer questions and decide issues and to give the historian the last word in a controversy."

The historian, Butterfield insists, must not exceed his competence. It is within that competence to say how a moral principle influenced some great actor. It is harder to judge the resulting behavior right or wrong under the aspect of eternity.

It may seem strange that a historian so keenly interested in moral judgment in history should so aggressively urge caution in exercising it—at least in its more facile forms; odd that such a moralist would scorn "the luxury and pleasing sensuousness of moral indignation." But what a wonderfully exact term! For indignation is often luxurious; and its indulgence does offer sensuous pleasure. It is the sordid pleasure that one noted Whig historian, Lord Macaulay, found repellent when he said there is "nothing so disgusting as the British public in one of its periodic fits of moral indignation." (No slouch at historical moralizing himself, he failed to see the irony of the remark.)

The answer to the riddle lies, I believe, in Butterfield's sense of the overwhelming importance and solemnity of historical justice—so vital, indeed, that (heeding the scriptural injunction on vengeance) it probably should be confided in the difficult cases to God himself. It is certainly not to be cheapened by historians handing out the equivalent of ten-dollar parking and speeding tickets and reducing historical judgment to the mundane level of the magistrate court's fine.

III

Finally and in closing, I return to the implications of this great essay for me, and for us all.

You may find yourself wondering whether *The Whig Interpretation of History* is really of any great consequence for those who are not professional historians. But I am no professional historian, and if I believed that Butterfield's lessons were restricted to the technical craft of historical writing, I would not write about it in these terms.

In his notable memoir *North toward Home,* Willie Morris recalls his first Oxford history tutorial—on the Reform Act of 1832:

> I had stayed up straight through one fog-filled night applying the finishing touches. My next-to-last sentence said, "Just how close the people of England came to revolution in 1832 is a question that we shall leave with the historians." I read this to my tutor, and from his vantage point in an easy chair two feet north of the floor he interrupted: "But Morris, we *are* the historians."

There is an impression—perhaps even among those of us who indulge occasionally in the formal study of history— that what historians do has little likeness or relevance to the judgments that you and I make in our workaday world. Oh, we might echo a few received platitudes—Santayana's dubious suggestion that those who do not remember history are condemned to repeat it or Charles A. Beard's distillation of history's lesson to the banal proposition that "the mills of the gods grind slow, but exceedingly fine." Otherwise, however, we are usually content to leave historical judgment calls to historians, as my friend Morris proposed to do. But the impression that historical judgment is something only specialists exercise is far from completely true. It is true in some ways but false in others; and the ways in which it is false are much the more important. Historians usually enjoy perspective, which is the defining characteristic of true history (as distinguished from journalism, say); and good historians are trained in special methods of analysis—of documents, memoirs, oral testimony and other forms of material evidence—as ordinary lay students of past and present may not be. But in the last analysis we no less than they attempt to construct coherent and plausible versions of the past, selective as to detail and judgmental as to what is or isn't significant. Otherwise we can have no sure sense of our individual or social bearings in time, or of national or religious identity.

So we all exercise such judgments; and to paraphrase a famous remark of Keynes: Practical men who believe themselves to be altogether exempt from historical judgment are often the slaves of some defunct historian.

What Butterfield's essay still says to me, with undiminished force, is how hard it is in the realm of affairs to make just and useful judgments. They are both inevitable and indispensable; but they are always problematical.

Indeed, one of the chief public vices of our time, in our

public discourse and often in my own trade of journalism, is an aggressive and superficial moralism. Often the results are perverse. By an effect familiar to all the great interpreters of our nature from Dante to Tolstoy, the actual result of this glib and promiscuous moralizing about political and social behavior (even as Butterfield anticipated) is less to sustain high standards of public behavior than to trivialize and debase them.

I think, for instance, of the recent Waldheim case. It was discovered not long before he was elected president of Austria that as a young Wehrmacht lieutenant the former United Nations secretary general had had guilty knowledge of German atrocities in the Balkans. He had served as a young officer in a unit implicated in the deportation of Greek Jews from Salonika. He was obviously not proud of this part of his past; and he sought for a long time to conceal and prettify it. Since more of the truth has emerged, many of my colleagues—and not they alone—have been quick to condemn Waldheim's behavior. The condemnation, if duly cognizant of the circumstances, may be appropriate. Yet there was little of the caution or compassion or sense of complexity that Butterfield would have asked us to exercise in bringing Waldheim to historical accounts—little mention, for instance, of the overbearing pressures brought upon Austrians by the *Anschluss* or the Hitlerian plebiscite or the drafting of young Austrians of Waldheim's generation into the German army. I do not know whether Waldheim served willingly or not; I have heard that his family had been strongly anti-Nazi so long as they dared.

It has been said that Waldheim— as a young lieutenant in the intelligence branch of the German army—had to know about the fate of 50,000 Greek Jews deported by his unit from Salonika. Perhaps he did know. It is less certain how effectively he could have resisted it. There were many during those years, in more exalted and powerful positions, whose knowedge of Nazi atrocities exceeded their power or willingness to act. In his book *The Terrible Secret,* Walter Laqueur has established that the deadly nature of Hitler's program for the extermination of the European Jews was widely known here and in Europe by 1942. Great figures such as Roosevelt and Churchill were pressed to stop the deportations—even by bombing the rail lines. They can hardly be accused of indifference. Yet they too took refuge in inattention, disbelief, evasion, and inaction.

My intention here is not to acquit Waldheim, merely to illustrate by example—a difficult and provocative one—the immense complexity of historical judgment that moved Herbert Butterfield, nearly sixty years ago, to assail the Whig interpretation of history with all its self-righteous and self-satisfied certainties. Butterfield's counsel can help us here; for the implication of all he says is that by the constant exercise of glib retrospective indignation we risk squandering the energies of just and accurate moral judgment.

Beyond that, Butterfield counsels us against the arrogant failure to inquire searchingly into the constraints that play on those whose acts later come to seem disagreeable, counter to the current of history, or even outright evil. It was Acton's argument, a formidable one, that pardoning too much in the past could sentimentalize or enervate judgment in the present. But Butterfield is not wrong to remind us of the contrary hazards.

And finally, there is the modesty of perspective. It is perilous to assume that we in our little moment of time have reached a plateau of moral distinction that licenses us to look upon the past in haughty condescension. Our ancestors had flaws and errors and evils to answer for; but so do we, and some of them undoubtedly do not as yet declare themselves to us.

In the end, *The Whig Interpretation of History* does not counsel a supine paralysis of judgment. It is, however, a powerful warning against our disposition to separate sheep from goats too easily, too quickly, and with too much delight when we should be trying to understand more accurately what happened—and what is happening even now. "By merely enquiring and explaining," Butterfield writes, the historian (and all of us) "increase human understanding, extending it to all the ages, and binding the world into one. . . . If we have not that understanding the history of all the ages . . . may only give us a larger canvas for our smudging, a wider world for our willfulness."

The great Dutch historian Pieter Geyl has put an allied point wonderfully well:

Comprehension, a distinterested understanding of what is alien to you—this is not the function of the mind which will supply the most trenchant weapons for the political rough-and-tumble. The man who has made up his mind for all contingencies will often be too quick for one who tries to understand. We live in a time when it is important to know your side and there are dangers involved in keeping an open mind. Yet if we all of us devote all our efforts to the struggle, what shall we in the end have struggled for? To understand is a function of the mind that not only enriches the life of the individual but is the very breath of the civilization we are called to defend.

2. American Uses of the Past

Edwin Arlington Robinson's "Miniver Cheevy" epitomizes a peculiarly American notion of the uses of the past—natural to a civilization that abruptly severed ties with the past at a strategic point in its history. And the tale it tells is implicit:

> . . . Miniver sighed for what was not,
>   And dreamed, and rested from his labors;
> He dreamed of Thebes and Camelot,
>   And Priam's neighbors. . . .
> Miniver mourned the ripe renown
>   That made so many a name so fragrant;
> He mourned Romance, now on the town,
>   And art, a vagrant. . . .

We get the point almost without trying: Miniver Cheevy is a classic failed American—a misfit whose plight perfectly flatters the view we inherit, almost as mother's milk, as children of the New World. It is the view that it is the future—or at any rate the vibrant and tangible present—that really counts, not the past. It is the view that to regret, with Miniver, "the days of old" is not only a vanity but very likely to lead to the un-American vices of vagrancy, Machiavellianism, snobbery, alienation, poverty, and eventually alcoholism. Miniver Cheevy—the very name suggests what a misfit he is—romanticizes those institutions and ideas our mythic forefathers are believed to have fled. He admires just those things whose subversive vortex Lambert Strether, in Henry James's *The Ambassadors,* senses with a comic shudder in the person of Miss Gostrey—"a Jesuit in petticoats":

> . . . . that was to say the enemy, the monster of bulging eyes and far-reaching quivering groping tentacles . . . exactly society, exactly the multiplication of shibboleths, exactly the discrimination of types and tones, exactly the wicked old rows of Chester, rank with feudalism; exactly in short Europe.

I have long harbored a secret sympathy for Cheevy, a sentiment that stole over me when as a boy of fourteen or so I first read of him in a high school English course. Where Robinson clearly intended us to feel a *frisson* at the wages of nostalgia, the poem misfired for me. If he is a failure, Miniver seems anything but wicked, harmless anyway, and certainly interesting. I resented Robinson's underhand way of suggesting that if you were interested in things historical—the past or chivalry or the Medici—you were on the slippery slope to vagrancy and the grog shop. Miniver's vice is his inordinate sense of the past; for by it he is immobilized, disabled, stripped of that pristine historical innocence that some see as the principal American virtue.

Certainly, the portrait of Miniver Cheevy implicitly expresses an important part of the conventional New World wisdom about the past—its corruptive potential, even its pathogenic power; and it may be interesting to investigate, briefly, a few repercussions of that notion.

It is nowadays not unusual to lament the poor quality of American school history, or the deficiencies of American historical understanding. The assumption is usually that it is a mechanical failing, a failure to teach history well. But the problem may be deeper—not mistraining so much as mistrust. Certainly we are historyless in unlikely places. Consider, for instance, what passes for American political conservatism. In older cultures conservatism is invariably tied to a sense of the past; but those who call themselves conservatives in America are rarely so in the classic sense. They are rather Manchester liberals, devotees of the Industrial Revolution with a profound faith in its social beneficence, so long as the meddlesome hand of state planners is stayed. This conception of conservatism would certainly have baffled Edmund Burke, the father of English-speaking political conservatism, to whom the American conservative's inveterate hostility to the state would be strange.

In the study of literature the most famous school of criticism, usually called the New Criticism, is very much an American hybrid, of which Lionel Trilling has remarked "the impulse . . . to deny that between Now and Then there is any essential difference, the spirit of man being one and continuous."

How does one explain this impulse to merge Now into Then? Robinson undoubtedly caught the central clue—that in a dynamic society in which speed, change, "development," progress, the moving frontier are all but worshipped, the past is potentially a virus that may hinder, retard, and even induce fatalism and dissipation. But it is also obvious that the past is not for us a vivid dimension because there is simply not very much of it—we are Crevecoeur's "new men," planted in a vast historyless emptiness. And the dimension of time is short as well. American historical destiny began with the Revolution, a mere second away from the present. At its longest it began at that instant now difficult to mark precisely when Americans ceased to think of themselves as English colonials and began to contemplate—to imagine—a separate destiny. "The land was ours," as Robert Frost put it, "before we were the land's."

Physically, the European past weighs palpably on the present, in ways impossible to conceive in most places in America. The American eye is captured by the contemporary, not least because the landscape hints at little else. Perhaps a few places—Bull Street, Savannah, St. Paul's churchyard in Edenton, a Nantucket whaler's cemetery—suggest age. But they are few and scattered in a landscape bristling with currency. We all remember Henry James's exclamation, almost of surprise, in his essay on Hawthorne:

> . . . No state, in the European sense of the word . . . No sovereign, no court, no personal loyalty, no aristocracy, no church, no clergy . . . no country gentlemen, no palaces, no castles, nor manors, nor old country houses . . . nor thatched cottages, nor ivied ruins; no cathedrals, nor abbeys, nor little Norman churches . . . no political society, no sporting class—no Epsom nor Ascot!

To which the detractors of the imaginary Miniver (and for that matter of the very real Henry James, the patronizing expatriate James) would no doubt respond: And good riddance!

But what about the treatment of history itself? It is helpful to recall Lionel Trilling's remark about the impulse "to deny that between Now and Then there is any essential difference." If it is Miniver Cheevy's undoing to create his own romantic past—not only "what was not" for him, but what never was for anyone—he stands in good company. It is not only our Minivers with their mythic Camelots but even historians who decline to take the past on its own, sometimes alien terms. I offer in evidence the case of three eminent American historians, all of whom have recently gone public with their musings on the nature of history. And their confessions suggest that as much as our historians may respect the past as raw material, they often wish it would behave itself a bit less strangely.

Fawn Brodie, biographer of the Civil War Republican leader Thaddeus Stevens, published two years ago in the *New York Times Book Review* a lengthy complaint, "Who Won the Civil War Anyway?" The gist of it is this—that Southern-born historians are winning, with pens, the war their ancestors lost with swords and guns. Mrs. Brodie particularly abhors "the glorification of the Southern hero . . . the minimization of the horrors and immorality of slavery . . . the pinioning of the abolitionist as the true villain." In Mrs. Brodie's view, good historians are those who are "not ashamed to be indignant over slavery"—as if retrospective wrath would break one rusty shackle or erase one whiplash scar from a back long since gone to dust. The bad historians are those who, like Douglas Southall Freeman, write of their heroes (even southerners who wickedly fought for the Confederacy) as if they too were human, driven by motives comprehensible by their lights if not by our own. It is difficult to say where in Mrs. Brodie the historian stops and the scold begins. In her irritation, she seldom pauses to ask whether, or in what circumstances, it is useful for the historian to sit in judgment. To be sure, it is astonishing to reflect that our ancestors of 1787, thinking slavery morally evil, should have condoned it in the Constitution, should have deferred to unionism as a higher principle than abolition. But that deference seemed to them the price of Union. Of course, it is equally surprising to recall that William E. Gladstone delivered his maiden speech in the Oxford Union in defense of the slave trade.

The related case of Barbara Tuchman, author of *The Guns of August,* is even more interesting. In her provocative article "Can History Be Served Up Hot?" she pretends, at least, to see no difference between the unexamined past, on the one hand, and history as we write it on the other. "In my innocence," she writes, " . . . I had simply assumed that history was past events existing independently, whether we examined them or not." It is hard not to think that such naiveté is a pose; but there is no evidence that she is joking.

Then there is the confession of Arthur Schlesinger Jr. in his article, "The Historian and History." After working in the White House during the first two years of the Kennedy administration, after watching the process by which powerful men make decisions, the eminent New Deal historian now shudders, he says, "when I think how confidently I have analyzed decisions in the ages of Jackson and Roosevelt, traced influences, assigned motives, evaluated roles, allocated responsibilities, and, in short, transformed a dishevelled and murky evolution into a tidy and ordered transaction." The sad fact, he continues, is "that in many cases, the basic evidence for the historian's reconstruction of the really hard cases does not exist—and the evidence that does exist is often incomplete, misleading or erroneous." His revised feeling is that while would-be makers and shakers in statecraft must have a sense of the past, a few months as an activist have shaken his former belief that the historian occupies "a quasi-priestly vocation, supposed to liberate him from the passions of his day . . . "

The confession is startling. Who, having read Mr. Schlesinger's three fluent volumes on the Age of Roosevelt, would have thought them the work of a writer "liberated" from "the passions of his day," serene in his perspective or "objective"? One might instead have assumed that a historian of his sophistication and party spirit would have questioned the myth of dispassion long before serving an apprenticeship as a White House aide.

What have these three historians in common? Isn't it that they all reveal some resistance to the notion that before the historian arrives on the scene to piece the clues together, the formless past has a certain stubborn integrity of its own? This is what they have difficulty accepting. But why?

One undercurrent in the popular conception of the American past is that in striking out anew, in creating a new historical covenant, in dispensing with that "multiplication of shibboleths" which alarmed Lambert Strether, Americans somehow fought free of the chains of the past. Perhaps it is not far-fetched to see in these historians a seeking of proof of that emancipation. Our three historians wanted to find the past malleable on their terms. And it is grudgingly, if at all, that Mrs. Brodie would admit that slavery was ever a debatable issue, or Mrs. Tuchman surrender the notion that some objective past is waiting patiently there to be captured, as if by a photograph; or that Mr. Schlesinger concedes that the Age of Jackson may have had its own distinct logic, defiant of the probing of the most dedicated historian.

Our historians apart, any number of popular conceptions of the American past might be revealing—for instance, the belief that the United States was never a colonialist power. The evidence is entirely to the contrary, but the feeling that we evaded the colonialist fever raging in late nineteenth century Europe is strong today. Why? It is clearly a question of consciousness, as Kipling recognized when, in urging the United States to "take up the white man's burden" in the Philippines, he urged Americans in effect to recognize their de facto colonialist status. Kipling did not understand the difficulty, did not understand the urge to exempt ourselves from the real past. And similarly, consider the great problem of race in America, our "American dilemma." It was not until Vann Woodward reminded us of the fact in a memorable book that it was accepted that Jim Crow laws actually had a history: that segregation's strange career as the guiding spirit of laws really took root only some twenty years after Appomattox.

If these three historians are representatitive, might one say that Americans believe the past should be plastic enough to be molded, to be accessible and intelligible and accommodating to the present? A past that refuses to conform to this condition may safely be minimized or ignored. Emerson, that patron saint of the ahistorical American, thought that when the currency of history is not freely convertible into the currency of the present observer, it is negligible. Again and again his essay "History" echoes the idea:

> I have no expectation that any man will read history aright who thinks that what was done in a remote age, by men whose names have resounded far, has any deeper sense than what he is doing today . . . All inquiry into antiquity, all curiosity respecting the Pyramids, the excavated cities . . . is the desire to do away this wild, savage, and preposterous There or Then and introduce in its place the Here and the Now.

This impulse to assimilate the past to the present must be carefully distinguished from what George Orwell called "doublethink"—a tampering with the integrity of the past for immediate and political purposes. The impulse to tamper with the past implicitly concedes the power of the past. The American instinct, by contrast, is usually to ignore it as if, ignored, it might cease to influence us. This attitude may be related to the attitude that produced "doublethink," though it is by no means so sinister in its implications. It is merely impoverishing and disorienting.

But why, after all, risk being too fond of the past? Why court the Cheevyan handicap? Admittedly, the risk associated with history-mindedness is precisely nostalgia; and nostalgia may easily become a form of "iron clothing" that weighs us down and impedes our supercharged national genius. It is also the foe of innocence, and of the dangerous delusion of American exceptionalism. Adding the grace of history-mindedness places much at risk; and that would seem, to some Americans, a prohibitive cost.

Yet perhaps it is equally mistaken, a product of the Cheevy myth, to think that there can be no dynamism in the true sense of the past, along with its grace. To witness the roles played in our own time by the likes of Winston Churchill and Charles De Gaulle, both of them steeped in the past, is to see how grace may be mingled with, and even generate, a vaulting energy that is anything but debilitating. The uses of the past may be inspiring and not crippling, and are always clarifying.

The dignified impartiality of the past is not always reassuring for those who would use history crudely to reinforce their political prejudices. But it can provide a basis both stable and humane for national and personal judgment. A nation that acts in lucid knowledge of its best traditions, which knows the origins of its aberrations from them, is forearmed against that excessive self-righteousness with which Americans so often astound the world.

3. The Madisonian Persuasion

It is impossible to venture far into the writings of James Madison without suspecting, to understate the situation, that in what is perhaps the most crucial of all debates about government Madison clearly stands with the Augustinians, not the Pelagians.

In the fourth century a Welsh monk, known to the history books as Pelagius, put forward an enticing vision of potential human perfection. The key to it for Pelagius was man's freedom of will. If the will is free, it follows that there is no theoretical limit to self-improvement, personal or social. If original sin might be conquered, so might its effects. And since perfection requires no supervision, Pelagius's was among the first of those post-Christian philosophies envisioning—or at least providing a rationale for—the rule of saints on earth or the withering away of the state.

Now, Saint Augustine regarded this view as quite fundamentally dangerous and wrong. I think Madison would have taken Augustine's side. With Augustine, Madison would have said that human nature is so far flawed as to make government both inevitable, as a regulator of the appetites, and, as to its form and rules, very problematical.

Any reader of Madison's work—especially the familiar *Federalist Papers* Numbers 10 and 51—will note that Madison's thoughts about government are linked to basic reflections on human nature. He clearly assumes that human nature (or, if you prefer more empirical language, observed human behavior) is flawed, so that the exercise of power by men over other men is invariably perilous and, to repeat an inescapable term, problematical.

To rest political argument on basic assumptions of this sort would not have been viewed as remarkable in Madison's day. The habit merely situates Madison in the great stream of political theory, stretching back to antiquity. In Madison's day people of learning would have assumed that serious political thought must begin with a theory—a theology, if you like—of human nature. If we are no longer so rigorous in political argument, that is perhaps a mark of the inferiority of our habits of argument to those prevalent in the 1780s.

There has been much knowledgeable speculation on Madison's views of human nature. Invariably, however, scholars cite the influence on the young Madison of Dr. John Witherspoon, the Scots theologian who taught him at Princeton. Witherspoon's thought had a distinctly Calvinist cast, as might be expected of a dour Presbyterian. On the great issue of free will and perfectionism, Witherspoon would no doubt have leaned toward the Augustinian position. And notwithstanding his own Anglican heritage, Madison apparently did not find Witherspoon's views uncongenial. But by all accounts Witherspoon's Calvinism lacked the harshness we associate with the earlier and bleaker Calvinism of John Knox.

No more than most Virginians of his time and rank did Madison make a parade of his personal religious views. But even without open or especially revealing professions of faith, certain features of Madison's outlook may be glimpsed, or pieced together from fragments. And no feature is, I think, more striking than his conviction that man in society is likely to misbehave and to tread on the toes and liberties of his neighbor. In his political speculations you find little of that airy talk of human innocence characteristic of utopian thinkers. Witness, for instance, Madison in the *Federalist* Number 10: There is, he tells us, a "connection between . . . reason and . . . self-love." Inflamed by party spirit (or the spirit of "faction," as he calls it) men will be "much more disposed to vex and oppress each other than to co-operate for their common good." We live in no earthly Eden; it is rather a place replete with "mutual animosities . . .unfriendly passions . . . [and] violent conflicts."

Notwithstanding these sentiments—and bearing in mind that they served the immediate polemical end of persuading New York to ratify the Constitution—it would be misleading to think of Madison as a pessimist about human nature in society. He was instead a realist. Like his mentor Witherspoon, he took the guarded view that the human condition might indeed be improved by effort—so long as the effort is firmly anchored in a healthy respect for the strength and variety of human appetite and, above all, in some wariness of the perils of concentrated appetite. He did not expect people to reach some state of earthly harmony by charitable self-sacrifice and forbearance.

In this respect it is instructive to compare Madison with his lifelong friend and collaborator, Thomas Jefferson. No two colleagues in politics were ever more loyal to one another; and for the most part their goals for the new republican America harmonized. Yet at the heart of this working alliance was an affinity of opposites, of com-plementary views. Jefferson's characteristic note is philo-sophical and visionary, and sometimes his optimism seems almost giddy. Madison's tone is concrete, institutional, and sober. Jefferson seems to have entertained at least some of the typical Enlightenment hopes for human progress, pro-vided that his new "empire of liberty" avoid the snares of city life and cultivate the soil. Madison has far less to say about such speculative matters. He was not given to what Dr. Johnson called "attitudinizing." His writings do not glow with that peculiar Jeffersonian patina. It is as hard to imagine Madison writing the early paragraphs of the Declaration of Independence as it is to imagine Jefferson writing the *Federalist* Number 10.

This distinction is serviceable. It helps us define and grasp Madison's distinctive contribution to the shaping of the Republic. Jefferson said and did many great things. But he was finally more a theorist than a builder of institutions. I picture him, for instance, as an edgy and impatient delegate to the constitutional convention, had he been there and not attending to his ambassadorial duties in Paris. There was a streak of the romantic in Jefferson—a hint that man-made institutions tend to contaminate our native innocence and freedom. One can imagine Jefferson fidgeting in his chair during those long, stuffy summer afternoons in Philadelphia, as connoisseurs of the fine detail of government (James Wilson, for instance) droned and quarreled over the structure of congress and how it should be elected; or on what basis to levy taxes; or how to choose presidents. These were Madison's food and drink. He liked to deal with the fine print of governance. Every sentence he ever wrote about government radiates his conviction that political institutions are not impediments to the good life but the only means by which the willful and self-regarding inclinations of man may be tamed—civilized, in the literal sense. As such, they were worthy of an infinite investment of patience and thought.

This, I think, is the implication of Madison's frequent reflections in *The Federalist* on the complex barriers essential to free and just government. Because people are self-interested, they will combine in "factions" to get their way. And unless these combinations are checked and refined, they will often override the weak, producing injustice and tyranny. The great advantage of an "extensive republic" is that factions—despotic concentrations of power and will—may be controlled in a variety of ways. Federalism controls by apportioning powers and duties at more than one level. Checks and balances and the separation of powers serve the same aim in different ways.

The Madisonian persuasion, as I have called it, is consummately summed up in *The Federalist* Number 51. In this great state paper, Madison struck off many of those phrases for which we remember him: that "ambition must be made to counteract ambition," for instance; that the structure of government must, as he puts it, "supply, by opposite and rival interests, the defect of better motives." Its great passages, familiar in this bicentennial season, nonetheless bear endless repeating:

> But what is government itself, but the greatest of all reflections on human nature? If men were angels, no government would be necessary. If angels were to govern men, neither external nor internal controls on government would be necessary. In framing a government of men over men, the great difficulty lies in this: you must first enable the government to control the governed: and in the next place oblige it to control itself.

But Madisonianism has not entirely held the field. Indeed, it is far from doing so. Americans are by nature a bouyant people; and the Pelagian tendency has been strong among us. Maybe we perceive in lucid intervals that men are not angels; but we have sometimes permitted ourselves to suspect that angels do sometimes slip down from the higher realms, if not to govern us, at least to whisper in the ears of those who do. Or so we dare think when we approve of their measures.

There is, in other words, a certain irrepressible millennialist tendency in our history, a strange blend of puritan moral certainty and Jeffersonian optimism. It finds expression in the persistent view that America is an exemplary land—the exceptional and deserving beneficiary of a special providence and dispensation. According to this exceptionalist mythology, we have escaped the terrible penalties history has imposed on less favored lands—not because we are lucky or geographically isolated but because we believe in the steady improvement of man and because our motives are good.

One might observe (with impartiality) that our last two presidents have shown signs of Pelagian views. President Carter told us in 1976 that the national shocks and humiliations of the terrible 1960s and after could be accounted for by the failure of government to achieve a level of rectitude commensurate with our private behavior—to be "as good as the people themselves," as he occasionally put it. President Reagan, for his part, often quoted a saying of that irrepressible revolutionary, Thomas Paine: "We have it in our power to begin the world over again." Paine learned to question the sentiment. Mr. Reagan did not.

In any case, this astonishing belief in the easy dispensability of the past runs directly contrary to the soberer views of the founder of Mr. Reagan's party, who said: "We cannot escape history." And indeed, Lincoln was right; we cannot. It is perfectionist to believe that we can wipe away the mingled errors and injustices of the past—the legacy of slavery, for instance—escaping the consequences of all that has gone before. It is as perfectionist, in fact, as believing with Mr. Carter that states fail to be moral only when and because they fall short of the private morality of their citizens.

These attitudes must have a certain attraction, since millions of Americans have heard and applauded them. The point to be made here, however, is that they are deeply un-Madisonian. Concealed in both—in the idea that government fails because and to the extent that it is faithless to the goodness of "the people"; or that we can make the world anew every morning—is the Pelagian heresy: Government and social institutions are not refining but inhibiting mechanisms. It hardly matters what special ideology of the moment, liberal or conservative, is thought to be served by these naive sentiments. Either would be far from the views of James Madison and equally far, therefore, from the philosophy of man and society implicit in the Constitution of the United States.

If you believe what these two recent presidents say they believe, it follows that the political problem is simply to find the best way to emancipate our natural instincts from institutional bondage, to discover the best and fastest way to channel popular sentiment into law and action. If you are Pelagian enough, you must believe not as Madison did in representative government but in something quite different: plebiscitary government. Far from being suspicious of unrefined majoritarianism, you must regard it as the essence of just government.

But of course Madison's much reiterated point is that a government protective of public liberty must look to checks and balances, delay and dilution of popular spirit. Any easy or rapid concentration of political will, however pure the motive or exalted the purpose, is potentially if not actually tyrannical. It is faction by definition; and it threatens liberty for the reasons Madison so patiently explains. The Madisonian persuasion, moreover, is incompatible with the view that government itself is inherently undesirable, whether misshapen or not. "Government," said Mr. Reagan in his First Inaugural address, "is not part of the solution to our problem. It is the problem." But Madison would not have said so. No idea more alien to his own system and outlook can be imagined.

Surely, one clear lesson of our eventful century is that government is often the great teacher, the great licenser of behavior, for good or evil. When it is designed to protect personal liberty and promote the general welfare, its civilizing influence can be great. But a good match between means and effect in government is a rarity. Most of the world has been misgoverned most of the time throughout most of its history. Only those who are blind to the implications of that fact will sneer at government that works tolerably well, as if it were a barely tolerable inconvenience. It has become fashionable in recent years to derogate the arts of government; but it is not an indulgence Madison would have encouraged in a free people.

Behind the "parchment barriers" erected in Philadelphia in the summer of 1787 lay James Madison's unflinching realism. He was realistic about our nature, though far from lacking in hopes for its future. He hoped that sound institutions might restrain, direct, and civilize it. Like most faiths that matter, Madison's was no geometric proposition capable of precise or rigorous demonstration. It was a creed to be tested by time and trial and turmoil. And so tested, notwithstanding the failure even of eminent public men to grasp its inner genius and rationale, it survives. Considering the mutability of governments and constitutions, that fact is perhaps the great testimonial of all to the enduring relevance of the Madisonian persuasion.

4. The Centrality of Institutions

When I was growing up in a small North Carolina town thirty or more years ago—and even later when I was a student in Chapel Hill—American society seemed strikingly stable. I was a "Depression baby," born in 1934, and while the great slump and the world war that followed ruffled the surface of things they did not much alter deeper currents—so far as one could see.

The collapse and discrediting of the free-wheeling business order of the 1920s spawned some revolutionary impulses. But they were confined to the political fringes. This confinement of revolutionary consciousness undoubtedly was in part the result of Franklin D. Roosevelt's reassuring authority. From 1932 to his sudden death in 1945, FDR remained the commanding presence of American politics, to a degree not to be repeated. Roosevelt struck some as a menacing and radical figure, though no close examination of his political style and ideas would sustain that impression. His approach to the discontents of his time was activist and sometimes even aggressive, but he threatened no traditional institution. The ferment was in his willingness to experiment and to thrust government into a larger role in the everyday life of ordinary people, usually by means of programs that transferred to the national arena experiments already tested in the states.

Certainly he had programs enough—programs for the farmers, for the South, for the regulation of business, for public power. This programmatic approach to the nation's problems set what has continued to be the pattern of our political culture. No president is deemed respectable unless he has a "program"; and if he doesn't, the press and political activists will taunt him until he puts one together. It is almost a quantitative test of political seriousness; and it reached a high water mark in Lyndon B. Johnson's "Great Society" agenda in the mid-1960s. Before the Vietnam War engulfed him, Johnson saw himself as building upon, but vastly extending what FDR had begun. So much did programs become the norm, the ultimate test, of political seriousness that we are still under the spell today. If something is wrong—and something usually is—the answer is a program.

In this respect, however, I must confess to an unfashionable state of mind. I used to be a believer in programs; and only an idiot would deny that some (Social Security is an obvious example) are of essential value. Now, however, in political midlife, I find myself increasingly skeptical of the programmatic approach to politics and far more absorbed in the role and fate of institutions. No successful society can afford to disregard either; but at the moment, an imbalance needs righting.

I have said that the atmosphere in which I grew up was—as surely it continues to be—one of inordinate faith in the power of programs to keep the society stable and straight. Institutions, for their part, seem to take care of themselves handily enough. Their stability is nowhere better illustrated than in a famous confrontation of the Roosevelt years. In 1937, President Roosevelt launched his most aggressive foray into institutional reform. He proposed that Congress enlarge the membership of the Supreme Court, having watched as the Court found a number of his experimental programs unconstitutional. For every justice reaching the age of seventy but choosing not to retire, the president could appoint another, up to the number of six. But despite his commanding political position, the nation recoiled and FDR suffered a decisive defeat.

It was, I think, natural for one nurtured and conditioned in this climate—where ferment expressed itself programmatically, and where the Court was far from being the only all but untouchable institution—to think of it as the natural equilibrium. But from the perspective of political midlife this assumption seems almost a handicap, typically American and perhaps typically twentieth century. For surely the political crisis of our time is not a crisis of programs; it is a crisis of institutions.

In fact, it is difficult to think of an institution, small or large, that isn't in trouble. The presidency is imperial and bureaucratic. Congress is corrupt at the edges, also bureaucratic, also—worst of all—lacking in responsiveness and efficiency and filled with "entrepreneurial" members who owe no deep allegiance to party or congressional leadership. The courts are accused, often with justice, of usurping the legislative function. The nation's intelligence agencies are correctly thought to have been insufficiently restrained by law. The schools and universities, having lost their poise and coherence in the student rebellions of the 1960s, have not regained them. The military services, deprived of the draft and increasingly bewitched by high-tech weapons, are not what they should be. And in the more intimate and private realm there is disintegration enough—divorce equalling marriage, the nuclear family falling apart. One might expect in the face of all this that there would be some cosmic shift of our intellectual gears—away from a preoccupation with programs and toward a more sophisticated scrutiny of institutions. So far, it hasn't happened. Why not?

History, after all, is chiefly a study of institutions and their shifting relationships. Schematically, one could say that ancient history is the story of three great institutions—Jewish monotheism, the Greek city-state and the Roman Empire; that its sequel, culminating in the Middle Ages, is the story of two great institutions, feudalism and the church, interacting. As one moves on, beyond the scientific, industrial, and democratic revolutions, the picture becomes more complex and the vital institutions multiply; yet they remain at the center.

Consider, for instance, something of paramount importance: the institutions of political liberty. A few years ago the Carter administration adopted "human rights" as a cardinal plank of American foreign policy—surely a worthy cause in principle. Yet in many of its specific applications the policy quickly ran into difficulties; for rights tend to flourish in complex institutional settings. So far, no universalizable set of "human rights" has been discovered that will root itself simultaneously in Iran, the Soviet Union, Korea, and Brazil. It is characteristic of the programmatic approach to politics to ignore the world's variety. We should know from our own experience that the ideal of ordered personal liberty (what *we* usually mean, in the main, by "human rights") is not a code that can be handed about or easily transplanted. It was not so, after all, even in our own development. The Anglo-American conception of liberty is bound up with complex institutions—constitutional supremacy, the rule of law, the limitation of power, checks and balances among competing authorities, federalism, the Bill of Rights; and all have a story behind them.

To grasp these indispensable elements in mere outline, you must understand something of the English common law judges, like Sir Edward Coke, who attempted to wrestle an independent "due process" from the shadow of kingly will. You must understand the struggle of the seventeenth century between the English House of Commons and the Stuarts to differentiate a popular political will from that of the

Crown. You would need to understand the classic consideration of liberties in the writings of Edmund Burke, both when
he supported the American Revolution and, later, when he
argued quite as passionately against what he properly saw as
a great heresy: the tendency of dissenting preachers in
England to confuse the utopian ideas of the French rev-
olutionaries with the knotty particularities of English liberty:
the rights of man confused with the rights of Englishmen. In
Burke's day, it was important to grasp the difference between
a liberty rooted in institutions and events, and a concept of
liberty that springs from the abstract notion of the rights of
man in the large. It is no less so today. Burke himself said it
best:

> The nature of man is intricate; the objects of society are
> of the greatest possible complexity; and therefore no
> single disposition of power can be suitable either to man's
> nature or to the quality of his affairs. When I hear the
> simplicity of contrivance aimed at and boasted of in any
> new political constitutions, I am at no loss to decide that
> the artificers are grossly ignorant of their trade, or totally
> negligent of their duty. The simple governments are
> fundamentally defective, to say no more of them.

Indeed, the frailty of a simple liberty is easily established,
whether one thinks of the reaction that followed the French
Revolution or the upheavals of our own time. Today Marxist
thinkers invent their own "objective" version of history and
define rights as mere rationalizations of class standing or
privilege, as before them the Jacobins had deduced them
from a romantic conception of the innocent natural man. No
idea of liberty so conceived can be thought to depend on the
durability of institutions or on a grasp of their history; to the
contrary, institutions are thought of (as by Rousseau) as
inherently corrupting. Romantic rights derive instead

from the proclamation of a prophetic vision, an all-encompassing theory of human nature which often as not views institutions as barriers to, not buttresses of, human freedom.

Again, it is impossible to improve on what the historic defenders of ordered liberty have said of it, distinguishing it from the programmatic and prophetic sort. In *The Old Regime and the French Revolution,* for instance, Alexis de Tocqueville says:

> Our revolutionaries [he is speaking of the French revolutionaries, the apostles of programmatic liberty] had the same fondness for broad generalizations, cut-and-dried legislative systems, and a pedantic symmetry; the same contempt for hard facts; the same taste for reshaping institutions on novel, ingenious original lines; the same desire to reconstruct the entire constitution according to the rules of logic and a preconceived system instead of trying to rectify its faulty parts. The result was nothing short of disastrous; for what is a merit in the writer may well be a vice in the statesman and the very qualities which go to make great literature can lead to catastrophic revolutions.

All this—and more could be cited—and yet the institutional mode of exploring social and political values today seems remarkably passé. Today the typical prejudice is that the failures and dissatisfactions of our time flow from some lapse of moral principle. Indeed, a term floats up to mind from the early history of disputation in the Christian West: gnosticism. This early heresy held that religious conversion was essentially a process of knowing and understanding. The gnostics sought to strip Christianity of its historical, institutional, sacramental elements and to impose in their stead a test of initiation or apprehension. It was wisdom, not faith, it was cognition, not instructed intuition, that would distinguish the faithful. Is there not some parallel with the anti-institutional and antihistorical style of thought—the pro-grammatic style—I have been describing? Consider again what Tocqueville says of the French literary intellectuals, of their fondness for generalizations, for formulas, for "pedan-tic symmetry," for reconstructing systems by the rules of logic; it is precisely a sort of secular gnosticism.

I think with some amusement of the recent memoir by the editor of *Commentary* magazine, Norman Podhoretz's *Breaking Ranks*. Some have called it the most significant political memoir of the 1960s. Mr. Podhoretz is not, I think, an anti-institutionalist in politics. But in the book—which takes the form of a letter to his college-age son—Podhoretz attempts to explain his own careening journey into and out of political radicalism. He describes a wild succession of causes, positions, notions, nostrums, attitudes, to which he in dizzying succession attached himself. As Podhoretz relates these cycles of affiliation and disillusionment, one might have thought he had subscribed to a cause-of-the-month club. As he moved through all these radical fashions, one gathers, it scarcely occurred to Mr. Podhoretz to ask himself how many of them were reinventions of the wheel, and whether the institutional constraints of American society and politics rendered them of dubious relevance. It was political gnos-ticism in high gear: a desperate search for illumination.

Of course, this disposition for the abstract, even among usually prudent men, has been enormously reinforced in the century and a half since Tocqueville wrote—by the rise of the social sciences. A science of society is conceivable; and it may even teach us things of value. What it cannot teach are values themselves. Recall, for instance, the misuse of the several Coleman Reports, in which a distinguished sociologist told us in the most methodical way what social and educational results to expect from the equalization of school opportu-nities by busing. Recall, also, the ensuing reconsideration of the earlier findings. This is all the more the tendency of the social sciences when delicate institutions fall under their scrutiny. For every sensitive and appreciative study, there seem to be dozens that conceal, between the lines of critical description, a thoughtless and subtle denigration. The denigration may be appropriate on occasion. But since it is implicit in scientific method to emphasize the values of logic, objectivity, symmetry, clarity, and order, and to neglect the values of custom, symbolism, predictability, and habit, the thrust is often mindlessly destructive.

This influence has been reinforced by an extensive permeation of popular journalism by popularized social science—I say it as a journalist. This is particularly the case with journalism in its "investigative" mode, which tends to measure institutional realities (insofar as they can be grasped at a brief glance) by some idealized model that has no known embodiment in history. A university, a foundation, a government agency, a military service, a court—these find themselves exposed for the practice of some traditional habit to which inertia has accustomed them, but which is seen not to measure up to an abstract ideal of democracy, equality, or openness. Investigative journalists jerk trees up by the roots to prune them or grade their fruit. And the social horticulturists who perform these—literally radical—investigations often have no direct personal experience of the institutions from the inside.

There is, for instance, the Bob Woodward-Scott Armstrong book about the U. S. Supreme Court, called *The Brethren*. This book, a best-seller, handily illustrates all the hazards of superficial institutional investigation. The Supreme Court is among the few remaining institutions that conducts its deliberations confidentially—for a number of compelling reasons. One is as important as it is mundane: Justices sometimes change their minds, and reserve the right to change their votes even on the very brink of an announced decision.

Messrs. Woodward and Armstrong, enthralled by the current prejudice that what is hidden must for that reason be suspect, amassed documents, rumors, and hearsay about the Court's internal deliberations in the years 1969-75: a time of important rulings. From this patchy evidence they constructed a picture of the Court in action which, among other defects, presents the nine justices as a nest of vipers, fighting among themselves and subordinating great judicial considerations to undignified prejudices. I know of no serious scholar of the Court, however, including many who have clerked there, who regards the book as a true or useful portrait of the institution. Yet the book slakes that thirst we share for an "inside" look at, an exposé of, a venerable institution with its hair down—and disheveled. Not altogether in jest, George Will suggested that the nation may have to choose between having a functioning government and having an investigative reporter as shrewd and diligent as Bob Woodward. This is, I guess, an entertaining way of wondering how much of the arcana of our vital institutions we can afford to bring to light while expecting those institutions to function and to command public confidence.

In this instance as in others—the leaking and publication of the so-called "Pentagon Papers" regarding the origins and conduct of the Vietnam War is another example—the threat to the institution lies not in the revelation of truth, or in the critical spirit, but in the illusion that truth is easily discovered. Most institutions have their dirty little secrets, capable of being misunderstood or magnified when exposed. But it is not the spilling of secrets but the tendency to misconstrue from them the inner nature and function of institutions that is the threat. When suspicion and skepticism are driven by the impulse to measure the worth of everything by the latest dogmatic abstraction or slogan (for instance, "the right to know" or "freedom of information"), trouble lies ahead.

It is not my submission that we ought to sentimentalize institutions. But institutions do suffer a disadvantage when placed under the strain of relentlessly rationalistic or "scientific" analysis, precisely because their values and strengths are never altogether rational or scientific. What indeed is the utility of a system in which nine elderly lawyers, appointed for life during good behavior, may declare unconstitutional a law passed by 535 elected legislators? What is the utility of those scientific and humane studies that for hundreds of years have formed the centerpiece of humanistic education in the West? To ask these questions is to bring to light the truth, disturbing to many these days, that certain things are done in certain ways for reasons that go beyond rational analysis and are simply buried in the seedbeds of history, and in the wisdom of cultural traditions. A nation, said Burke—and he might have said the same of any long-established collection of institutions,

> ... is not an idea only of local extent, and individual momentary aggregation, but it is an idea of continuity, which extends in time as well as in numbers, and in space. And this is a choice not of one day, or one set of people, not a tumultuary and giddy choice; it is a deliberate election of ages and of generations; it is a constitution made by what is ten thousand times better than a choice, it is made by the peculiar circumstances, occasions, tempers, dispositions, and moral, civil and social habitudes of the people, which disclose themselves only in a long space of time.

What we ought to investigate more frequently than we do these days is the utility of "utility" as the sovereign measure of institutions. Custom, habit, predictability, lore—these are crucial to the morale of institutions and have their place in a society whose needs are not merely those of the useful but also of the symbolic, the psychological, even the theatrical and ceremonial. If these needs are scanted in the programmatic fury of our time, it may be for want of sufficient historical sense or experience. If you know something of the role of the Royal Society in the scientific revolution, if you have read Walter Bagehot on the English constitution or James Madison on our own, even if you have read the recent delightful biography of the founding editor of the *Oxford English Dictionary*, you are likely to learn more about institutions as the carriers of values than you can learn by merely examining those values as detached abstractions, ripped from their settings.

The programmatic mind asks: "Who thought of it and who is for it?" The institutional mind asks: "What is its history? Has it been tried before and did it work?" The programmatic mind values motives, aims, purposes, causes; the institutional mind must always be haunted by thoughts of consequence. In this world it is the latter by which our efforts are judged. It never has been or can be otherwise.

5. Whose Constitution Is It Anyway?

My own answer to the question is an emphatic "no one's." The Constitution is essentially a trust between generations—neither yours nor mine—and we are bound as temporary stewards not to bend it to self-serving or transitory advantage. From this principle it follows—at least for those who follow Edmund Burke's admonitions—that "popular perceptions" of the Constitution are of secondary importance. The Constitution of the United States is not a subject of referendum; and a good thing, too.

According to one recent poll, 80 percent of Americans favor a constitutional amendment guaranteeing the right of organized prayer in the public schools. But here, numbers seem to me unimportant, if not irrelevant. Surgery on the First Amendment, whatever the strength of the popular clamor for it, is too delicate to be performed by plebiscite.

When I was a college student thirty years ago, someone did a survey to discover the depth of public attachment to the basic principles of the Bill of Rights—a pertinent subject at the time, which was the era of so-called McCarthyism. Without exception, the respondents professed their dedication to the Bill of Rights in principle. But many respondents could not have known what rights it guaranteed, because they overwhelmingly repudiated their application. Even today—I suppose eras do not differ much in this—there are surprising gaps in public knowledge of the Constitution. Many associate it with Thomas Jefferson, a confusion probably arising from Jefferson's authorship of the Declaration of Independence. But very few people seem to be clear on the difference between the two documents. How many people in the street today could say whether the sentiment, "all men are created equal, and endowed by their Creator with certain unalienable rights" appears in the Declaration or the Constitution? Not many. The casual attitudes toward our basic instruments of government are depressing—an unflattering reflection of our failure to teach our own history well, to say nothing of the history of the wider world.

What it comes down to, then, is that the Constitution is inescapably an "elitist" document, to use a term that today carries a somewhat negative charge. But this is no condemnation. The Constitution was the work of an elite, less of birth or wealth than of public spirit and talent, the natural *aristoi* of whom Jefferson often spoke. An elite has remained its guardian and interpreter; and those guardians have done a praiseworthy job, too, considering the vicissitudes that have befallen so many nations and political systems over the past two hundred years. Yet it does not follow that the Constitution was written to serve, or does serve, only the few. Sometimes it has, but had that been invariably the case, the Constitution of 1787 would long since have proved too inflexible to accommodate the robust growth of twentieth-century democracy.

The belief that the Constitution is elitist in the negative rather than the positive (or neutral) sense has persisted in our history. It was articulated in the state ratifying conventions by the able men calling themselves, or known to historians as, "Anti-Federalists." In the modern era, in the 1920s, the historian Charles A. Beard popularized a theory that men of property had written the Constitution primarily as a bulwark of property values. He provided elaborate tabulations to support the theory that the Constitutional Convention of 1787 had staged a sort of bloodless *coup d'etat*, by and for the rich.

Most historians today view Beard's famous theory as a period piece which, in common with most materialist explanations of history and human behavior, rests on selective evidence. The truth is that the propertied classes of the 1780s were sharply divided over the virtues of the Constitution, many fearing it as a threat to their wealth, not insurance for it. The Beard theory told less about the origins of the Constitution than about the political climate of Beard's own time. The Progressives, to whom Beard the citizen was devoutly attached (sometimes pulling Beard the historian in tow), believed that a conservative legal system, rooted in the Constitution, had hindered political and regulatory reform. There was substance to that belief. But the Constitution, or even the Fourteenth Amendment, wasn't the basic problem. The hindrance was political, not constitutional. Attitudes needed changing, not constitutional articles.

The Progressives were, to be sure, right about one thing. The Constitution was designed to temper and delay change. It explicitly acknowledges that the people are sovereign; and popular sovereignty was a daring idea when the Framers embraced it. Yet they were sufficiently apprehensive of democratic excess to draw up complicated rules of political procedure. The doctrine was liberal, especially for its time; the structure was conservative. Lord Macaulay, the popular nineteenth century British historian, reflected the Whiggish misconception of the day when he declared the American system "all sail and no anchor"—a spectacular misjudgment. Many have found it the reverse.

And there is yet another fundamental point. The Constitution of the United States is now among the oldest written constitutions still in force, if not the very oldest. Its nearly two-hundred-year lifespan is the more remarkable when you consider that most constitutions have not endured, even for an era. Most constitutions, like most nation-states, are new, post-World War II or later. Many are so prolix, so catalog-like in their lists of guarantees, that the human mind can hardly master them, even in a lifetime of study. Our own, at some seven thousand words, is not simple. Yet its main lines may be grasped rather easily at a reading.

What does the contrast suggest? Many recent constitutions are prolix because they take an expansive view of the obligations of government and, moreover, treat those obligations as organic. Many of them, for instance, incorporate at a gulp the United Nations Universal Declaration of Human Rights and proclaim encyclopedic pledges and promises. But since government is always flawed, many of these high-minded pledges are mere wallpapering. The more grandiose the promises, in fact, the farther the performance will—of necessity—fall short of them. Many recent constitutions, for example, guarantee a human right to work, even as the U.S. Constitution guarantees rights of speech, press, assembly, and religion. But it is easier to place limits on what government may do than to guarantee what it will do. That is where more recent conceptions of constitutionalism stumble and flounder. It is true that entitlement to a job for everyone who wishes to work is an admirable political ideal, and indeed an obligation under United States statutory law. But it is not a constitutional right; and trying to entrench it as a right when "full employment" cannot be literally full in a dynamic economy is an invitation to disillusionment and cynicism.

II

From time to time—and ours may be such an age—Americans grow restless with the modesty of our Constitution and long for something a bit racier—a bit longer on the sort of modern entitlements at which the Brazilian and Argentinian constitutions beat ours all hollow. Underlying this impulse there is a certain failure to absorb the teachings of historical experience. The framers of the U. S. Constitution omitted social and economic policy from the text for both political and philosophical reasons.

In spite of their precautions, issues of policy do occasionally become constitutional battlegrounds. Slavery, the income tax, the consumption of alcoholic beverages, and, more recently, the chronic insolvency of the Treasury, are examples. But the turmoil and confusion that have usually marked the incursion of social and economic policy into the constitutional arena dramatically demonstrate why such incursions are better avoided. Often enough—the fiasco of the Eighteenth Amendment is the classic example—an attempt to make social policy constitutional causes more trouble than it cures. There are historians who believe that the Civil War might have been averted but for the "constitutionalization" of the quarrel over the extension of slavery between 1854 and 1857. I am not sure they are right; but whether they are right or wrong, the consequences of this development were catastrophic enough in themselves.

Less explosive, though in some ways similar, was the growing belief that measures taken to revive business prosperity during the Great Depression of the 1930s threatened constitutional values. By 1935 or thereabouts, President Roosevelt and the Congress had reached accord on the need for an experimental program aimed at economic recovery. But the Supreme Court majority of that day was wedded to the view that certain economic doctrines had been embedded in the Constitution: "sanctity of contract," for example. Invoking those doctrines, the Court precipitated a crisis by blocking a number of congressional policies and frustrating the president's popular mandate for experimentation. At issue here, as we now so plainly see, were not systemic issues but issues of public policy. The Court was levering proximate social and economic arrangements into constitutional issues. Instead of guarding the rules, it sought to shape the outcome of the game. The impasse was abruptly broken by the timely change of one justice's mind and by the retirement of others; and the Court withdrew from its attempt to regulate economic life under the mystique of "substantive due process." Today, we are surprised to recall that eminent judges and scholars of that day saw issues of constitutional dimension in farm price supports or the legislative regulation of the gold content of the dollar. Few today would regard them as other than debatable issues of policy.

The capacity of the Constitution to shed the barnacles of substantive due process (in its economic phase, at any rate) is, to my mind, a vindication of the Framers' wisdom—specifically, their wisdom in regarding economic and social issues as political rather than constitutional. To be sure, this was in part pure accident; for the men of 1787 envisioned a far more limited role for federal government than has become our current expectation. But the accident was fortunate. What so many of the slick latest model constitutions view as entitlements, we are content to submit to the rough and tumble of voting and debate.

But are we not in some danger of drifting away from this fundamental principle of American constitutionalism? There are some warning signals.

One notable trend today is what one might call, not very originally, the atomization of American society. We are becoming less a community than a nation of claimants. Far more than in the past, or so it often seems, Americans are sensitive to ethnic, social, racial, class and other group distinctions—and to the claims that spring from them. The occasion for this trend is not, or not usually admitted to be,

conflict or strife. It is the popular idea of group entitlements—rights that belong to us not as persons or individuals,
but as members of some group or other. A former colleague
of mine, the late Anne Crutcher of the *Washington Star,* once
brilliantly summed up the idea: *E pluribus plus,* a witty pun
on the national motto. Not "one from many" but "more from
many." She was summarizing an interesting development—
the addition to the 1980 census forms of questions about
ethnic background and ancestry. For the first time Americans were asked to identify themselves by ethnic origin: a
minor but significant symptom of the new atomization. At an
earlier time in our history, this bother about group rights
and group claims and group pride would have been
regarded as a bit discreditable, going against the American
ideal of the melting pot. "Hyphenated Americanism," as
Theodore Roosevelt called it, was frowned upon. But the
melting pot ideal has fallen today into some disfavor—no
doubt because it melted some more easily than others. Now
it is an accepted practice to assert rights and claims not as
citizens or individuals but as members of various unmeltable
groups. My Constitution or yours? You take your part, and
I'll take mine.

Thus the self-consciousness of youth, at first a function
of numbers as the "Baby Boom" generation came of age,
helped obtain the vote (which is rarely exercised) for
eighteen-year-olds. The assertiveness of women as women,
blacks as blacks, Hispanics as Hispanics, Asians as Asians, or
even Aleuts as Aleuts is historically understandable; but the
outcome of all this scrambling for visibility is yet to be seen.
Whether the outcome is wholesome or not, group-conscious-
ness can hardly fail to affect our view of the Constitution,
what we owe it and what it owes us.

If the new vogue of group-based rights and claims
fosters an assertive parochialism, a tendency to see the
Constitution as a grab-bag of promises and entitlements

rather than as a modest charter of liberty and self-government, it could do harm. Our political parties, once an inducement to coalition politics, have been enfeebled by television and other forces making for an entrepreneurial and atomistic politics. Coalitions are harder to form and hold together, surely one reason why so many Americans have plunged headlong into "single-issue" politics. Basic institutions seem almost too feeble to reach principled, timely, and effective resolutions of urgent problems—problems like assuring the solvency of the Social Security system, or the integrity of the federal budget. The *E pluribus plus* mode is part of the problem, though not the whole of it. But we know from the experience of some Third World and Latin American nations that the more numerous, specialized, and exalted the expectations encouraged by a constitution, the greater the room for—indeed, the certainty of—disappointment. And after disappointment, cynicism will follow.

Those who wrote the Constitution of the United States viewed it primarily as a rule book, enabling effective government. It enshrined and promoted wholesome, even noble, values. But the crucial and central values are procedural and neutral: order, continuity, liberty, and equity. A good constitution, the Framers seem to have thought, should declare the rules of the game and tell us how the players qualify to play it. But save for the grand generalities of the Preamble ("the general welfare . . . domestic tranquillity") it withdraws from the scramble and does not attempt to draw a blueprint for the good society. Had it done so, it would have been a blueprint that cramped each succeeding generation, weighing them down with the dead hand of the past.

For the sometimes frustrating way in which the Constitution slows and tempers change, even desirable change, it compensates with a wonderful tensile strength. Its recent monument is the great revolution in civil rights. It is not much more than ninety years since "separate but equal" was declared to be the rule of the Fourteenth Amendment, hence of law and practice; and it is only 132 years since the *Dred Scott* decision held that blacks had never been, and could not be, citizens. Ours is another and immeasurably better world on this score; yet the Constitution was not wrenched out of shape or recognition by the change.

"Popular perceptions" of the Constitution may matter in one way, even when misguided. They galvanize the discontented to attempt improvement. Thousands of amendments are thought of, hundreds written, only a handful ever presented or ratified. Yet times do change; things do move. It is essential that the Constitution not undertake to settle, let alone entrench, what passes in a passing age for social and economic wisdom and justice. We leave that sort of wisdom to the statute books which, by majority vote, are more easily blotted and rewritten. The Constitution of the United States is a promissory document only to the extent that it promises liberty to the person and representative government to the people.

6. Privacy: The Search in the Shadows

It requires no very exacting scrutiny of American ideas of personal liberty—especially those embedded in the Bill of Rights—to see that "privacy" is in some sense paramount. The First Amendment "right to assemble" implies a right of private association. The Fourth Amendment right to be secure in one's "person, papers and effects" from "unreasonable searches and seizures" assumes a privacy which may be invaded only on suspicion of crime, and then only by warrant. The Fifth Amendment privilege against self-incrimination, with the privileges that stem from it (for instance, the confidentiality of one's disclosures to priest or physician or lawyer) also reinforces this sense of privacy.

Still, it exists only in some sense—the words of hesitation and qualification must be emphasized. Americans have long argued intensely over the nature and extent of the privacy which all of us more or less assume. In a noted *Harvard Law Review* article of December 1890, Samuel D. Warren and Louis D. Brandeis (later, of course, Justice Brandeis) pleaded for the legal recognition of "the right to be let alone." Dissenting years later in the *Olmstead* wiretapping case, Brandeis would name privacy as "the right most valued by civilized men."

Yet a century later, this assumed sphere of personal privacy continues to be problematical—its scope and dimensions in law widely and heatedly debated. Once one goes beyond the enumerated constitutional liberties—once one begins to ask questions about the derivation, scope, and variety of privacy rights—one enters one of the most unsettled of all constitutional terrains.

It might be thought odd that so late in the twentieth century some Americans—and some of them not the least solicitous friends of personal liberty—would be troubled by the assertion of a legal right of privacy. I say odd, because the twentieth century has witnessed so many of the horrors of the totalist state—the society that treats the citizen as a cipher, allowing no personal autonomy and no zone of privacy which the government is bound to respect. The atomized society satirized in George Orwell's ominous novel *Nineteen Eighty-four,* which systematically extinguishes personal loyalties and intimacies the better to foster state- and leader-worship, is not a mere fantasy. The twentieth century, moreover, has been marked by the swift development of invasive technologies—the long-range microphone, fingerprint, the polygraph, urine sampling for drugs—all of which, unless rigorously controlled, threaten the integrity of the person.

It is hard to square these two great facts—first, that a due regard for privacy is clearly among the key distinctions between a free and a totalitarian state; and that we nonetheless experience a vexing difficulty in reaching a consensus about the nature and reach—even the existence—of American constitutional privacy. There is custom, to be sure, and it is valuable; but custom can be a weak reed, not always withstanding the pressure of popular excitement and official expediency.

That Americans are still far short of agreement on this matter was apparent as recently as the summer of 1985, when the Supreme Court, in the case of *Bowers v. Hardwick,* upheld Georgia's statute prohibiting consensual sodomy in private between adults. In his impassioned dissent, Justice Harry Blackmun protested that "the right of an individual to conduct intimate relationships in the intimacy of his or her own home seems to me to be the heart of the Constitution's protection of privacy." Yet Justice Byron White rejected the very idea of constitutional privacy as a "substantive gloss" on the Constitution, cousin, he tartly suggested, to the "economic liberty" glosses read into its words by the pre-FDR Supreme Court of the 1930s. Here, in fresh form, are all the old arguments about whether privacy is implicit in the Constitution or merely springs from the over-generous imagination of judges.

Yet while Justice White and others raised the usual questions about the competence of judges to define the sphere of personal privacy, one doubts that even skeptics would say that constitutional privacy is altogether a figment of the judicial imagination. We come, inevitably, to an inescapable fact: The most revealing disputes of recent years about the nature of personal privacy have more often than not sprung from noted Supreme Court cases, especially those touching so-called "reproductive rights." This merely vindicates again Tocqueville's shrewd observation that all great political issues in this country eventually become judicial issues. But Tocqueville's truth is at once a convenience and a problem. It is a convenience because the facts of "cases or controversies" do often handily frame the issue. It is also a problem because few of us would concede that American constitutionalism is coextensive with what judges say. Chief Justice Hughes's famous quip notwithstanding, the Constitution is often a good deal more (if sometimes somewhat less) than what the judges of the day say it is.

Most of the dispute over privacy begins with the difficulty that it is only inferentially, if at all, protected in the

Constitution. Perhaps that is because the late eighteenth century was not a time when people worried about their privacy, or supposed that it might someday need specific constitutional protection, like, say, the right of bail or habeas corpus. Privacy is not only a new worry; it is a relatively new subject for serious legal inquiry. In the card catalog listings at the library of the U.S. Supreme Court, all of scores of citations pertain to materials of the last century and less. The Warren-Brandeis article of 1890 is the Ur-document. It was only twelve years ago that Congress passed a "privacy act" so named. And even the Warren-Brandeis article came equipped with a long fuse.

The need for an explicit safeguard of privacy may not have occurred to the constitutional draftsmen of a pre-industrial state of vast extent with a moving frontier, a keen sense of individualism, and plenty of extra space for those who took exception to (or were taken exception to by) their neighbors. Perhaps not every suspected witch or warlock escaped Massachusetts Bay ahead of the witch-burners. But with the exception of such quasi-authoritarian colonies as the soi-disant "city on a hill," early American settlements for the most part seem to have adhered to a doctrine of live and let live. Government was often far away; and early American officials who wished to scrutinize the private behavior of citizens lacked the proximity and technological means to do it very effectively.

The threat to privacy that spurred Warren and Brandeis to new thoughts and worries in 1890 was not the approach-ing menace of electronic technology; it was the new mobility of people carrying cameras. Warren and Brandeis cite as a particular outrage the case of a certain Miss Marion Merona, an actress. While performing on Broadway in a dramatic piece that required her to appear in tights, Miss Merona was, without her leave, photographed by a Mr. Stevens with a "flash-light" camera. She sought and was granted an uncontested court order prohibiting the circulation of the photograph. Warren and Brandeis saw the incident as the essence of a current assault on the integrity and sensibilities of the person. They beheld with horror the fact that "gossip is no longer the resource of the idle and of the vicious but has become a trade ... pursued with industry as well as effrontery." "Numerous mechanical devices," they warned, "threaten to make good the prediction that 'what is whispered in the closet shall be proclaimed from the housetops.'"

Volumes of changing American social history are implicit in the indignation with which these two young nineteenth century Bostonians cried alarm at violations of privacy which are all too common in our time. What "Isaiah" (as Justice Brandeis would come to be called in his later prophetic days as a venerable Supreme Court justice) would have had to say about the great hordes with hand-held TV cameras, staking out the victims of tragedy, one can only guess. They were careful to admit some exceptions to the legally protected sphere of privacy they advocated. But "the right to be left alone" (as they called it, quoting Judge Thomas Cooley's treatise on torts) was to be ample. Their inspiration was the menace of gossip-mongering journalism, in the dawning age of the "yellow press." Their argument is of its time, and many of its assumptions are distinctly antithetical to the First-Amendment glosses that underlie today's ideas about freedom of the press. In any event, the sneaky photographer and the gossip, though enthroned, were soon to be overshadowed by intrusive government. Brandeis would later borrow for his *Olmstead* dissent the essence of his 1890 privacy doctrine, but with a revealing variation: The justice would say that the framers of the Constitution "conferred, as against the government, the right to be let alone—the most comprehensive of rights and the right most valued by civilized men." But for the moment the effort failed to implant such a right by judicial edict in the form of a ban on wiretapping.

In fact, we must jump a very long way forward in American history to find the constitutional doctrine of privacy finally achieving a firm judicial foothold. It came with the Supreme Court's decision in *Griswold v. Connecticut* (1965). The decision is often cited among the notable landmarks of the Warren Court and, by some, as an example of what they view as its besetting vice: "liberal activism." In fact, the usual alignments are missing. No case that found the "conservative" John Marshall Harlan declaring himself foursquare for a privacy doctrine, while the "liberal" Hugo Black strenuously dissented, can be taken as representative.

The *Griswold* case involved a 1958 Connecticut statute regulating the use of contraceptives. It reveals the deeper, more elusive currents of dissidence within the Warren Court. Griswold, executive director of the Planned Parenthood League of Connecticut, had joined with a Yale professor of medicine to counsel married couples on the use of appropriate birth-control devices. After barely ten days, they both were arrested and charged with violating the prohibitory law and the law making it a crime to "aid and abet" another in the commission of a misdemeanor.

The case became a high-water mark in the development of a constitutional doctrine of privacy. The Court threw out the intrusive Connecticut statute; but that was in some ways the least significant fact about the decision. The sale of contraceptives for "prevention of disease" was anyway perfectly legal in Connecticut. The declared aim of the law was to prevent the use of contraceptives as an aid to promiscuity.

In 1965 the Court was composed—not only in Harlan and Black but in William O. Douglas—of exceptionally articulate justices with firm views, capable of clothing those views in weighty and sometimes flashy phrases. It is accordingly from the *Griswold* case that we draw even today much of the language in which constitutional privacy has subsequently been debated.

Justice Douglas, writing for the Court, cited several recent decisions in which privacy had been recognized, at least implicitly. (For instance, the membership lists of the Alabama NAACP had been shielded from state authorities wishing to use such lists to put economic pressure on NAACP members.) "In other words," Douglas went on, invoking a vivid figure of speech destined to have a continuing life, "the First Amendment has a penumbra where privacy is protected from government intrusion." Since specified rights are sterile without the means of giving them robust effect, Douglas argued, "the foregoing cases [that is, cases like the Alabama NAACP case] suggest that specific guarantees in the Bill of Rights have penumbras, formed by emanation from those guarantees that help give them life and substance. . . . Various guarantees create zones of privacy." Indeed, Douglas continued, resorting to one of the broad-brush sweeps of declaratory history that frequently adorned his judicial opinions, "we deal with a right of privacy older than the Bill of Rights—older than our political parties, older than our school system."

Here, as plainly and starkly laid down as it could be, was a creed that is probably half-consciously shared by most Americans, more or less without stopping to think about where it might come from. Lacking Douglas's metaphorical flair and glibness, not everyone would think of privacy in terms of shadows and "emanations" and "zones." But the idea seems disarmingly plain and appealing, a sort of motherhood-and-apple-pie proposition. Was it not reasonable to assume a preconstitutional stratum of preexisting rights (cousin, perhaps, to the "life, liberty and the pursuit of happiness" mentioned in the Declaration of Independence) which no subsequent political act could have alienated or expunged? Possibly. But to assume or assert it is one thing; to derive it persuasively from the history or words of the Constitution (a task Douglas airily shunned, at least in the *Griswold* opinion) has proved an immensely more challenging task. The fact was that neither Douglas nor anyone else could say precisely where this right of privacy came from—it seemed a "Topsy" among constitutional doctrines, one which appeared one day without birth certificate or known parentage. Indeed, any doctrine dependent on "penumbras" was by definition shadowy.

Nor was Justice Black slow to supply the classic articulation of the other side of the coin. It might be useful to say a parenthetical word or two about Black's views, for he was considerably misunderstood. Out of his independent searches of the classic political theorists and philosophers, out of his practical experience as an Alabama judge and New Deal senator, Black had over the years developed a sternly positivist doctrine of constitutional construction. For Black, what counted and all that counted was what framers and legislators literally wrote down: the stuff in black ink. This literalism was allied to a fierce hostility to all natural-law flourishes; and these were the threads that bound together so many apparently inconsistent positions. As his wife's recently published diaries reveal, Black was all but obsessed with judicial positivism. He conducted a one-man crusade within the Court against the subjectivism which to his mind was invited by expressions like "civilized conscience" and "values implicit in the concept of ordered liberty." (That these phrases were great favorites, sometimes even coinages, of his rival Felix Frankfurter did not diminish his objection to them.)

It was Black's contention, strenuously argued for years, that natural-law interpretations of the great phrases of the Bill of Rights were out of place—a facade for judicial caprice. This went double for any judicial gloss that rested on the discovery of such novel and elusive quiddities as "penumbras" or "emanations" in the specific provisions of the Constitution. "Privacy," wrote Black in his *Griswold* dissent, "is a broad, abstract and ambiguous concept. . . . Use of any such broad unbounded judicial authority would make of this Court's members a day-to-day constitutional convention." He appealed to the words of Justice James Iredell, in the early case of *Calder v. Bull:* "The ideas of natural justice are regulating by no fixed standard: the ablest and the purest men have differed upon the subject; and all the Court could properly say . . . would be that the legislature (possessing an equal right of opinion) had passed an act which, in the opinion of the judges, was inconsistent with the abstract principles of natural justice."

As Black attached "absolute" value to the word "no" in the First Amendment ("Congress shall make no law . . ."), he also attached near-absolute value to what the Constitution did not say, what it was silent about. And it made not the slightest mention of the word "privacy." Even the Fourth Amendment, where privacy values are implicit if they are anywhere, could only be stretched into a charter of privacy by judges operating on their own hook. That was not the proper function of judges. Black had fought back when the "penumbras" sheltered notions like "sanctity of contract" or "economic freedom" in the 1930s. Thirty-five years later, he resisted again when other justices discovered emanations of privacy there.

With this inspection of the major opinions in the *Griswold* case, one comes full circle. I said earlier that while the rise of the totalitarian state (which a man like Hugo Black could hardly be suspected of admiring) seems to give ever greater urgency to the recognition of a privacy doctrine, the necessity does not of itself create a constitutional fact—not, at least, in the eyes of eminent positivists like Justice Hugo Lafayette Black. But—and this is the key question—if privacy is not to rest on ingenious formulas such as Douglas's "penumbras," what is the alternative? Is there one? Are privacy and other unstated but important values assumed by Americans as their historic legacy to be regarded as imaginary unless spelled out in chapter and verse at some "canonical moment" by the Philadelphia convention or the First Congress? Do the canonical moments begin only with the Constitutional Convention, or do they reach back to the Continental Congress or the clear embrace of natural-rights doctrine in the Declaration of Independence? In *The Federalist* (admittedly to forestall an embarrassing challenge to the proposed Constitution), Alexander Hamilton argued that bills of rights can be dangerous because they may encourage the assumption that rights not specified are inferior or have no legal standing.

The privacy issue, like the *Griswold* case which so clearly exhibits it in microcosm, points to the paradoxical nature of a society governed by a written constitution and written laws. Few of us today, however we may feel about some of the more exotic or unusual claims of sexual privacy, would concede that our expectations of personal privacy are confined and limited by the literal chapter and verse of the Bill of Rights. Hugo Black's questions do, admittedly, have a haunting resonance: Who is licensed to search the shadows and declare the nature and extent of any valuable right? If judges may do it with only their personal sense of natural justice to guide them, does that mean that constitutions are subject to change when judges change, or judges change their minds? If privacy—or "the right to be let alone"—is indeed the right most valued by civilized men, how then did so eminently civilized a group of men as those who wrote the U.S. Constitution overlook the need to name and secure it? Is a value of such importance to be no more than a continuing apple of discord for jurists, journalists, and scholars?

The questions are endless; and some of them are probably not answerable. Justice Black liked to warn against the danger of consigning constitutional liberties to the subjective whim of a "bevy of Platonic Guardians," yet one must weigh the hazards of judicial subjectivism against the perhaps equal dangers of an arid positivism—a doctrine that finds no more in the Constitution than parade-ground commands. When all is said we cannot, I think, dispense with the age-old substrata of natural law out of which modern democracy and personal freedom emerged—and "the right to be let alone" along with them. Without some civilized consensus about these universal political values, the often meager prohibitions of the Bill of Rights may lose life and vibrancy. Indeed, there is no guarantee at all that literal readings are the same for every literalist. I admit, speaking for myself as a citizen's committee of one, to finding it repugnant to think that one's expectations of privacy are little more than whims, without solid constitutional footing. Until a more fetching metaphor comes along, perhaps Justice Douglas's mysterious "emanations" and "penumbras" must take their place along with the notion that homes are castles. Constitutional privacy is there, somewhere, in the shadows, is it not? As the late Justice Potter Stewart once said of certain kinds of pornography, we may not be able to define it but we know it when we see it—and, as importantly, when we miss it.

7. The State of the Constitution, 1987

> So great at times has been the emphasis on the purely negative characteristics of a constitution, on prohibitions of the exercise of power rather than on the giving of power, as to create the false impression that the primary function of a constitution is negative rather than positive. . . .
>
> Carl Brent Swisher, in *The Growth of Constitutional Power in the U.S.*

Let us begin with a homely maxim. The state of the Constitution at any given moment, like beauty, is largely in the eye of the beholder. The maxim implies no flaccid relativism about constitutional meanings—no more, at least, than the *de gustibus* maxim implies a total absence of objective standards in esthetics. There obviously are essential and abiding features of the constitutional system; and we would tamper with them only at our peril.

Examples are fortunately more easily imagined than recalled. A president, let us say, displeased with a Supreme Court decision curtailing "executive privilege," might invoke the Jeffersonian doctrine that each coordinate branch is the final arbiter of its own constitutional powers. Accordingly, he might say to the justices: You have made your decision, now enforce it. If he did so, a true constitutional crisis would arise. But in the real case, Richard Nixon, withstanding his habit of claiming extravagant implied powers, shrank from challenging the justices when they ruled that he must surrender the tell-tale Watergate tapes. And such self-restraint has been more typical in the American experience than not.

Why then do Americans frequently complain that the Constitution is, or soon may be, a thing of shreds and tatters? The answer seems to me rather obvious. In the absence of clear cases of usurpation (which, like hard-core pornography, according to the late Justice Potter Stewart, might be more readily identified at sight than defined in the abstract), most of us use the terms "constitutional" and "unconstitutional" in a subjective, almost Pickwickian fashion.

There is also the factor of political convenience. The late Senator Sam Ervin used to say that in constitutional matters we run with the hare and hunt with the hounds, as suits the occasion. One's sense of the state of the Constitution often depends on the opportuneness of a certain constitutional theory, restrictive or expansive. We are strict or loose constructionists by seasons. When the president seems too assertive, we turn very Whiggish and speak dolefully of the "imperial presidency." Then some strong action is suddenly required—the cry of 1973 was, "give us more gasoline, Mr. President"—and no one but the president seems able to perform it. Then we grow impatient with congressional or judicial finicking. No good constitutionalist could applaud Theodore Roosevelt's immortal boast: "I took the Canal and let Congress debate; and while the debate goes on, so does the Canal." But it is entertaining; and there is in it an amusing truth about our constitutional tolerances.

Examine almost any period of political tension or party

conflict in American history—from the undeclared war with France of 1798, to the Civil War and Reconstruction, to the undeclared war in the North Atlantic on the eve of World War II, to Vietnam. In every instance, one's sense of constitutional limits is not so much the starting point as a by-product, perhaps even an embellishment, of political loyalties or some urgent programmatic agenda.

This is no less true today and no less characteristic of journalistic rhetoric. Consider a recent *New York Times* column by the highly regarded Anthony Lewis. "The imperial presidency," Mr. Lewis warns, "is on the rise again. . . . As before in history, the delicate balance at the heart of our constitution is under threat." And what, exactly, are the symptoms of this threat to constitutional balance? A U.S. Court of Appeals judge, sitting in Washington, has declined to block an expropriation in Honduras—yes, Honduras, where the writ of even the most activist American judge may falter. Had this act of judicial restraint not been explained, I suspect that Mr. Lewis would have found it less alarming. But Judge Antonin Scalia—now Mr. Justice Scalia of the Supreme Court—rationalized his ruling by saying that courts "do not intrude on the conduct of foreign affairs," a doctrine usually true in practice that one would not want to freeze at so high a level of generality. Judge Scalia may overstate the rule, but not by much.

Another threat to the constitutional balance, to Mr. Lewis's sense, is President Reagan's insistence that Congress lacks the power to "limit his commitment of Marines in Lebanon." It is unclear what is meant here, for President Reagan followed the statutory process for the commitment of American armed forces prescribed by the 1973 War Powers Resolution. The Marine presence in Lebanon was not established by presidential fiat, but after negotiation between the White House and congressional leaders. Whether it could be extended indefinitely in the face of congressional displeasure, as the president believes, is a question that may not be tested. Mr. Lewis perhaps refers to Mr. Reagan's expression of reservations about the War Powers Act itself. But those reservations are consistent with those expressed by all his predecessors in the years the resolution has been on the books.

So despite the alarmist language, what is at stake here is not the delicacy but the tilt of the constitutional balance. That tilt changes from era to era; no doubt about that. The Framers knew it would and were content to leave its exact bias at any given time to the clash of ambitions and powers, more than to legal metaphysics. Ambition would be the "auxiliary precaution," more powerful than any parchment barrier, checking competing ambitions.

At all events, it is interesting that Anthony Lewis invokes, as fit warning for presidents, Justice Robert Jackson's admonition in the Steel Seizure case of Korean War days. "The Constitution," wrote Justice Jackson, with his usual incisiveness, "did not contemplate that the title of Commander in Chief of the Army and Navy will constitute [the president] also Commander in Chief of the country." (If General Alexander Haig had grasped the distinction on the evening of the "Saturday Night Massacre" of Watergate days, when he told Attorney General Elliot Richardson that his "commander in chief" had given him an "order," he might have spared himself some derision.) Let it be noted, however, that the Justice Jackson who joined the hounds of restraint in the Steel Seizure case was the same Jackson who had also run with the hares. As Franklin D. Roosevelt's attorney general some years earlier, he had worked out the legal rationale for an expansive exercise in implied executive powers—the famous swap of "overaged" U.S. destroyers for British bases. That Jackson had been denounced as an evil counselor and, of course, as a constitution-wrecker. A further illustration of the hare and hounds rule.

It is easier to understand the worry about the constitutional balance if one assumes that it has something to do with policy preferences. Mr. Lewis would like the Marines withdrawn from Lebanon, and he does not approve of United States intervention in Central America. These are honorable and responsible views, but surely more in the nature of policy than constitutional principle. One does not transmute them into the latter by portraying a given president as a constitutional aggressor when he vigorously asserts traditional executive claims. And the time will inevitably return when those who now fret over the resurgence of an "imperial presidency" will long for a strong hand in some now unforeseeable emergency.

I don't mean to sound cavalier. The anxieties echoed in Mr. Lewis's column are no doubt very real. A few weeks ago many of my colleagues of the press were charging that it was grossly unconstitutional—a violation of the First Amendment—for the Pentagon to restrict coverage of the Grenada operation. It would be a hard case to prove, as hard as the recent assertion that the appointment of an American ambassador to the Vatican violates the First Amendment principle of the separation of church and state.

At this point I should pause for a confession. I write from some personal experience on the hare-and-hounds theme. In 1970, weary with the Vietnam War, I was among those who took a favorable view of legislation (such as the Cooper-Church resolution) as a legitimate way of curtailing out-of-hand presidential authority. I found it offensive to hear the Gulf of Tonkin Resolution of 1964 described (by then-Attorney General Nicholas Katzenbach) as the "functional equivalent" of a congressional declaration of war. But by 1973 I had come to share the view that the so-called Clark Amendment, restricting CIA operations in Angola, was an ill-advised infringement of presidential discretion. In truth, it would have to be said that there was little obvious

difference in principle between the two pieces of legislation—the end-the-war resolution or the later one on Angola.
It may only be said that at least I did not claim that my
shifting views represented the essence of constitutional
propriety.

I have always had my doubts about theories of constitutional construction which imply that the great constitutional
phrases are, beyond the most literal and obvious, self-
interpreting. The text often settles the easier questions. But
those are seldom the questions that provoke serious or
difficult constitutional dispute. Even in its documentary
aspect, the Constitution is far more than a legal code. Recall,
in that connection, the famous admonition on the nature of
the Constitution by Chief Justice John Marshall in *McCulloch
v. Maryland* (1819). At stake was the dispute between the
Federalists and the Jeffersonians over the implied power of
the federal government to charter a bank, to facilitate the
regulation of money and credit. Speaking for the Federalist
view, Marshall undertook to refute the "strict construc-
tionist" view of good Jeffersonians about the "necessary and
proper" clause:

> A constitution, to contain an accurate detail of all the
> subdivisions of which its great powers will admit, and all
> the means by which they may be carried into execution,
> would partake of the prolixity of a legal code, and could
> scarcely be embraced by the human mind. . . . Its nature,
> therefore, requires that only its great outlines should be
> marked, its important objects designated, and the minor
> ingredients . . . be deduced from the nature of the ob-
> jects. . . . We must never forget, that it is a constitution we
> are expounding.

That seems to me very nearly the last word, as it was
almost the very first, on the subject. A constitution made to

last must combine structural features of great integrity with sufficient flexibility to accommodate changing goals and needs. Have we lost sight of Marshall's vision of the difference between constitutionality and legalism? There is now in the air a bit of what I would call constitutional mandarinism, whose clearest symptom is the recent struggle for advantage between the president and Congress. This is nothing new. What is new is that Congress has developed the urge to substitute legalism for struggle and comity.

It has been a long time since Congress moved to check a major executive initiative by the ancient method of cutting off funds, "refusing supply." The preferred instrument of congressional resistance today is the insertion of legislative veto provisions into law, requiring presidents in many matters—a good example is the sale of arms to foreign powers—to function *ad referendum*. This would be appropriate in areas clearly subject to congressional authority, or even to joint authority—for instance, the negotiation and ratification of treaties. But legislative veto provisions have invaded almost every corner of the relationship. The Supreme Court has recently cast doubt on the constitutionality of legislative vetoes in a minor immigration case (*INS v. Chadha*, 1983). We do not yet know, however, whether this is a raid or an onslaught. One indication, which I myself do not expect to see, would be a Supreme Court ruling on the 1973 War Powers Resolution or some other major claim of congressional "veto" authority.

The legislative veto has been an established feature of some legislation since the early 1930s. But of the 250 or so existing legislative veto provisions, more than half date from the 1970s—the decade of Vietnam and Watergate that brought us the myth of the imperial presidency. Of all these enactments, the most assertive is indeed the War Powers Resolution, which purports to make Congress a full and equal partner in all foreign military operations. Like the

Liliputians, Congress has been moved to see itself as a band of weaklings struggling to tie down a drowsy but dangerously strong and impulsive giant. It has spun a great web of statutory strings, perhaps the chief example of the shift from the Marshall to the mandarin view of constitutional relationships.

Another salient example of mandarinism is the impoundment restrictions of the 1974 Budget and Impoundment Control Act. Experts partial to the congressional view tell me that I am wrong about these provisions; but this is the way it looks, anyway. Until the great clashes between President Nixon and Congress in the early 1970s, impoundment—by which the executive declined to spend some appropriated sum—was one of those more or less rogue practices, nowhere mentioned in the Constitution, which had been useful at times. It had never been codified. It sometimes caused friction, but it had rarely worked without the implied consent of Congress. The mutual assessment of its legitimacy and usefulness shifted from era to era. But then, inflamed by Mr. Nixon's aggressive impoundments for policy and ideological ends, Congress moved to codify the rules. It distinguished between various kinds of impoundments and defined timetables and procedures for handling each kind. Without intending to do so, however, Congress not only cured an abuse but tossed away a device that was often as helpful to Congress as to economy-minded presidents. It may be more than coincidence that following the statutory restriction of impoundments, budget deficits have swollen inordinately and that we now find President Reagan and some of his congressional allies dreaming of an item veto.

You will by now have read my theme. The state of the Constitution is sound; but the rhetoric and the recent outburst of legislative codification both threaten to get out of control. The idea of "mandarinization" seems to me to capture the spirit of what is going on—a tendency to exchange the Marshall view, which has high politics at its core, for something like a legal code: to forget that "it is a constitution we are expounding." Spin a web of law thick and intricate, we seem to suppose, and Gulliver will have no choice but to lie still. Now Gulliver often has trouble moving at all. Lord Macaulay's famous warning that the Constitution was "all sail and no anchor" was inaccurate enough when he issued it; but it is spectacularly off the mark today. The anchor is heavy; the sail is small.

Action on all the great issues, from proper pay for upper-level government scientists to Social Security reform, has been so balked that nearly every decision has recently had to be referred to an appointive commission, in the hope that an independent forum might bypass the jammed and clogged channels of government. We have had commissions not only on Social Security financing but on the MX missile, Central American policy, and one on deficits seems inevitable sooner or later. What could provide more embarrassing evidence of the incapacity of the constitutional machinery, as we are now using it, to produce vigorous, decisive and accountable government? It isn't, in my view, the fault of the Constitution; it is a study in the evolution of the American political culture away from the harsh necessities of governance and choice. Perhaps the Constitution needs some tinkering here and there, as plenty of thoughtful people from time to time suggest. But the main problem is that we are shrinking it, from a document designed to order and regulate government by consent to a code that too often seems to *prevent* the act of governing.

8. The Myth of the Fourth Estate

It was Edmund Burke, gazing up at the reporters' gallery in the House of Commons, who supposedly said: "Yonder sits the Fourth Estate, more important than them all"—more important than the lords spiritual and temporal or the Commons themselves. When he said it no one could possibly have taken him seriously. It is otherwise today, at least in America.

The problem for a press powerful enough to be called an estate of any realm is accountability—the exercise of large power to do hurt, coupled with a constitutional exemption from responsibility.

It is fair to note that this expansive role, and its temptations, have been to some degree thrust unsought upon the press. When the First Amendment was written in 1791, no such role could be foreseen. Indeed, with the rise of party divisions in George Washington's first administration, newspapers quickly became viciously partisan. Their usual tone is suggested in an early and famous libel case (*People v. Croswell*, 1804) which sprang from a charge against Thomas Jefferson: Jefferson was said to have paid the scurrilous journalist James Callendar to call Washington "a traitor, a robber and a perjuror" and John Adams "a hoary-headed incendiary"—and this while president. Jefferson was scandalized by the charge; and he had every right to be.

Such mudslinging was typical of the American party press in its infancy. It would have been absurd to suggest a quasi-official function for so blunt and crude an instrument. Yet a system of government of which the separation of powers is a key principle was, by its own internal logic, likely to demand some "public" function of the press. This was not at first recognized. Well over a century passed before the implications of the First Amendment and the separation of powers sorted themselves out; and the surrogate duty, even when recognized, has been exercised in a haphazard and uncodified fashion. The development, moreover, has by no means been steady; and there has even been some degeneration. The presidential news conference, once a sober and informative exercise in news-gathering, has ballooned in recent years into a grotesque television spectacular in which network news personalities jostle one another for attention—and, worse, from which no useful information emerges. The press conference is no more than a pale shadow of the parliamentary question time, with which for a time the more hopeful students of its possibilities once compared it.

Yet changes of law and technology have emboldened the press in the past quarter-century or so to expand its claims. We journalists have raised the shibboleth of "the people's right to know," often clothing self-interest in the dress of public interest. The trend towards a more expansive version of the First Amendment is welcome, if only to counteract the growing mania for official secrecy. But it is important to recall how nearly accidental the "fourth estate" role is; and equally important to bear in mind its problematical nature in a system operating under democratic theory. Is it more than myth?

The starting point is to understand that no official role was at first foreseen or intended. But that is only a fragment of the story. As nearly as can be told, the aim of the First Amendment was to assure the protection of the press against prior restraint. The initial theory stemmed directly from Blackstone. In his famous *Commentaries on the Law of England,* Blackstone, a near contemporary of the Framers, had written:

> . . . Where blasphemous, immoral, treasonable, schismatical, seditious or scandalous libels are punished by English law . . . the liberty of the press, properly understood, is by no means infringed or violated. The liberty of the press is indeed essential to the nature of a free state: but this consists in laying no previous restraints upon publications, and not in censure from criminal matter when published. Every freeman has an undoubted right to lay what sentiments he pleases before the public: to forbid this, is to destroy the freedom of the press: but if he publishes what is improper, mischievous or illegal, he must take the consequences of his own temerity.

To an ear attuned to recent and more expansive notions of press freedom, Blackstone's analysis sounds almost timid. Note all the qualifications that have disappeared, at least in American law. In Blackstone's time and before there had no doubt been isolated philosophers of freedom who distinguished between truth and opinion, the better to assert that some play of undisciplined opinion is essential to free government. But that was an advanced view, at least in the English law of the mid-eighteenth century. Seditious libel remained a working restraint. Journalists were not at liberty to write with abandon about officials; far from it. Nothing like a theory of the relativism of opinion had arisen, under which it might be supposed that the views of this or that pamphleteer could matter as much as the view of an official or magistrate.

No other conclusion is possible when one looks into the terms in which seditious libel—the defamation of officials—

was discussed at the time of the First Amendment. On August 28, 1789, Jefferson writes to Madison from Paris to say that the new Constitution would have suited him better if Article 4 had included these words—this was, of course, before the first Congress had written the First Amendment: "The people shall not be deprived or abridged of their right to speak, to write, or otherwise to publish anything but false facts affecting injuriously the life, property, or reputation of others or affecting the peace of the confederacy with foreign nations." Even Jefferson, our premier philosopher, assumed that even a free press must observe distinct limits when it infringed on reputation or even, it would appear, conditions of war or peace. Opinion, to say nothing of truth, is not for him a relative term; and "false facts" would be exempt from constitutional protection, leaving it to judges to say what is true and false and also, interestingly, to announce what expressions of opinion might "affect the peace of the confederacy with foreign nations."

It seems to have been far from the minds of the libertarians who initially chartered our liberties to regard falsehood (or slander) as worthy of legal protection. The best historical evidence is that less than a decade after writing the First Amendment, Congress enacted the notorious Sedition Act, under which a number of editors were prosecuted—and some fined or imprisoned—for publishing critical sentiments about officials that would be regarded as tame today. To be sure, Jefferson and Madison immediately and energetically assailed the Sedition Act on constitutional grounds, in the Virginia and Kentucky Resolutions. But their argument wasn't libertarian; they resorted to the doctrine of reserved powers, arguing that the act was a trespass against powers clearly left to the states. Under the Jeffersonian theory, then, the punishment of seditious libel was in a funny way a privilege reserved to the states. If officials were going to protect themselves against the slanders of impudent editors, they would have to do so by going to the state courts.

The same dismal picture—dismal, anyway, from the standpoint of later notions of press freedom—appears in the next significant chapter of the story: the energetic and widespread attack on "Copperhead" journals and journalism by the Lincoln administration, and sometimes even by military tribunals of the Union Army. Even before that, which at least had proceeded under color of wartime emergency powers, the precedent had been set in the stifling of dissident views, North and South, during the acrimonious quarrel over abolition and the fugitive slave laws. In times of trouble, the press was regularly harassed on a legal theory (of which we still hear echoes) that in matters of public policy the magistrates are ex-officio wiser than ink-stained wretches. The myth of a Fourth Estate might survive, as myth. As reality it played no visible role in the daily life of the Republic.

Later, things changed drastically; but that was much later. The first constitutional landmark in which a modern theory of press freedom may be discerned was the Supreme Court decision of 1931 in *Near v. Minnesota*. That ruling, odd as it may seem today, marked the Court's first significant venture into press law. A Minnesota "gag law" had been used to restrain an obstreperous newspaper, occasionally anti-Semitic and defamatory in tone, which was exposing municipal corruption in Saint Paul: a "Minnesota rag," as Fred Friendly calls it in his monograph on the case. Here, six years after the Court had first applied the First Amendment to the states, the Court affirmed the Blackstonian doctrine—no prior restraint. Chief Justice Hughes took judicial notice of what he called "a baleful influence" of "reckless assaults upon public men." But he also said that "the opportunities for malfeasance and corruption have multiplied, crime has grown to most serious proportions, and the danger of its protection by unfaithful officials . . . emphasizes the primary need of a vigilant and courageous press, especially in great cities."

These were the first of many murmurings friendly to the

press from the federal bench; but the main point is that the doctrine scarcely went beyond Blackstone. Blackstone was merely implanted in the First Amendment and applied against a state padlocking law. (It is incorrect, then, to say that Prohibition and the wave of mobsterism and corruption it spawned had no positive side-effects: It gave us, albeit indirectly, a broadened protection of press freedom.)

But there was almost no further judicial intervention of note for thirty-three years—not until that red-letter day in 1964 when the Warren Court ruled in *New York Times v. Sullivan*. With that decision, a new and vastly expanded doctrine of press freedom emerged—and rather abruptly. The facts of the case are somewhat humdrum. For one thing, the publication the Court decided to protect took the form of a paid advertisement, not a flaming pamphlet or man-ifesto. A city police commissioner of Montgomery claimed that he had been libeled in a pro-civil rights ad in *The Times*—some of whose copy reported "false facts," to recall Jeffer-son's oxymoron. The immensely more important fact is that the *Sullivan* decision marked the burial on these shores of the last traces of the ancient doctrine of seditious libel. The new doctrine is that public debate can flourish only through a "robust" tolerance of variety—a tolerance which includes the absolute right to print falsehoods, even defamatory false-hoods, against officials so long as they are printed in good faith. The *Sullivan* decision at a single stroke deposed the old presumption that officials know best, and replaced it with a doctrine of the relativity of opinion. Public officials would thenceforward have to take their chances as targets of the press; and few holds would be barred. Claims of libel would be sustained only if "actual malice"—deliberate and knowing misrepresentation of fact—could be proved.

The theory underlying the *Sullivan* revolution is, I think, a respectable and compelling one. Perhaps it is necessary as well, since it is often more important to expose a scandal than to get every single fact and inference right. But it ought to be noted that with that landmark there collapsed, on these shores, the appealing old Miltonian doctrine that the discovery of "truth" is the paramount rationale of press freedom. In the *Areopagitica,* his great protest against licensing of the press, John Milton had rested his case on the faith that when truth and falsehood grapple, truth will win; "for whoever knew truth put to flight in a free and open encounter?"

The *Sullivan* precedent is now a quarter-century old. It will soon be as distant from us as it was from *Near v. Minnesota.* But already its assumptions are firmly settled in the ethos of the American press and judiciary—even, remarkably, among most politicians. It is increasingly hard to recall what a revolution it was—the overthrow at a stroke of centuries of legal doctrine. Together with the rise of television as a major news source (or at least of impressions about the news) and companioned by "investigative journalism," the *Sullivan* doctrine is one leg of the tripod on which the press sits enthroned. There are problems, of course. Officials are bringing more libel suits, to get their stories told if not to win. Juries are returning some very large damages, which are not infrequently set aside on appeal. The Supreme Court has held that the "malice" standard—involving as it does a state of mind—may justify the judicial scrutiny of journalists' notes (or "work product," as some justices quaintly called them). And Renata Adler argues in her important book *Reckless Disregard* that the demands of the *Sullivan* defense in big libel trials have brought about a situation in which journalists must beat tactical and self-serving retreats from their professed dedication to the discovery of fact. Even with these qualifications, however, few journalists would willingly turn the clock back or revive the doctrine of seditious libel.

But the story as I have briefly laid it out so far is not one that ends, in fairy-tale fashion, "and they all lived (or wrote) happily ever after." Maybe it was inevitable that the old presumption of the magistrate's wisdom would be dethroned and opinion relativized. Maybe those tendencies were implicit in the First Amendment, like those grains of wheat from pharaohs' tombs that are said to germinate successfully after thousands of years. After all, the press is not the only institution in modern America whose habits of deference are vanishing; the more inquisitorial manner is in the air in America today. But the main worry is that even as an enlarged and perhaps necessary doctrine of freedom has flourished, no companion doctrine of accountability has come with it.

"To whom then are columnists accountable?" a friend asked me one day. "God," I said in a rare burst of quick-wittedness. Everyone had a good laugh, but is the issue of accountability so easy to laugh away? I can find nothing in the First Amendment to require it; but some of us are beginning to be uneasy with the cavalier attitude that the press never needs to explain itself persuasively in a democratic society. In a theory of government that demands earthly and tangible standards of accountability for all powerful institutions, it will hardly do for the press to claim, *Vox auctoris, vox Dei.* I haven't worked all this out. But it is clear to me that the press should either establish some standard of self-disciplined accountability or drastically gear down—not its constitutional freedom, but the immodest boast that everything it does is *ipso facto* in the public interest.

A true fourth estate would not only acknowledge a theory of accountability. It would need competences—capacities for seasoned judgment—for which journalists often are not trained. There are those who say that our job is just to print the facts, without explanation or apology. But there are notorious cases when the facts as they appeared yesterday are not the facts as they appear today. David Broder has noted, for instance, the case of the weeping Edmund Muskie in 1972. The senator was in that year the odds-on favorite to win the Democratic presidential nomination—until he mounted a truck at the doorstep of the offices of the Manchester *Union-Leader* to denounce its publisher. Muskie's grievance was an item, lifted from *Newsweek* magazine, reporting that Mrs. Muskie used salty language and took a drink or two. It was snowing and darkness was closing in; and the senator appeared to weep. The episode, reported with heavy insinuations about the senator's emotional volatility, was thought to have finished off his candidacy. What we were not able to report would certainly have included, if we had known it, the fact that Muskie was the target at the time of a furtive "dirty tricks" operation by the Nixon reelection campaign.

This was the first striking instance in which a drastically important fact about modern American presidential campaigning made itself evident: The press has now practically supplanted political parties as makers and breakers of candidacies. Many of my colleagues are comfortable with this function, which has filled the political reporters as a group with a sense of boldness and self-importance. But there is a world of difference between reporters, who represent only themselves and their publications or networks, and political parties, which represent a diversity of experiences, interests and attitudes.

No less daunting is the thought that the press, now addicted to leaked information whose provenance (and possible ulterior purposes) it is not always equipped to evaluate on a short timetable, could become the unwitting instrument of distortion. That the Iran-Contra scandal was at the long end of a string that began to be pulled when one hostage was released does not mean that every string leads to a scandal rather than to a sensitive initiative to which confidentiality is vital. Most official secrets of which we have recent experience have been guilty secrets. The stark and overriding fact is that government usually classifies information for reasons of political self-protection rather than "national security." But we cannot assume that all secrets are unworthy of being kept.

Unfortunately, while we certainly know the workaday difference between good news and bad news, no identifiable principle has emerged to guide us in distinguishing good exposure from bad exposure. And maybe in a system in which interim accountability is often difficult to impose even on those who are constitutionally accountable, imperfections in the performance of the fourth estate are worth what they cost. But if the self-important sobriquet we inherit from Burke were to be expunged from history tomorrow, and the dangerous flattery implicit in it wholly forgotten, I would not mourn its disappearance. We are well rid of the myth of official infallibility, whose gradual relinquishment I have described. Is the idea of official infallibility now to be replaced by an equally dubious myth of the infallibility of an unfettered and quasi-official press?

9. Harry Truman and the Lessons of History

It is one of our civic pieties that a statesman—an American president, especially—must have the past "in his bones," in C. P. Snow's phrase. By that we mean that the office requires a working sense of history. Of all our recent presidents, Harry S. Truman seemed above all to meet that exalted standard. And yet how did he meet it? He was not, like Theodore Roosevelt, a practicing historian, although he once said that had he not gotten "mixed up in politics" he might have been a history teacher.

Mr. Truman's consciousness of what we bravely call "the lessons of history" was by his own testimony constant and pervasive. The testimony is largely to be found in his two-volume memoir of the presidential years; and it is on the whole credible. Yet few of his associates were aware of the dimension of historical consciousness while he was in the White House. On the contrary, conventional wisdom had it that he was a "smaller" man than the majestic Franklin D. Roosevelt. It was a popular superstition that this plucky autodidact was essentially unlettered. So much, as usual, for conventional wisdom. We know better now.

Indeed, a distinguished historian, John Lukacs, has paid

an extraordinary tribute to Harry Truman and his early history teachers in his book *1945: Year Zero:*

> Among the benefactors of the United States and the Western world in the 20th century, two unknown women ought to be given places of high honor. They are Miss Maggie Phelps and Miss Tillie Brown, two teachers in the Columbian High School in Independence, Missouri, who inspired the boy Harry Truman's interest in history and biography. He felt it proper and just to record his debt to them in the political biography of his presidency. "My debt to history cannot be calculated," he wrote. Our debt to his knowledge of history cannot be calculated either. Few American presidents knew as much history as Harry Truman. Few presidents understood it better. His understanding . . . was the traditional biographical one, exemplified by writers such as Plutarch. . . . Men made history rather than history made men.

As a longstanding admirer of Harry Truman (even before his virtues came to be generally acclaimed), I join in Mr. Lukacs' high praise. Yet this is only the threshold of an interesting inquiry, bringing all sorts of questions to mind. What form, apart from the heroic and biographical, did Mr. Truman's historical knowledge take? Where and how, apart from the early tutelage of the Misses Phelps and Brown of Independence, Mo., did he acquire it? Was it historical knowledge of the sort that professional historians would recognize? Or was it of a slightly more rough and ready sort? And, most importantly, how and in what ways did it shape the critical decisions of the Truman presidency—if it shaped them? What did history tell Harry Truman that affected his view of the tumultuous world of 1945-53, or prompted him to seize his problems in a certain way?

The main evidence, such as it is, lies in the presidential memoirs. I counted well over a hundred references to history, historical events and historical figures in the index.

Bear in mind that Truman had left office when he wrote these memoirs; so this is a retrospective glance at what he thought—or thought he had thought. Yet even if one suspects that the record is embellished here and there, the range of references leaves absolutely no doubt that history was vitally important to Harry Truman. "I had trained myself," he writes, "to look back into history for precedents, because instinctively I sought perspective in the span of history for decisions I had to make. . . . Most of the problems a president has to face have their roots in the past."

When, for instance, Harry Truman was contemplating what came to be known as the Truman Doctrine—the doctrine that the United States would resist armed aggression and subversion abroad, against free but weak peoples— he amplified his underlying thoughts in a speech at Baylor University—this was the spring of 1947. "The lesson of history, I said, was plain: Freedom of international trade would provide the atmosphere necessary to peace." Later, canvassing his clouded political prospects in 1948, he "realized that my position was historically nothing new. . . . Since the election of Jefferson in 1800 there had been 36 presidential campaigns in which the press had supposedly played an important part. In 18 of these campaigns the press had supported the losing candidate, and in the other 18 it had been behind the winner. This was the clearest proof I needed that I had nothing to fear."

When a year later he promoted the Point Four program—the first program of U. S. economic aid to underdeveloped lands—he "knew from my study of American history that this country was developed by the investment of foreign capital by the British, the Dutch, the Germans, and the French. . . . The first packing house west of the Mississippi River was built by a Frenchman, a count in Napoleon's army."

When he sought to sell NATO—the nation's first

peacetime alliance—to a historically isolationist American people, he "always kept in mind the lesson of Wilson's failure in 1920. I meant to have legislative co-operation."

And yet again, as he charted a response to what eventually came to be known as McCarthyism, he tells us that his mind ran back to "periods of mass hysteria. . . . For example, when the French Revolution reached its height with the Jacobins in power. . . . Jefferson was accused of being a Jacobin and therefore disloyal."

As he emplaned to leave Kansas City for Washington on the Sunday in June 1950 following the North Korean attack on South Korea, and great decisions impended, he reflected that "in my generation, this was not the first occasion when the strong had attacked the weak." He thought of Manchuria, Ethiopia and Austria, and how the failure of democracies to act "had encouraged the aggressors to keep going ahead. Communism was acting in Korea just as Hitler, Mussolini and the Japanese had acted ten, fifteen and 20 years earlier." Later, having committed American forces to that war and placed General Douglas MacArthur in command, and having wearied of the general's insubordination, Mr. Truman—as one might expect—remembered history. It was Lincoln and McClellan all over again: "The general had his own ideas on how the war, and even the country, should be run. . . . Lincoln was patient . . . but at long last he was compelled to relieve the Union Army's principal commander." Truman, as we know, did likewise; he cashiered General MacArthur.

These references—and these are but a few of the many Harry Truman makes—do sustain John Lukacs's contention that Harry Truman approached public tasks with the voice of history at his ear. For the most part it was a voice offering enviably clear counsel. It was, as one historian a bit patronizingly calls it, "storybook history," the kind that seems to teach unambiguous "lessons."

One may, in fact, search Mr. Truman's reminiscences pretty thoroughly without finding the slightest evidence that the mysteries of history, its perversities or ironies or ambiguities, ever weighed on him. He speaks of history as if it had been an open book, holding no fugitive secrets. After all, as he explained to Merle Miller, "there's nothing new in human nature. . . . If you want to understand the 20th century, read the lives of the Roman emperors. . . . Men don't change. The only thing new in the world is the history you don't know."

These lessons without riddles are the gist of practically all the Truman musings on history. There is an implicit view, which we usually associate with antiquity, that time is not linear but cyclical; that identical situations and challenges recur, reflecting and testing an essentially unchanging human character. Mr. Truman was aware, as any omnivorous reader would be, that more than one view might be taken of almost any historical episode. But that did not lessen his confidence in the usefulness of the message. "No two historians," he told Merle Miller, "ever agree on what happened, and the damned thing is that they both think they're telling the truth."

For purposes of this inquiry, however, far the most important of Mr. Truman's beliefs about history was that, as he put it, "it is the man who makes history," that "the greatest strides occur when courageous and gifted leaders either seize the opportunity or create it." It followed that a statesman of character and willpower need not fear defeat by the imponderables of fate or circumstance. It was because James Buchanan was a "do-nothing" president that he failed to stop the outbreak of the Civil War. Buchanan, Truman thought, "could have stopped the Civil War in South Carolina, just as easy as old Jackson did it about 20 years before that. Jackson told South Carolina that if they did not enforce the laws in their state, he'd come down and hang every one of them . . . " We know from other memoirs how strongly Mr. Truman condemned Buchanan's delinquency. On November 20, 1950, the historian Herbert Feis visited the president in connection with an article he was writing about great presidential decisions. At the suggestion of the White House press secretary, Charles Ross, Feis handed the president a carbon of the rough draft. He watched as Harry Truman read through it, coming to the part about Lincoln. "Need never have been, never," Mr. Truman said, "if Buchanan had done what he should have. . . . Hard to understand—he had great experience in public affairs—ambassador to Russia—secretary of state. Something lacking . . . hard."

There is a certain starkness, not to say simplicity, in this faith that men shape history at will; that intentions matter so much. No one can say that Mr. Truman was wrong—that had Buchanan been a Jackson secessionism might have been stifled in its cradle. What we can say, however, is that Lincoln, who soon tried to do what Buchanan failed to do, found himself with a civil war on his hands. Had Lincoln lived to write his presidential memoirs (and what a book it would have been), it would surely have offered a darker, more guarded assessment of the possibilities of human mastery over events. Lincoln's soberer view of the role of fate, chance, destiny, providence in the affairs of men is reflected in a great passage of the Second Inaugural Address. As an account of the coming of the Civil War, it has not been exceeded for succinctness and penetration:

> All dreaded it, all sought to avert it. While the inaugural address was being delivered from this place, devoted altogether to saving the Union without war, insurgent agents were in the city seeking to destroy it without war—seeking to dissolve the Union and divide effects by negotiation. Both parties deprecated war, but one of them would make war rather than let the nation survive, and the other would accept war rather than let it perish, and the war came.

II

The greatest of all the choices President Truman faced in those years had to do, of course, with Europe. Between April of 1945 and June of 1950 he made most of the decisions that defined, at least for America's part, what we know as the Cold War. What guidance did his historical memories offer?

Once he had found his footing, Harry Truman was not the sort of president who could be blown about by strong-minded advisers, though he certainly had them, and though he seems to have delegated authority easily. Yet if one expects Mr. Truman's decisions always to be drenched in historical self-consciousness, there are gaps and puzzles in the record. There was, for instance, the notable episode when Secretary of State James F. Byrnes, negotiating at the Paris peace conference, felt himself undercut by the public pronouncements of Secretary of Commerce Henry A. Wallace. Byrnes complained bitterly and soon insisted that Mr. Truman choose between the two of them. Henry Wallace was arguing for a sort of live-and-let-live policy towards the Soviet Union, an argument that soon proved to be well outside the political consensus. At first, however, Mr. Truman pretended that Wallace's views were not inconsistent with his own, or even with Secretary Byrnes's, though in fact they plainly were.

Henry Wallace accepted with equanimity that the price of good relations with the Russians would be acquiescence in a Soviet sphere of influence in those neighboring countries whose political control she deemed vital to her security. In this he believed himself to be adhering to the FDR tradition, implicit in the Yalta agreements, in which Russian paramountcy in the borderlands of Eastern Europe would be conceded. Henry Wallace's turned out to be a minority view within the administration and some thought it sappy and even outrageous. But even the historical Truman was slow to see the inconsistency. As Daniel Yergen observes, "Truman was . . . very much a traditional Wilsonian. . . . The ideas of spheres of influence and a big power peace were abhorrent to him." His failure to see from the outset the very un-Wilsonian implications of the Wallace position is a sort of mystery—but then perhaps no more so than his casually unhistorical, and naive, remark that Josef Stalin is "more like Tom Pendergast [the Democratic political boss of Kansas City, and Truman's sometime political patron] than any man I have ever known." That is, Stalin was essentially a ward-heeling politician whose good instincts were being obstructed by the Politburo much as Truman's own were being obstructed (so he claimed) by the Eightieth Congress.

The paramount issues making for Cold War tensions were from the outset those of history and geopolitics. Perhaps Russian intentions were, as Churchill had said, enigmatic. But what weight was to be assigned to traditional Russian imperial preoccupations, and what weight to a revolutionary ideology? What principles were to govern Truman's policy? Wilsonian universalism assumed the sovereign right of all countries, wherever situated, to choose their political destinies freely. On the other hand, the more cautious realism which, though inexplicit, seemed to govern Roosevelt's negotiations at Yalta would militate in the direction Henry Wallace favored. Peace would be bought by conciliation, sometimes at the expense of principle. These were, in retrospect, the crucial issues of policy. Yet for all his close reading of history, one finds little evidence that President Truman consciously reflected upon them. It may be that for Harry Truman (as Daniel Yergin suggests) the "sphere of influence" questions came with answers already predetermined by a Wilsonian cast of mind.

There was, for instance, the quarrel over the postwar government of Poland—the Anglo-American support of the government in exile in London versus the so-called "Lublin government" established by the Russian armies. It now seems doubtful that any traditional American statesman could have been other than instinctively outraged by what was unfolding in Poland: a straightforward tale of Soviet bad faith. And there was the yet greater question of Germany. Germany, to quote Daniel Yergin once again, "presented an infinitely complex problem which was, at the same time, a very simple one—neither side could take the risk that a reunited Germany might become the ally of the other." For perhaps two years after 1945 some hope lingered on both sides that a four-power agreement on the future of an undivided Germany might be attained. But irreconcilable tensions, some natural and others manufactured, soon emerged. The Russians, their economy shattered, insisted on the $20 billion in German "reparations" that had been vaguely promised—or at least spoken of—in wartime conferences. For their part the Western Europeans and the Americans, having shelved the dreamy foolishness of the Morgenthau Plan, had recognized that to drain Germany's resources, to make her a permanent ward and captive, would be economically self-defeating—that the sooner Germany could be restored to productive self-sufficiency the less insistent would be its pressure on U.S. and hard-pressed European resources. For the Russians, Germany was primarily a security problem, while for the United States and Britain—and later and more gradually, for France—Germany soon became an economic problem. In this divergence of interest and perception there lay the seeds of conflict—of the clash of policies that by 1948-49 led to a divided Germany, the Berlin blockade, and, yes, the acceptance of de facto spheres of influence.

Again, one finds little evidence that Mr. Truman's sense of history led him to so abstract or Olympian an analysis. If Mr. Truman's historical views influenced policy on Germany, it was because he strongly believed in the "lesson" of the 1920s and 1930s. And that lesson, he believed, was the folly of trade restrictions and reparations—and appeasement. His views made it all but certain that he would go along with the decision to restore Germany to economic health and later to seek its integration into the Western political community. The key episodes that generated the Cold War—the events that widened every small fissure—sprang from differences over Poland, over Germany, and over the ultimate disposition of atomic weapons. The Berlin blockade and the Czechoslovakian coup of March 1948 confirmed suspicions sown by those germinal problems.

Then in June 1950 the outbreak of the war in Korea set a seal of bloodshed on this unfolding tragedy. The Russians, as we know now, assumed that South Korea had been placed outside our "defense perimeter," as U.S. officials had said. But they missed the telling significance of the qualifying term, "in case of global war." Harry Truman's resolute response in Korea apparently surprised Stalin. But the response seems remarkably predictable, for it was a classic example of the kind of decision in which Mr. Truman felt the weight of historical warnings: of Manchuria, Ethiopia and Munich. As Ernest May has observed: "The members of the Truman administration appear to have thought about the issues before them in a frame of reference made up in part of historical analogies, parallels, and presumed trends and . . . the history employed for this purpose was narrowly selected and subjected to no deliberate scrutiny or analysis."

Undoubtedly. And as time passed, the analytical subtleties that at an earlier stage might have suggested important distinctions between Soviet and Nazi behavior grew dim. The operating assumption came to be that all aggressors are alike and, unless firmly resisted, will find in every success an invitation to move on to the next hunting ground. There was without doubt a hardening and coarsening of the historical consciousness, such as it was, in Mr. Truman and those who advised him. This must be conceded, but without conceding that the analogizing was in any sense perverse, or out of character. This latter needs adding because a school of revisionist historians has challenged our earlier reading of the onset of the Cold War, some even claiming that it was more the fault of U. S. provocations and misreadings than of the Soviet Union.

It is necessarily the premise of these revisionists that the Cold War was in some sense avoidable, and avoidable on sensible terms. Was it? One is uncannily reminded of the revisionist arguments of an earlier historical controversy—the famous debate about the origins of the American Civil War that J. G. Randall touched off an age ago with his celebrated essay, "A Blundering Generation." He took the view (it has odd parallels with the view Harry Truman took of James Buchanan's failure) that no such tragic conflict was "irrepressible"; that the American Civil War was the result of a breakdown of the arts of statecraft in an atmosphere of hysteria and extremism. Of this thesis there are interesting echoes in the literature on the origins of the Cold War—allegations of "hysteria," blundering, miscalculation and shortsightedness. That there was some blundering is undeniable; it was far from being the essence of the matter.

It was not the essence of the matter for precisely the same reasons that historians like Pieter Geyl and Bernard De Voto noted in response to Randall's "Blundering Generation" thesis about the outbreak of the Civil War. Geyl speaks in a telling phrase of the "despiritualization" of historical causation that began with the Beards' economic determinism. De Voto, for his part, writes:

> In its concern to show that the Civil War was a product
> of hotheads, radical agitators, and their propaganda, an
> almost incidental result which could have been avoided if

some extremists could have been induced to hold their
tongues, history is in eminent danger of forgetting that
slavery had anything whatever to do with the
war. . . . [This] history will not put itself in the position of
saying that any thesis may have been wrong, any cause
evil, or any group of men heretical. . . . [and] will not deal
with moral values.

Similarly, revisionist history of the Cold War—much of
it, anyway—discounts honest moral passion having at its core
a concern for personal liberties and self-determination and
what one might call, perhaps without excessive presumption,
elementary civil decencies—such as not provoking the
murder or suicide of Czech statesmen. To try to grasp the
origins of the Cold War without taking account of the
differences between a philosophy of freedom and popular
sovereignty on the one hand, and a philosophy of historical
"realism" and collectivism on the other, seems unhistorical.

Professor Ernest May, a wise and learned diplomatic
historian who is not a revisionist, says that President Truman
and his advisers "should have recognized the important role
that historical evidence played in their reasoning. . . . [and]
that they were fixing on only one piece of history—and that
a piece which had as yet been subjected to little detached
examination."

True. Yet there is a further complication. Perhaps, to be
of use to the statesman facing some immediate and confusing
challenge, history must offer striking and salient lessons;
perhaps it must even be a bit simplistic in what it tells him.
Historians have the luxury of leisurely reflection after the
fact. Presidents must act quickly, and on imperfect evidence.
Indeed, analysis may even paralyze the will to act so that
decisive opportunities pass while the analysts shuffle their
position papers.

History was important to Harry Truman because it

seemed to him to suggest clearly defined choices. History obviously played a material role in the choices he had to make, as well as in his recollection of them. Yet I wonder whether, even in so history-minded a president, we who expect an elegant marriage of history and policy are not cherishing a pleasant myth. The thoroughly analyzed history for which Ernest May calls is desirable in principle but in practice it may be elusive. History is more likely to explain a powerful subliminal predisposition. It is not, even for Mr. Truman, an ever-illuminating lamp. Perhaps the more important thing is that Harry Truman was not bemused by the fear that statesmen could not control outcomes by acts of will, were in effect prisoners of onrushing events. That was his strength, though as the contrast with Lincoln suggests, what was a strength in the statesman was also a sort of frailty in the amateur historian. The dimensions of irony and tragedy seem missing or minimized. In the end the inquiry only seems to deepen the mystery it sought to penetrate. Historical consciousness is an asset for the practical states-man. It affects, but cannot really supersede, his felt sense of the moral and practical questions he must answer with time's implacable deadlines approaching.

10. W.J. Cash and
'The Mind of the South'

Forty-four years after its appearance in the war-darkened year 1941, Wilbur J. Cash's *The Mind of the South* seems ripe for some such pro-and-con examination as Professor Pieter Geyl once arranged for the historical reputation of Napoleon. No enterprise could be more appropriate, since the book has itself become very much a part of the South's recent history.

Cash: For or against?

On the positive side of the ledger, the book has won votaries in great number among southern intellectuals— jurists, journalists, historians and statesmen, many of whom do not hesitate to identify it as the touchstone of the modern southern political sensibility. I have to count myself among the epigones of Cash. As a college student of nineteen, on summer vacation, I came by a recently issued paperback edition of *Mind* and devoured it, thunderstruck, as if by almost supernatural revelation. What one had dimly sensed or felt as a matter of personal experience underwent sharp and sudden clarification. Like the Molière character who was astonished to discover that he had been speaking prose, we were all startled to find, so crisply exposed, the historical roots and causes of what we had been vaguely thinking, sensing and feeling all our days.

Yet along with the praise and thanksgiving one would also have to note, and account for, a loyal opposition to the book—loyal in the sense of giving Cash his due as a voice of prophecy, and of recognizing his genius, but opposition none the less. And a distinguished one. It has been led by the most eminent of all recent historians of the South, the Arkansas-born Professor C. Vann Woodward, and by the most original and provocative student of the slave South in our time, Professor Eugene Genovese. Both have been troubled by Cash's liberties (as they see it) with the southern past. Before proceeding to a closer inspection of the qualities that have given permanence and fame to Cash's book, a preliminary glance at the opposition may be in order.

In a 1969 essay, "The Elusive Mind of the South," Woodward questioned outright Cash's two dominant themes—the unity and continuity of the Southern historical experience. To the contrary, Woodward insists, the disruption of hopes and plans, a sharp *discontinuity* of political and social experience, have been more the rule for the South down through time:

> Southerners, unlike other Americans, repeatedly felt the solid ground of continuity give way under their feet. An old order of slave society solidly supported by constitution, state, church and the authority of law and learning and cherished by a majority of the people, collapsed, perished and disappeared. So did the short-lived experiment in national independence. So also the short-lived experiment in Radical Reconstruction. The succeeding order of Redeemers, the New South, lasted longer, but it too seems destined for the dump heap of history.

The point, buttressed by important examples, cuts right

across Cash's central theme. For Cash, as we shall see, held that the key to southern experience for at least a century and a quarter, hence to an understanding of its "mind," was a nearly unaltered rhythm of challenge and response. Challenges to the southern way of life might vary. But invariably those challenges were marked by the same failure to achieve true transformation, accompanied by the same dismal slide back into accustomed patterns of reaction, romance and evasion.

As for another central preoccupation—Cash's obsessive concern to deflate the romantic Cavalier legend of the Old South, to kill off the *seigneurs* of fond romance and replace them with graceless, uncouth, grasping and socially irresponsible parvenus—Professor Genovese has his doubts. He has asked a challenging question: When has any ruling class, any "aristocracy," been other than acquisitive, pushing and often uncouth? Where did Cash get his idea that master classes are otherwise? And whence, in any event, might an aristocracy arise, if not out of the primal struggle for gain and advantage? Cash, insists Genovese, asks the wrong question. The question isn't whether the upstart squirarchy or "cotton snobs" of antebellum days were ill-bred or avaricious. It is whether the aspirations of that nascent ruling class were to the bourgeois, commercial life or to the spacious seigneurial life—or as Genovese puts it, to Massachusetts or Virginia?

Woodward, finally, has drawn attention to another curious shortcoming, or at least paradox: That having set for himself the task of portraying the southern "mind," Cash argues that the typical southerner—"the man at the center"—entirely lacked intellectual and analytical capacity, hence presumably any capacity to develop a mind worthy of the name. Cash's prototype southerner—one shrinks from the word "stereotype," though the book abounds with schematic figures—is a simple, impulsive fellow, incapable of analyzing in depth the social and economic forces that affect and at times victimize him. The model is Henry Adams's very patronizing portrait of Rooney Lee, the son of General Lee, as a student at Harvard:

> . . . The habit of command was not enough, and the Virginian had little else. He was simple beyond analysis; so simple that even the simple New England student could not realize him. No one knew enough to know how ignorant he was; how childlike; how helpless before the relative complexity of a school. . . . Strictly, the southerner had no mind; he had temperament. He was not a scholar; he had no intellectual training; he could not analyze an idea and he could not even conceive of admitting two . . .

Far from asking himself how truly representative this acid sketch might be (or even, which is certainly in question, whether it were accurate as to Rooney Lee himself), Cash bends it to his purpose and accepts it as a pattern. "It was," Cash elaborates, "the total effect of Southern conditions . . . to preserve the southerner's original simplicity of character as if it were in perpetual suspension. . . . And whether he was a Virginian or a nouveau, he did not (typically speaking) think; he felt; and discharging his feelings immediately, he developed no need or desire for intellectual culture. . . . " Could so sweeping a characterization really apply "typically speaking" to a whole region, of which one might expect the normal distribution of brainpower and sensibility? Had not psychological probability (considering that harsh experience is more likely to deepen and complicate than to simplify human natures) been sacrificed to a regional thesis? Certainly the Rooney Lee pattern would be demonstrably inapplicable, as Woodward notes, to any number of Southern intellectuals, from the great age of Madison, Jefferson, Marshall and Taylor of Caroline, down through Calhoun.

After nearly half a century, then, the balance sheet on Cash and *The Mind of the South*—considered as history—would not necessarily be longer on credits than debits. The book has inspired and nourished two or three generations of native critics. Yet it was problematical in what it claimed about the Southern past. Indeed, one might ask whether in the light of the foregoing criticisms by eminent historians, *Mind* would continue to qualify as history at all. But if not history, what? The projection of a brilliant but troubled and parochial imagination upon random, often half-digested raw materials of history? A form of retrospective anthropology or sociology? Impressionistic journalism, whose ingenious formulations wither under close analysis?

One way, and I think the most fruitful way, to face the problem of Cash and his book is to set aside the unsettled argument over historicity and to view the book as serving essentially extrahistorical (or metahistorical) purposes. Obviously, that was the role Cash himself hoped for. We know that the book, and some of its themes, were a long time in the making—incubating over a decade or more as Cash labored at his daily newspaper chores. Cash was groping above all for insights into the South's experience as a region and a people which would make sense of the South's present. It was a discouraging and stormy present—the world of the late 1920s and 1930s—in which acute economic misery, lynching, labor conflict and violence, and a resurgent Ku Klux Klan might have been taken, to the despair of a decent progressive, as portents of the South to come. There was every reason, in external events of Cash's mature years, why it might seem that the worst experiences of Reconstruction and other "frontiers" were repeating themselves; and from that it could be a tempting inference that this was precisely what had been going on in the South for well over a century.

That would explain the plaintive note of exasperation and impatience, bordering on rage, with which Cash recounts the struggle of the South to transform itself into a modern (or at least modernizing) society. No sooner did the region seem to arrive at the threshold of a realized ideal, aristocratic or agrarian or, later, industrial, than some assault, often as not instigated by Yankees (the "tariff gang" or whatnot) would push it back yet again into the rough-edged ways of the frontier. Time and again, it seemed to Cash, the dog-eat-dog spirit of the frontier, briefly driven underground, would be reborn. For Cash, the South is Sisyphus, eternally pushing the boulder up the hill but never quite to the top; or Tantalus, stooping to drink from the spring that always sinks before his lips. Time and again *The Mind of the South* returns to this dominant note: that of the frustrated seeker of realized chivalric ideals. Ironically, it was the pretense among Southern nostalgics that these ideals had once been realized that drew Cash's most heated scorn. Perhaps no historian pursuing the prosaic matter of "the past as it really was" can afford so tortured and personal an affair with his subject. For in the eternal search for the static ideal, he may miss, or misinterpret, the transformations in which the essence and interest of history usually reside.

As others have noted, moreover, Cash's South was not the only South in the dimension of space, as it was not in the dimension of time. Cash's was a limited, some would say insular, sub-South. As Woodward wryly observes, Cash took it as his mission to write "an unbiased history of the South from the hill-country point of view." Of that special corner of the mid-South Cash would be the historian, as the North Carolina novelist Thomas Wolfe had been the poet and the Tennessean James Agee, of the Luce magazines, the reporter. Cash's horizons were narrow, even in southern terms, though of their narrowness he seems at times nearly unconscious.

Cash's enterprise, finally, was to analyze and evoke a "mind"—"a fairly definite mental pattern, associated with a fairly definite social pattern," as he defines it. But his enterprise departs in a striking way from recent attempts (for instance, by annalists of the French historical school) to recapture past "mentalités." For them, the essential point of going in quest of a bygone cast of mind is to identify and savor its strangeness, its utter distance from the way present people would think or believe. But this was precisely what Cash did not seek and did not achieve. Nothing, in fact, seems to have been further from his intent. His approach is to sound enduring themes, persistent through time, whose significance lies in their stubborn resistance to extinction or even transformation. The South's "mind" is above all notable, as Cash evokes it, for changelessness and endurance. No wonder that even when it purports to be most historical Cash's book has about it an air of anthropology or sociology, or even meteorology: at one notable (and eloquent) point, Cash traces to the weather certain lingering qualities of the southern religious temperament. Much more often than documents or archives, or historians, Cash cities as authorities eminent contemporaries of his, sociologists like Howard Odum of Chapel Hill, or Broadus Mitchell of Baltimore: scholars who in his time were performing statistical analyses of the region.

To say all this is neither to patronize Cash nor to suggest that history is susceptible of only one definition, or yields its secrets only to one technique. It is to say that in his search for lasting patterns in the southern experience that would make sense of the South's temper in his own time, Cash's book is purposeful, directed to an identifiable end. The past as he uses it points to, and explains, the present. *The Mind of the South* indeed bears the telltale marks of that "Whig interpretation of history," that history-through-the-moralist's eye, examined and censured in a notable essay by Herbert Butterfield. It is characteristic of this "Whig interpretation" as Butterfield described it, to weigh in on the side of the progressives and winners, to assume that people in the past must answer to present moral standards. Insofar as they fail to live up to those standards, they deserve the wrath and judgment of the historian. A bit waspishly, but with point, Professor Genovese complains that Cash bears "heavy responsibility for the spread of guiltomania," the apologetic and defensive air which in his view stands in the way of an accurate view of the past. From the guilt stemming from the admitted moral evil of human slavery has flowed a certain censoriousness of the antebellum slaveholding South which may blind us to the poise and serenity with which the slaveholders (some of them at least) lived at ease with the conditions of their time, and were far from thinking of themselves as evil or immoral for doing so.

If we are right, then, in insisting on a more personal perspective on Cash's book, it follows that to understand it fully we must understand the tortured young journalist who wrote it, the two being inseparable. But alas, it is easier to infer Cash from the book than to learn things about the book from the life of Cash. For while Cash must by any standard be counted a major figure in American historical writing—even with the reservations noted above—we know little of his life apart from the typewriter. And in any case that life was short, forty years. The late Joseph L. Morrison, in preparing a brief biography twenty years ago, was hard put to find very much of interest to say about Cash the man.

Of Cash the legend, however, as distinguished from the more obscure Cash the man, I had some indirect experience. When I moved to Charlotte, North Carolina, in the autumn of 1958 to write for Cash's old newspaper, *The Charlotte News*, local legends were easy to come by. The revival of Cash's fame and note was then at its height, signalled, for instance, by the extravagant praise *The Mind of the South* had drawn from an anonymous reviewer of recent American historical writing in the *Times Literary Supplement* of London. Old hands around the *News,* an evening paper, claimed to remember Cash personally; and all had tales to tell about him. The reminiscences ran to a pattern. They tended to stress his moodiness, his heavy drinking, his precarious health. One had the feeling they were colored by his tragic suicide. For Cash, having published his book to wide acclaim and having won the traveling fellowship he had sought for so long, had gone to Mexico City in the summer of 1941 to work on a novel. (Like many very successful writers of nonfiction, he seems to have looked to fiction as the highest form of self-expression.) There, unaccountably, he had hanged himself one July evening in a bathroom at the Hotel Reforma.

In the recollections that abounded in Charlotte news-paper circles, one could choose among a wide assortment of theories. "Jack" Cash, it was confidently said, had been the victim of an inoperable brain tumor, or exhaustion, or even epilepsy. Or he had become so deeply depressed by the sweep of Hitler's hordes across Europe, in a tide of unending conquest, that he had despaired of the future of civilization. One of the more intriguing and colorful stories, impossible to verify, was that upon reading news of the Munich Agreement and the dismemberment of Czechoslovakia on the wire, in September 1938, Cash had fallen to the floor in the *News*'s telegraph room in a sort of catatonic seizure. What was missing from these stories, unfortunately, was any vivid or particular sense of what Cash the man had been like: his habits (other than prodigious reading, writing and drinking) or his temperament, his circle of friends. Which naturally suggests that the author of *The Mind of the South* spent most of his spare hours, as he did his working time, reading and writing.

And perhaps brooding as well. Cash, so far as I know, left only one slight and teasing fragment of autobiography:

an identification note which was to accompany the publication of one of his earlier pieces of journalism in H.L. Mencken's *American Mercury* magazine. The note is veiled and a bit self-dramatizing. Cash's father had operated a company store for one of the textile mills in Gaffney, South Carolina, where Cash was born and spent his boyhood. A characteristic sound of that upland Piedmont South was the sound of company whistles, punctuating the workday, summoning workers to the looms and spindles and later dismissing them. "The keening of the five o'clock whistle," Cash told Mencken, "drilled me in sorrow." Moreover, in the churches of his fundamentalist boyhood, he said that he was haunted by "the Baptist preacher's too graphic account of the Second Coming."

These arch and histrionic self-descriptions tell us very little; but they are richly suggestive. The South that Cash knew best, as we have noted, was the cotton-mill South of the uplands where the "fall line" of the rivers had originally provided power to drive the looms. And despite Cash's heroic effort to give it the color of a reincarnation of the plantation, this was on the whole a bleak and culturally impoverished South. By reading, reflection and the exercise of his lively imagination, Cash had contrived to lift his own vision well beyond it. Yet the vestiges of this peculiar subculture may be detected in the book. Consider, for instance, his all but obsessive attention to the battle between religious fundamentalism and Darwinism. The small but serious Baptist denominational college of which Cash was a graduate, Wake Forest in North Carolina, had been a battleground of the struggle to preserve academic inquiry from the smothering "savage ideal" of cultural and intellectual conformity. Under the leadership of the biologist William Louis Poteat, Wake Forest was often at bay, as Cash notes, in the fight for intellectual inquiry against the antimodernists. No doubt—we would say more cautiously, perhaps—Cash would have felt himself less threatened by the recurring "savage ideal" (and the South with him) had he been a son of cosmopolitan New Orleans rather than of Gaffney, South Carolina.

It is also likely that Cash's embittered quest for patrician ease, large-mindedness, for aristocracy in the old South outside the coastal fringes, had personal resonances as well. His labored and contemptuous dismissal of the pretensions of the upland gentry may tell us more of what Cash himself was like, of his secret aspirations and snobberies, than it does about that class of southerners.

And yet when all the notes of reservation have been duly sounded, we are left, in this man and his lasting book, with a formidable achievement. Whatever its limits as history, whatever the marks of personal and autobiographical projection upon the stuff of history, it is not hard to say why *The Mind of the South* has lasted and has exerted a powerful and continuing influence: Why, for instance, such a figure as the late Judge Waities Waring of Charleston could say that the book had been the foremost influence shaping his noted decision striking down the so-called "white primaries" that preserved the supremacy of the Democratic Party. And why many such tales could be told.

The continuing force of the book is primarily to be explained, I believe, by two qualities, one intrinsic and the other circumstantial. The intrinsic quality is the enchantment of Cash's prose at its best. To the modern ear, it rings on occasion a bit false. It is mannered and overripe at times, as southern rhetoric often is. But its haunting rhythms precisely fit the questing, inquiring strategy and spirit of the book. The writing propels us ever onward, now asking a question, now proposing a thesis, now doubting or qualifying it or affirming it in a new way, and finally arriving at the achieved synthesis. Always, there is a kind of coiled tension.

Another compelling quality, more circumstantial, is the accident that *The Mind of the South* came to be reissued in paperback at a propitious moment. Anchor Books, in one of the series that touched off the "paperback revolution" in American trade publishing, brought out the reprint just as the Supreme Court of the United States was poised to strike down the "separate but equal" doctrine, the underpinning of racial segregation in the South. By May of 1954, all eyes were turned with unusual interest to the region and to the Court's mandate ordering an end to the dual school system—a system that had grown up with the twentieth century and was indeed the only public school system the South had known. However clouded the future, however unforeseeable the ultimate scope of what would become the "civil rights revolution," the South again faced fundamental challenge. What could be more useful at such a time than a book, already acknowledged as a classic, which took as its foremost topic the ways in which "the mind of the South" had responded to challenge?

Moreover, Cash's skeptical and questioning temperament, his sometimes querulous impatience with the South's penchant for romance and evasion in the face of challenge— all this very much suited the mood of the new generation of southerners coming of age in the 1950s: liberals certainly, but not liberals alone. Cash's voice was attractive, too, in that his strategy was not the broadside attack but the measured appreciation. He described himself as the South's "loyal son." He seemed as keen to celebrate its generous and attractive qualities as to condemn, in caustic terms, its faults. And in speaking scaldingly of "the frontier the Yankee made" (Reconstruction, as he viewed it) or of "the tariff gang" of more recent times, he could skewer the hereditary enemies of the South as zestfully as anyone.

Nor was this all. However doubtful its history, at least in the academic sense, *The Mind of the South* breathed an undoubted originality. It might fail the more critical test of analysis in some ways. But it was in many other ways far more useful, for a region in ferment, than more formal academic history might be. The book carried a persuasive explanatory power at a time when explanation was needed, when it was thirsted for. For instance, touching the perennial question of the "one-party South," now again put in jeopardy by racial and civil rights ferment, Cash had written with great insight. He knew how the Democratic Party of the so-called "Redeemers" and "Bourbons" (depending on whether friends or foes were describing them) had maintained its grip by crassly exploiting a sense of racial solidarity among whites of all classes, master and man, to stifle insurgency and keep Republicanism from power. This mechanism, this "proto-Dorian convention," in the rococo label Cash gave it, was by no means dead. It would continue to be a useful instrument of political analysis throughout the 1950s, 1960s and beyond.

And on top of this there was Cash's astute estimate of that familiar bane of the region, the southern demagogue. Under the challenge of the Supreme Court's antisegregation decisions, that type was to flourish anew, especially in the Gulf South. Cash had deplored the type; but he had distinguished among its better and worse varieties, had noted the difference between, say, a Huey Long of Louisiana (who had in some ways served the poor as well as himself, and had not resorted to race-baiting as a political weapon) and such egregious types as Cole Blease of South Carolina and Theodore Bilbo of Mississippi, who had battened on the vilest racism. Cash's careful discriminations were to sharpen the vision of observers of the demagogic animal in the new era. And they were to be sustained by and large (as his grander themes sometimes were not) by the new scholarship.

And finally, there seemed a painful but undeniable truth in Cash's insistence on the durability of the "savage ideal," the persistent resort to an enforced tribal solidarity in response to challenge and inquiry—whether it had been that of the abolitionists before the Civil War, the Yankee reconstructionists just after it, or the claims of modern science in the 1920s. The "savage ideal" was to rear its head again, with savagery indeed, as near police-state atmospheres prevailed in some states of the Deep South in the 1960s, before being decisively overborne by federal authority.

Thus the book, with its enduring virtues, reborn like a phoenix in the turbulent South of the 1950s, claimed further generations of readers, admirers and converts. Notwithstanding its polemical and querulous tone, the power of the prose will no doubt guarantee it new readers and devotees so long as there is a South to be puzzled over and a southern mind to be sized up—so long, that is to say, as there are readers who in seeking the identity of the region are, like W.J. Cash, in large measure seeking their own.

11. Fundamentalism

It all began, according to the historians, some sixty years ago with a series of tracts called The Fundamentals, to which many eminent theologians of the day contributed. For both proponents and detractors the word itself—"fundamental-ism"—seems to have become current about 1920. Since then, to quote one eminent scholar, "its fate in historiography has been worse than its lot in history."

In so saying, the late Ernest Sandeen of Macalaster College meant that fundamentalism has been treated by historians "primarily as a negative force," a disruption of "denominational machinery," or as an outdated vestige of nineteenth century Christianity rather than as a distinctive religious movement with a unique focus of its own.

However defined, it is clear to any follower of the news that fundamentalism is flourishing in America today. In fact, its propagation by cable television may expose more Americans than ever before to its blandishments. But the impact goes well beyond television. The stained-glass tone in politics, so characteristic of the fundamentalist approach, is a constant of the age. Not long ago in Mobile, Alabama, Judge Brevard Hand of the U.S. district court ejected a long list of history, social science and even home economics textbooks from the school curriculum. He explained that they promote "secular humanism," which is a religion according to the judge's definition and thus cannot be taught in the schools. This interesting judgment (subsequently, and not very ceremoniously, reversed by higher courts) is a true oddity. It is one of the rare instances in which the alleged negation of religious belief has been treated as a religion—a new thing in American jurisprudence. (Was it Anatole France who exclaimed, regarding Deism, "A religion with God? My God, what a religion!")

Perhaps not all of the six hundred or more plaintiffs in the Mobile case may accurately be classed as fundamentalists. But pressure of this sort on schools, school boards, textbook publishers and textbook adoption authorities has been more typical than not of the recent fundamentalist agenda. In their latest incarnation, fundamentalists are confident and even aggressive. They won a related legal victory in Tennessee, when another federal judge allowed parents in Greenville to absent their children from elementary reading classes whose primers they objected to as ungodly. (This decision, too, was later reversed.)

The Reverend Pat Robertson, impresario of the "700 Club," was an active if not very successful campaigner for the 1988 Republican presidential nomination and unblushingly identified his cause with that of "the Kingdom," presumably of Heaven. Everywhere, biblical Christians (as they like to call themselves) are engaged in political activities they might once have avoided as an earthly vanity.

I know the danger of lumping together what may be, beneath the surface, a variety of distinguishable views and sects. But one can hardly discuss any broad religious issue without doing some violence to its subtleties as an adherent would see them. Even with that disclaimer, it may be said that the many schools of religious fundamentalism do bear a single common stamp, almost a sine qua non. Now as before it is biblical literalism. Fundamentalism has changed very little in this respect since the term entered ordinary speech about seventy years ago. Much of today's fundamentalism reiterates, in its patterns of belief and affirmation, in expression and form, patterns now a century and more old. Literal interpretation of the Bible, its reading as a source of propositional truths little distinguishable from those you might see in the daily newspaper, is what links the two great pillars of fundamentalist cosmology: creationism and apocalypticism.

The theories of biblical inerrancy may be as subtle as the doctrine of "verbal inspiration of the original autographs." More usually, they are quite starkly simple. A few years ago, there was a great and divisive uproar at one fundamentalist seminary. It was caused by the discovery that the mustard seed is not, after all, as one of the New Testament parables had it, "the smallest seed in nature." The discovery that nature had inconsiderately produced still smaller seeds posed a theological dilemma. The existence of the smaller seeds could be denied; or the seeds could be reclassified as nonseeds; or the strictest theory of literal inerrancy of the Bible could be modified. To those of us who come from other traditions, it seems bizarre that momentous issues could turn on so small and historically contingent a point as the size of seeds. But common sense is rarely the hallmark of biblical literalism. And indeed the mustard-seed story is symptomatic of a larger problem—the unconditional rejection of historical method, of the insights of form criticism and other recent techniques of biblical study, all of it leading to the impoverishment of discourse. And, so far as one can see, with few obvious gains for piety or faith.

But back, briefly, to the past. The great crisis of biblical literalism on these shores surely came that steamy summer day in Dayton, Tennessee, some seven decades ago, when William Jennings Bryan—taking the fundamentalist side in the famous "monkey law" trial—agreed to an impromptu examination on biblical inerrancy. It was, to borrow a useful Freudian term, the primal scene: the scar in the memory that never healed. It is worth remembering because it tells us that simple stories aren't always so simple as our memories. Bryan, a tragic figure, embodies much of what is best and worst in the fundamentalist set of mind. No social reformer of his time worked more tirelessly for social and economic justice. He is not vulnerable, moreover, to the usual charge that fundamentalism is necessarily a privatizing version of religion, lacking social consequence or content. Bryan's life, writes his biographer Louis Koenig, was an "eloquent repudiation" of that idea. "Driven by faith in God's word and purpose," Koenig writes, "[Bryan] had worked for decades, courageously and against crushing odds, to overcome America's social injustices and the murderous strife . . . called war."

That charitable evaluation tends to be obscured in most history books by the ruder words of H.L. Mencken, whose caustic journalistic dispatches from Dayton to the *Baltimore Sun* set the tone of sophisticated reaction to the Scopes trial. "Wherever the flambeaux of chautauqua smoked and guttered," wrote Mencken, "and the bilge of idealism ran in the veins, and Baptist pastors dammed the brooks with the sanctified, and men gathered who were weary and heavy laden, and their wives who were full of Peruna and fecund as the shad . . . there the indefatigable Jennings set up his traps and spread his bait."

This is vivid and funny but neither balanced nor fair; but then fair play was not Mencken's idea of good journalism. It was, however, because Bryan was a man of social conscience who valued kindness and charity that he feared the corruption of religious belief by the demon of "modernism," and especially by the Darwinian theory of natural selection. In his 1921 lecture "The Menace of Darwinism," Bryan asserted that Darwin's theory advanced the Nietzschean cult of the superman. It was "a string of guesses" emphasizing "the blood of the brute"; it was "a jungle creed," rationalizing appetite and ruthlessness. As to the social creeds extracted from the theory of natural selection—usually known as "Social Darwinism"—this was not altogether inaccurate, though it had little to do with Darwin himself—far more, indeed, to do with his popularizers. But it remains a central motif of the fundamentalist assault on evolutionary biology. The tendency to confuse Darwinism with Social Darwinism, the ideological derivative, and science with scientism, endures.

Again, the crucial event was Bryan's defense of biblical inerrancy against Clarence Darrow's crafty interrogation. The flavor is suggested by some of the more memorable exchanges:

> *Darrow:* Do you claim that everything in the Bible should be literally interpreted?
> *Bryan:* I believe everything in the Bible should be accepted as it is given there. Some of the Bible is given illustratively. For instance, "Ye are the salt of the earth." I would not insist that man was actually salt.
> *Darrow:* But when you read that . . . the whale swallowed Jonah . . . How do you literally interpret that?
> *Bryan:* I believe in a God who can make a whale and can make a man and can make both do what he pleases.
> *Darrow:* The Bible says Joshua commanded the sun to stand still for the purpose of lengthening the day, doesn't it? And you believe it?
> *Bryan:* I do . . .
> *Darrow:* Did you ever discover where Cain got his wife?
> *Bryan:* No sir, I leave the agnostics to hunt for her.

After recounting the story of the temptation of Eve, and the curse upon the serpent, Darrow asked: "Do you think that is why the serpent is compelled to crawl on its belly?"

Bryan answered that he did. "Have you any idea how the snake went before that time? . . . Do you know whether he walked on his tail or not?" Bryan said he had no way of knowing.

This famous exchange on a southern courthouse lawn—the weather was so hot that the court had moved outdoors—seems in substance more than a bit sophomoric. Yet the issues still enthrall millions; and for that the persistence of biblical literalism is largely responsible.

To the abiding worry over Darwinism there has now been added another element—the revival, in popular forms, of nineteenth century Darbyist dispensationalism, or millennialism. Hal Lindsey's book, *The Late Great Planet Earth,* projects, from a mixed bag of Bible texts, an approaching end of earthly days. According to what is now usually called "Bible prophecy," the establishment of the State of Israel in 1948 (albeit under secular auspices) set the world in irreversible motion toward the "end-times" when earthly history will culminate with a bang; when the faithful will be "raptured" into the sky and the great war of Armageddon will be waged on or near the ancient banks of the Jordan.

Again, the common denominator is clear. Just as fundamentalists usually insist on reading the majestic creation myth of Genesis as science, so they interpret the apocalyptic texts of Daniel and Revelation—and various passages from the Pauline epistles—as a sort of super Jeane Dixon forecast of things to come. So far as I can see, Mr. Lindsey's book is innocent of serious attention to the historical context of the apocalyptic writings: their well-established setting and purpose. That they were probably written to console and hearten ancient peoples—the Israelites under the Babylonian captivity or early Christians under the Neronic persecutions—the consensus judgment of recent Bible scholarship—is far from the point of *The Late Great Planet Earth.* Rather, by torturing the texts out of their settings and authorial objectives, we are given an emergency bulletin on the immediate future of Israel, the Soviet Union and China, spiced with chilling premonitions of nuclear war. Here is a typical passage:

> After the Antichrist assembles the forces of the rest of the world . . . they meet the onrushing charge of the Kings of the East in a battle line which will extend throughout Israel. . . . Terrible fighting will center around the city of Jerusalem (Zechariah 12:2,3). . . . The apostle John predicts that so many people will be slaughtered that the blood will stand to the horses' bridles for a total distance of 200 miles northward and southward of Jerusalem. . . . The conflict will not be limited to the Middle East. The apostle John warns that when these two great forces meet in battle the greatest shock wave ever to hit earth will occur . . . John says that all the cities of the nations will be destroyed (Revelation 16:19). Imagine, cities like London, Paris, Tokyo, New York, Los Angeles, Chicago—obliterated! John says that the Eastern force alone will wipe out a third of the earth's population. . . . that entire islands and mountains would be blown off the map. It seems to indicate an all-out attack of ballistic missiles upon the great metropolitan areas of the world.

After nearly a century of controversy, fundamentalists— whether heirs of William Jennings Bryan in the war against a monkey ancestry for mankind or latter-day Darbyists like Mr. Lindsey and his eighteen million readers—have neither diluted nor relinquished their views. The wine is old. Some of the wineskins have a sleek new look, an ingratiating mink or sable, say, rather than ordinary goat. But even with the sleek new packaging, the contents haven't varied. The most notable change, perhaps, is that fundamentalists are boldly carrying the fight for their version of orthodoxy into many arenas they once avoided.

Given the American instinct for fair play, and our sometimes lazy and misplaced intellectual egalitarianism, there is a good-natured tendency to ignore quite basic differences; to say that even if they are important, there's plenty of room in the ark for variety. Tolerance is a high value in our system of religious pluralism; but this isn't an issue of tolerance. There is a difference between forbearance and sloth. And the difference can have serious consequences.

Recent polls suggest, for instance, that a substantial majority of Americans—as many of 60 percent of those asked—believe that so-called "creation science" should enjoy the same footing with biology in school classrooms—should, in effect, receive "equal time." The Supreme Court has indicated, however, that religious views posing as "creation science" will be denied that equal footing, and a good thing too. Should the Court relax that view, we could look forward to a degradation of both science and religion. The young man who sold me a paperback copy of *The Late Great Planet Earth* one day in a bookstore in Alexandria, Virginia, probably speaks for millions. I was, I admit, faintly embarrassed to ask for it—"I'm interested in it as a curiosity," I pompously told the clerk. He did not share my embarrassment. "Good book," he said. "Makes you think."

Makes you think? Now, whatever a book like *The Late Great Planet Earth* makes you do, thinking isn't one of them. According to the short biography of Hal Lindsey in the back of the book, he "served for eight years on the staff of the Campus Crusade for Christ, speaking to tens of thousands of students on major university campuses. . . . " I wonder what he told them, and how many he sent away burdened with a crude, unhistorical (and scarcely faithful) fatalism about the prospects of the earth.

It is no violation of charity for those who do not take the fundamentalist view of things to speak as boldly as the fundamentalists do—about the false idea that science and religion must be enemies (or, in the case of "creation science," false friends); about the nature of biblical language and prophetic revelation; about the nature of history and the evidence of divine intervention in it. There is much to dispute. For the fundamentalist, the creation account in Genesis is not a grand and stirring effort to interpret, in metaphorical language, man's origins and nature, his relationship to the sovereign source of life and energy. Instead, to its loss, it is shrunk to the same petty and protean discursive plane as bad "science," even though even the most pretentious science long ago surrendered its interest in metaphysical judgments and "final causes."

Here is precisely that impoverishment of discourse I spoke of. As Alan Richardson has said, "religious truth can be expressed more adequately under the forms of imagination—symbol, image, myth, drama, parable, liturgical rite and sacramental action—than in the propositional sentences of the intellect." When you insist that biblical discourse, in all its manifest variety, is as flatly "propositional" as a newspaper or a science textbook, you fatally cripple its power to mediate the transcendental to our earthbound imaginations. Do not remarkable claims require exceptional signs and symbols? By scrambling science, which is about processes, with story, which is about ends, fundamentalists commit a tragic crime against mind and spirit.

As for the kindred fascination with apocalyptic forecasts, it is likewise a disquieting commentary on the failure to teach rudimentary history and historical method—to tutor our children in the ways we distinguish in the temporal world between the real and the fanciful. In the absence of some elementary grasp of historical thinking, people are left to be dazzled by spectacular muddles like *The Late Great Planet Earth*, wild hybrids of fact, speculation and oracular fantasy. These imposters supplant that clear historical understanding which is essential to an accurate grasp of the Christianity of the apostles, the historical religion par excellence. Lurid theories of the imminent "end times" seduce the credulous from the story of a God who acts in and through time and history, though in ways no more fully intelligible to us than they were to Job. In the new apocalypticism, divine justice emerges not as grand but as whimsical and arbitrary and—dare one say it?—even nihilistic.

The onset of this mighty thirst for future apocalypses to contemplate is puzzling. Our century has given us enough for a lifetime's contemplation—the slaughter of millions in the static trench warfare of 1914-18; the death camps of World War II; Hiroshima; the ongoing blights of poverty, tribalism and race hatred, breeding their daily slaughters so fierce as to numb the civilized imagination. The preference for a fanciful futurism in lieu of real sequences of cause and effect, real historical events, real showcases of the endless perversities of human society and character—all this is nothing if not escapist. In it mankind is not so much acting as acted upon, a puppet in a foreordained melodrama, presided over by a god who suspiciously resembles some earthly martinet, perhaps Charlie Chaplin as the Great Dictator. Is this the religion of the Bible? And if it isn't, what is to explain the error? Inspiration or vanity? Vanity is the more likely suspect. Many years ago in a famous passage in his *Introductory Lectures on Psychoanalysis*, Sigmund Freud wrote:

> Humanity has in the course of time had to endure from the hands of science two great outrages upon its self-love. The first was when it realized that our earth was not the center of the universe. . . . The second was when biological research robbed man of his peculiar privilege of having been specially created, and relegated him to descent from the animal world, implying an ineradicable animal nature in him. . . . But man's craving for grand-

iosity is now suffering the third and most bitter blow from present-day psychological research, which is endeavoring to prove to the ego in each one of us that he is not even master in his own house, but that he must remain content with the veriest scraps of information about what is going on unconsciously in his own mind.

Freud was not a modest man. As the chief explorer of the dynamic unconscious, he did not shrink from equating his explorations with those of Copernicus and Darwin. But he has something here, all the same; and it is not merely a premonition of that epidemic self-absorption, that universal narcissism, which is today so commonplace. All religious belief systems must be on their guard against what is merely man-made and not eternal. Fundamentalism has, I believe, an unacknowledged agenda: to rescue us from that wounded vanity, to offer a refuge from those bitter blows to human self-love of which Freud spoke eighty years ago. Yet surely it is the small, man-centered universe, an earthly creation, that is vulnerable to these insults to ego, which seeks to build little shelters against them. The choice proffered to us by the fundamentalists between faith in an inerrant Bible and something called "secular humanism" is a false antithesis. If there is a choice, it is between the apostolic religion of the Bible, critically but faithfully interpreted, and these meager, man-centered refuges from the disturbing features and dimensions of the modern world.

12. Piety and Politics

If there was a primal scene in the recent American struggle over the appropriate relationship between church and state—or piety and politics—it was the U.S. Supreme Court decision of 1962 that held state-composed or sponsored prayer in the public schools unconstitutional. That decision in the case of *Engel v. Vitale* exposed a raw nerve.

I recall the decision day vividly. Having grown up in the small-town Protestant South, where before-class prayers and Bible readings were the usual practice, I was at first surprised by the ruling. We are creatures of conditioning; and my conditioning in the South had not prepared me for this new turn in constitutional law. There was little sectarian or ethnic variety in the North Carolina schools of my youth, little first-hand awareness of how Jews might feel about Christian prayers, or Roman Catholics about readings from the King James Bible. We had not felt the resentments that smolder when one, or one's children, are subjected involuntarily to unfamiliar rituals and doctrines.

And of course the Regents Prayer decision was only the beginning. The next year, 1963, saw Mrs. Madalyn Murray O'Hare challenge devotional Bible reading and win yet another landmark decision. I must confess that at the time Mrs. O'Hare struck me as at one with the puritanical killjoys who, in another age, could be imagined smashing stained glass windows or vandalizing pipe organs. Her worries seemed distinctly minor. How could she know that when Bible verses were routinely recited before class, in the schools I attended as a boy, the first to be called on would triumphantly intone, "Jesus wept," a verse so short that everyone knew it; the second, John 3:16; and so on until the familiar verses of the 23rd Psalm were exhausted and nothing was left? Mrs. O'Hare might have found much to object to in that scene. But it would hardly have looked very much like "an establishment of religion" in the making, or seriously menacing to minority religious views (had there been such). No one was in danger of being burned at the stake or branded on the forehead. Those of us who had grown up in that cozy and insular environment were thus ill-prepared for the anxieties and irritations that led to the prayer and Bible-reading decisions.

But that was then; and this is now. In the perspective of a quarter-century, my initial judgment seems to me quite mistaken, though my own change of heart seems exceptional. A large number of Americans, perhaps a majority, have not yet made their peace with the prayer decision or the constitutional philosophy underlying it. It remains an unhealed scar.

There are other signs of unease. Consider, for instance, the current attempt to regulate the use of school textbooks on grounds that they are permeated by "secular humanism"; or because they are said to disturb the innocent faith of children. It was reported—with what reliability I cannot say—that some of the Tennessee parents who challenged elementary reading primers recently in Greenville, Tennessee, objected to the story of "Goldilocks and the Three Bears." The tale involved unpunished breaking and entering, it was said; and there was the outright theft of a bowl of porridge! The contention over the place of religion in public, and public life, has become the continuing background music of our daily lives.

The school prayer decision presupposes a theory of strict church-state separation, classically expressed by Thomas Jefferson in the now-familiar letter to the Baptist congregation of Danbury, Connecticut—"an eternal wall of separation." Americans have mixed feelings about that lofty metaphor. In principle, most would probably endorse it—at least if it were not invoked, as it has been at times and in places, for petty or inappropriate purposes. But public schools in America have been—perhaps too much—the instruments of acculturation—"Americanization," as it used to be called. Part of that process was to be drilled in the pious view that our forefathers came to this land primarily to escape religious persecution and to worship as they pleased. The story was undoubtedly more complicated than that. As Daniel Boorstin has noted, one of the primary goals of the founders of Massachusetts Bay was to be free to persecute dissenters from the official orthodoxy without interference. Yet social myth can be mightier than fact; and one of the main problems with the Regents Prayer decision, as many saw it, was that it halted this long-established function of the public schools: religious acculturation.

Judge Brevard Hand of Alabama, author of the recent "secular humanism" textbook decision, has challenged the line of church-state decisions on the fairly radical ground that the Establishment Clause of the First Amendment is not binding on the states. At one time, that was accepted constitutional doctrine. But even most critics of the strict separationist view accept the now established doctrine that the Fourteenth Amendment "incorporated" the First Amendment, which originally restricted only Congress, as binding on the states. Certainly the Supreme Court shows no disposition to reopen debate on the issue.

Others, sometimes called "accommodationists," argue

that the Establishment Clause ("Congress shall make no law respecting an establishment of religion") imposes a strict neutrality on government's part as among faiths and sects. Otherwise, according to this argument, it may favor and even subsidize religion without constitutional offense. The accommodationists usually argue that rituals like school prayer, especially when not denominational, or the posting of the Ten Commandments on a classroom wall (another practice recently banned by the Supreme Court), or observing a moment of silence before the opening of classes, are not "an establishment of religion."

While I no longer share it, this is a view of respectable lineage, best articulated in a famous essay of more than forty years ago by Edward Corwin, the most eminent constitutional scholar of the period ("The Supreme Court as a National Board of Education," 1947). One might even go so far as to say that a more moderate—accommodationist—interpretation of the establishment clause might have proved to be a better way to keep the civil peace than the strict "wall of separation" doctrine. But the Supreme Court, beginning in 1947, took a different course; and there can be no doubt that it finds powerful backing in the writings of Madison, the major architect of the two religion clauses of the First Amendment.

To seek the elusive meaning of that amendment is to peer as far as we might into the mind and temperament of Madison. And when we do so, two points become unmistakably clear.

The first and most salient is that even as a young man, just out of Princeton, Madison had moved beyond the theory of "toleration" as the basis of church-state relations. That theory was current in the English law and tradition of his time. It assumed that there was a preferred religious truth and that it was the truth embraced by national law and by the great majority of citizens. The tolerationists had no quarrel, in principle, with the fostering of the state religion by civil law, so long as due allowance was made for those who could not conscientiously confess it. Where the theorists of toleration differed from the architects of earlier religious settlements was in thinking it preferable, for all sorts of reasons both humane and expedient, to suffer heterodoxy than to burn people for it. "Error" did, after all, have its rights. Toleration was characteristic of the relaxed temperament of the eighteeth century; it was the hallmark of the enlightened climate that shaped the religious ethos of our own founding generation.

Madison, however, distrusted toleration in both principle and practice. There is a searing letter from the young Madison, written from Virginia to a college friend in the North, and expressing his dismay that Baptist preachers in Virginia were still being hounded and persecuted:

> . . . . That diabolical Hell-conceived principle of persecution rages among some and to their eternal infamy the clergy can furnish their quota of imps for such business. . . . There are at this time in the adjacent county not less than 5 or 6 well meaning men in close jail for publishing their religious sentiments, which in the main are very orthodox. I have neither patience to hear talk nor think anything relative to this matter, for I have squabbled and scolded, abused and ridiculed, so long about it (to so little) purpose that I am without common patience. So . . . pity me and pray for liberty of conscience.

That was in 1774. Within a decade—the Revolution had intervened—Madison was stirred to write his great "Memorial and Remonstrance against Religious Assessments" (1784); and then to collaborate two years later with Jefferson on the Virginia Declaration of Religious Freedom (1786). Neither document can plausibly be read as a compromise or halfway house. Both are quite distinctly new in their implications for church-state policy; and the chief implication is that state and church must occupy two absolutely distinct spheres—must exist, for purposes of law, in worlds completely separate. What emerges in these documents, with precocious clarity, is a vision of utter separation—a wall indeed: a view that it is never the proper business of the state to encourage or discourage, promote or hinder, subsidize or penalize, anyone's religion.

Now, there is room for argument about the meaning of the *text* of the First Amendment religion clauses—especially the Establishment Clause. Leonard Levy has recently argued, and persuasively, that as Justice Hugo Black used to say, "no law" meant precisely that: The purpose of the clause was to put religious "establishments" (including schemes of impartial subsidy for all sects) outside the power of Congress to legislate. One will not find that view stated in the accommodationist Supreme Court opinions of the two most recent chief justices of the United States. Yet what we know of the mind of Madison suggests much about the "original intent" of the principal author of the First Amendment; and so does his early and strenuous opposition to the appointment of chaplains for Congress. If you believe Levy, and I do, the Establishment Clause is pregnant with considered contemporary meaning; and that meaning does not contemplate the mixture of church and state.

Certainly, it is hard to read Madison's words in the "Memorial and Remonstrance" as other than a new vision, radical in its implications for church-state separation. And this was more than policy; it accorded, as Madison saw it, with the self-sufficient strength of religion. Of Christianity, Madison remarks, for instance, that "every page of it disavows a dependence on the powers of this world . . . For a religion not invented by human policy must have pre-existed and been supported before it was established by human policy . . . "

Which is to say that Madison's view of the piety-politics issue was as much calculated to free piety from the coddling of politics as to free politics of intolerant collusions with piety. And this reading of Madison's intention seems to me reinforced by the prohibition of religious tests for office which the framers had already written into the text of the Constitution. In short, I have come to believe that Jefferson and Madison intended to bequeath to us a revolutionary ideal for the separation of church and state, of politics from piety, which we have been gradually and fitfully approaching for nearly two centuries.

If we haven't yet reached the summit, it may be because the air is thin on the mountain-top where prophets dwell. The Madisonian vision is so uncompromising that it leaves many people gasping for something a bit less rarified. That is perhaps why so many Americans see the solution to the dilemma in a broad, to-whom-it-may-concern form of public observance which scholars have called "civil religion." It is that bland if-there's-a-God-we're-for-him theology that engraves "In God We Trust" on the coins, that sings the hymnic verses of "America the Beautiful"; it is congressional chaplains praying over politicians and bailiffs crying, "God save the United States and this honorable court." In some of its milder forms, civil religion seems almost too innocuous to make an issue of, which is exactly Madison's quarrel with it. Civil religion is the kiss-your-sister religion, gesture without theological content or sacramental form: the worldly piety of the lowest common denominator. It is unoffending for the worst of reasons; it is too bland to be taken seriously, bless (to remember a phrase of Carlyle) its mealy mouth.

Apart from the rediscovery of Madison, there are other, entirely practical, arguments for strict separation. Look about at other societies and observe how many murderous divisions continue to be fostered by the inability to separate civil from religious policy. Consider Lebanon, with its infinite sects, or Iran with its Islamic fanaticism, or the Sudan, or Northern Ireland, the last battleground of the terrible sectarian strife between Catholics and Protestants that has raged from the early sixteenth century right into our own time. Consider even Israel, a secular state founded on Zionist principles, where ultra-orthodox religious communities insist on the control of marriages and divorce (and, more recently, the right to define legitimate conversion to Judaism). The variety of American colonial settlements, and the practical necessity of a rule of tolerance, have spared us those divisions. But others have been less fortunate; and it is arrogant to think that we would be immune to them. The late Senator Sam Ervin Jr., a tireless defender of the strict view of the Establishment Clause, liked to quote a famous statement by Chief Justice Walter Stacy of the North Carolina Supreme Court, written in 1930:

> . . . . It would be unbelievable, if history did not record the tragic fact, that men have gone to war and cut each other's throats because they could not agree as to what was to become of them after their throats were cut . . . For some reason, too deep to fathom, men contend more furiously over the road to heaven, which they cannot see, than over their visible walks on earth. . . .

The essential point of the current debate over church-state policy is a continuing blindness to the Madison vision—partly, as I have noted, because it is probably too austere for our easy-going, compromising habits of mind. But perhaps the problem has deeper roots. Even in a nation dedicated to the principle of religious pluralism, we crave the security of feeling that we are on God's side—or he on ours. You see this in the dubious creed which scholars have labeled

"American exceptionalism," a view deriving from the Puritan heritage: the idea of America as an exemplary and innocent "new Israel," a chosen people in a new Wilderness, a "city on a hill" called to exhibit before the world an exceptional godliness and piety. In less refined forms it degenerates into a crass identification of current political or economic norms with biblical mandates. In his book *Listen America,* the Reverend Jerry Falwell tells us that

> ... the free enterprise system is clearly outlined in the Book of Proverbs in the Bible. Jesus Christ made it clear that the work ethic was a part of his plan for man. Ownership of property is biblical. Ambitious and success-ful business management is clearly outlined as a part of God's plan for His people.

The peril of this thinking is that it sanctifies secular patterns of behavior and breaks down the tension between religious revelation and earthly ambition and spiritual arrogance. That is why most if not all political activity claiming some special religious sanction is troubling, whether it is the Moral Majority or Jesse Jackson's "Rainbow Coalition." Or, for that matter, the occasionally tiresome views of the National Council of Churches or the Catholic Bishops' Conference. It would be hazardous to take at face value the claim that church affiliation itself confers a special wisdom, or a commission to reveal divine purposes.

One must distinguish, to be sure. Is there no difference, for instance, between Jesse Jackson and Jerry Falwell—or Pat Robertson? Don't they all do essentially similar things? Aren't they all crossing the dim and twisting line that separates politics and piety? Yes, they are. But there are historical differences. The church was the only sanctioned means of political self-expression available to blacks during most of our history. That is changing now; and as it changes we may expect the heavier tones of piety to fade from black politics—or, when they linger, to be treated with the same skepticism as the stained-glass tone of some white politicians. But the civil rights movement as we knew it would have been unimaginable without the black church, and by no means so peaceful and productive. White preacher-politicians lack the excuse of a history of oppression. They are open to the suspicion of using clerical garb as a cover for worldly purposes.

All of us are free to moralize about political issues but we probably do better to wonder how so many worldly people learn so much about the heavenly political agenda. As Gillian Peele wryly observes in her recent book *Revival and Reaction,* the Reverend Pat Robertson's magazine *Perspective* "has . . . apparently derived from the Gospel clear views on wage and price controls, the size of the federal budget, and the desirability of national health insurance."

The continuing clamor over politics and piety shows no sign of subsiding; but there are encouraging signs that the sanctimonious tone that crept into presidential politics in the mid-1970s (a time of penitence, perhaps, for Vietnam and Watergate) has begun to weary the voters. We do make some strides toward the exhilarating Madisonian vision of religious pluralism and separation. Thirty years ago, no Roman Catholic had ever been elected president of the United States; and in view of the 1928 Al Smith fiasco many doubted that one ever could be. Then John F. Kennedy laid that issue to rest—permanently, it would seem, if not without effort. Kennedy's feat has not been repeated by other non-Protestants or non-Christians. Yet it could happen. The only constitutional restraint would be political; and that is for me the beauty of the legacy Madison and Jefferson left us. Our arguments grow noisy and bitter from time to time. But while the ballot is secret, and the courts sit to enforce the First Amendment, and the memory of Madison is strong and accurate, we are safe—or at least safer than most societies—from the consuming fires of religious strife.

13. The Storytelling Animal

Man is a storytelling animal—perhaps not the only one, but the only one whose tales we know. The human need for stories that make sense of our lives is among the most powerful of cravings. The novelist Reynolds Price may stretch that thirst a bit when he suggests that the need for story is "second in necessity after nourishment and before love and shelter." But by any measure, the need is fundamental. Stories, as Joseph Conrad has put it, offer finality—something, he says, "for which our hearts yearn with a longing greater than the longing for the loaves and fishes of this earth."Our basic stories vary. One might say: I am 170 pounds of carbon compounds, arrayed in complex cellular structures, programmed to react in predictable ways to certain stimuli. I occupy a small place on a burnt-out fragment of stellar material, related by the unalterable laws of gravity to other bodies in a mediocre galaxy, one of tens of thousands. Had I sufficient information, every move and perhaps even every thought might be explained by chemical or mechanical causes.

That story would be, in terms of the satisfactions we long for, barren and even a bit tedious for most tastes. Accordingly, I would prefer to say: I am one of an imaginative and mysterious species of which Hamlet exclaimed: "What a

247

piece of work is a man, how noble in reason, how infinite in faculties . . . how express and admirable in action . . . the beauty of the world; the paragon of animals." The stories I shall concentrate on, the oldest and most basic, are the humanistic and religious stories that have as their focus our peculiar standing as paragon of animals.

Five years ago, I began teaching a course at Georgetown University which I call "Great Narrators." At first, this was an excuse to teach books and writers that interest me— historians like Herodotus, Livy, Gibbon, Tacitus and Macaulay; novelists like James, Woolf, Turgenev, Tolstoy, Faulkner; scientists like Freud and Darwin; and other materials such as the biblical story of Joseph and his brothers. All stories demand organizing assumptions about the world, about destiny, about human nature. It gradually came to me that this enterprise, so self-indulgently begun, was leading in strange directions. You can't talk about stories and storytellers without asking yourself just how central they might be to spiritual survival. Or without asking the greatest question of all: Might narrative, might the way we tell ourselves our basic stories, offer a clue to the very structure of reality?

Recall a familiar sequence. We are all children for a long time; and among our earliest memories is the story hour. "Tell me a story" is the demand we seem to come to soon after the demand for milk or pabulum. The memory is shrouded with magic. Our minds were not yet burdened with niggling distinctions between the real and the fantastic, fact or fable or fiction. What Chesterton called "the logic of elfland" prevailed. Pinocchio and the Little Engine that Could, Greek myths and the Friendly Cow all Red and White, and the young Jesus astounding learned men in the Temple: Such stories merged in a fresh and undifferentiated world—a vivid panorama of fancy we would have found it impossible to distinguish from some "real world" even if we had wanted to.

If my memories of Anthropology I are accurate, this early and primitive state, this uncritical receptivity to stories, parallels the preliterate history of societies. Such societies rely on storytelling to root law and custom, ritual, totem and tabu, in a useful and meaningful sequence and order. Even for higher cultures and religions, storytelling remains the avenue to faith and belief in some ritualistic settings. What is lacking in the child's world, as, possibly, in primitive society, is neither complexity nor subtlety. It is self-consciousness, the curse attached to the knowledge of good and evil. The enchanted state remains undisturbed by the temptations of analysis, is without that murder by dissection of which Wordsworth spoke.

But there comes a time for us all—a growing-up time—when the magic fades. We begin to peer over the storyteller's shoulder and demand that he confess whether George Washington always told the truth, or whether dragon's teeth, sown like garden seeds, ever generated armed men. The early ease with story yields to the need to pull it apart. This is surely an essential stage; it is, so to say, the sophomore stage of our narrative life. Yet, just as some of us never press beyond the most literal credulity, others become snagged and arrested in a perpetual state of analysis—like Turgenev's character Rudin, who is described as having "the damned habit of pinning down every motion in life . . . as if he were pinning down a butterfly." All of us have something in us of the perpetual sophomore, the eternal village atheist.

There is, I think, a third stage. It is uncomfortable, there is no equilibrium in it, because it demands a wrestling with the angels of our nature far more strenuous than most transitions; and it has become all the harder in our age of statistical truth. Yet with effort, some of us grope our way beyond analysis because we have to; the demands of sanity require it. And having done so, we find that we at once transcend and return to the stage of receptivity. We come back to story as the key to meaning—not with untutored credulity but with the suspicion that it may finally be the only way of understanding that whose understanding makes us human; that it links all the unraveled strands of truth—not only cognitive but poetic, mythic, symbolic; not only personal but social and religious. It happens because coherence is a basic human need—greater, as Conrad would have it, than the hunger for loaves and fishes. But even as we accept the need, there is a part of us that continues to hector. What is the meaning of meaning?

There must be rules by which to test meaning, which is to say truth. My own baptism as a student of meaning was in the "new criticism" of the 1950s, new then if no longer; and its principal exponent then was Professor Cleanth Brooks, whose essays in *The Well Wrought Urn* constituted the authoritative text. The school had two axioms: that it was distracting and perhaps even pointless to pry into the historic origins of any work of poetry; and that ambiguity (a very big word) was a good thing. According to one eminent critic, there were at least seven types of ambiguity. It meant richness and *double entendre;* a poem or a story was good to the extent that it resonated for the reader or listener at many levels. Yeats's great apocalyptic question—

> And what rough beast, its hour come round at last,
> Slouches towards Bethlehem to be born?—

met the test to perfection.

Some quite alarming things appear to have happened to meaning (and the meaning of meaning) since those carefree days. We no longer read stories; we "decode" them, a term of art insinuating that the purpose of writers is not so much to give meaning to life as to encrypt and conceal it. The new critics of my youth praised ambiguity. But I don't think they contended that any text had no legitimate or definitive meaning, no hard and self-sufficient integrity of its own. Frederick Crews might parody the many schools of lit crit—Marxist, Freudian, new-critical, historicist—in his amusing book *The Pooh Perplex*. But no one would have suggested that the idiot's interpretation of the tale is as valid as the wise man's. Observers might revolve in orbit around the text, seeing it under many aspects and finding its disclosures different. But even as they revolved, it was the perspective that changed, not the authorial intent. The text itself endured.

To suppose otherwise implies a disconcerting anarchy, in literature and in life—a world in which stories have no agreed meanings, a world in which whim and subjectivity reign, where the storyteller's art serves amusement or politics but nothing fit to be called truth. If the deconstructionists and their tribe are right, we cannot understand our nature or destiny; for such understanding as ordered narrative might provide is invariably arbitrary, illusionary, but above all, programmatic in some sinister ideological way. The mirrors of self-recognition become fun-house mirrors that play tricks with our images but never cast back a reliable one.

More recently, the radical skepticism of the deconstructionists has begun to spread from literature into law. Bright iconoclasts, styling their art Critical Legal Studies, have reinvented what looks suspiciously like the lost wheel of legal realism. No doubt the first caveman who ever contemplated a law or a rule saw that it might in some special sense serve the interests of the rulemaker. But the contemplation of laws and rules did not halt with that threshold insight. Schools of legal realism tend to flourish at times of social and economic unsettlement. The Great Depression years of the 1930s gave us a bumper crop of village-atheist views of the law, featuring disguised class or economic interest; and the critique was not without point. Any suggestion that law might tell a useful tale about mankind's civilizing instincts, as Aristotle would have claimed; or about the enduring thirst for justice whose sounds we catch in the angry voices of the Old Testament prophets: all this was dismissed as hopeless naiveté. The old wine is today bottled differently, but it is still the brew of skepticism (100-proof Old Veblen, let's say), spiked with vulgar Marxism. The labels change; the thing itself does not.

Undoubtedly, the third stage—the stage of mature receptivity—involves a struggle. The problem is not a want of intelligence or ingenuity. Our earliest encounter is with simple stories, or stories that seem simple, and we wish they could remain so. There is something in us that resists truth, which in the hands of the master storytellers can be harsh and deflationary. To find repose in the stories they tell, we must attune ourselves not just to the cognitive but to the poetic. This is hardly subject to mathematical demonstration, after all. That storytelling is a portal to truth is something closer to an existential faith than a provable proposition.

And after all, such truth as there is in storytelling lies in the telling, not the story itself. That is one of the mysteries of the storytelling animal. Announce the plot alone and one could hardly distinguish *Anna Karenina* or *King Lear* from "Dallas." Try this one, for instance: A spoiled and precocious young man who dreams megalomanic dreams offends his duller brothers with his vanity and arrogance. They plot to murder him but instead sell him as a captive. There, in servitude, his gifts are refined and his character burnished by adversity. One day the tables turn and he holds the power of life or death over his treacherous brethren, and the power to play upon their lingering guilt and test them for moral growth; and then, in the end, to forgive them. Treated by a sentimental hand, it would make splendid soap opera; in the hands of the masterly redactor of Genesis (or of Thomas Mann), it becomes tragi-comic perfection.

Peter Taylor has recently published a short and much-praised novel, *A Summons to Memphis*. Taylor tells how a fragment of family history, become family myth—a father's betrayal by his business partner—endures and echoes unendingly in the lives of his children. We are shown how this primal event affects the way they act, how they dress, well into middle age. Then an astonishing thing happens. The father, now old, unexpectedly encounters the treacherous partner—the demon of family myth—in the dining room of a mountain resort. The two old men fall into one another's arms like lost brothers; the abandoned friendship renews itself as if never interrupted. Yet, having ordered their lives so completely around this primal enmity, the children are flabbergasted. They can't explain it, nor does Peter Taylor explain it. That isn't what storytellers do. They leave the telling to critics. They dramatize the ironies, the paradoxes, the improbabilities of life and leave it to us to make what we can of the story. Yet—and this is the point—not even the crowning irony of *A Summons to Memphis* renders the story in any sense confusing. Even Mr. Taylor has said that his aim was to explore what is, in part, still puzzling to him; but that does not suggest that all interpretations, however artless or bizarre, are equally valid. One can imagine the ultimate social-realist saying that the mythic betrayal was a trivial episode in the great history of twentieth century Tennessee capitalism; that the two old men finally come to see that and realize that their quarrel never mattered. One could imagine such a "decoding" these days; but it would be ridiculous.

We may be, from one point of view, mere biochemistry, or products of social or class origins. But for purposes of making sense of destiny we had better imagine, hope, that we are far more. Storytellers, therefore, as has been said of science, tell us things that are not only stranger than we imagine but stranger than we *can* imagine—without their help. They explore the frontiers. That is why they last, and why they are as necessary for us as food, drink and shelter.

Yet there are stories and stories. In the course of which I spoke, I have included Freud as a narrator. His great case histories—of Dora, of the Wolf Man; his astute and fascinating if fanciful psychobiography of Leonardo: this is great storytelling by any standard. Freud, archeologist of the psyche, taught us the value of the buried layers of our personal past, of the dream life, of excavating and arranging these lost layers in some satisfying and stabilizing order. The idea is to create narrative out of the disordered elements of the unconscious life; to draw together in coherent sequence the important inner progressions of which we are not conscious. The man or woman you are today may contain hidden parts of the child you were; almost certainly does. Freud in his rare moments of modesty acknowledged, as his followers do not always do, that the great storytellers had visited these obscure realms long before he sought to render their probing a science. He himself wanted to be a storyteller in the great tradition.

And there is history, which is to society as psychoanalysis is to the personality, orienting us in the stream of events and causes and effects so far beyond counting, so intimidating in their complexity and elusiveness, that Tolstoy could turn much of *War and Peace* into musing on historical cause as illusion. As a sort of immunization against historical silliness, it is hard even today to improve on Tolstoy's parody of the school textbooks of his youth. He grasped the absurdity of certain facile kinds of historical explanation long before the author of *1066 And All That:*

> . . . . The heirs of Louix XIV were . . . weak men, and also governed France badly. They had . . . such and such mistresses. Besides which, certain persons were at this time writing books. By the end of the 18th century there must have gathered in Paris two dozen or so persons who

started saying that all men were free and equal. Because
of this in the whole of France people began to slaughter
and drown each other. These people killed the king and
a good many others. At this time there was a man of
genius in France—Napoleon. He conquered everyone
everywhere . . . and killed them so well, and was so clever
and cunning, that, having arrived in France, he ordered
everyone to obey him, which they did. . . .

Ridiculous, of course. Yet such rubbish is still, it seems,
what many otherwise literate people think of when you say
the word "history." Yet silly as it is, this simpleminded
reordering of the past does at least recognize in its feeble way
that making sequential order of disorder is history's purpose;
that it is, after all, a story—*historia*. Which is more than can
be said of much that has succeeded it—history which in its
passion for daily documentation or quantification or some
other scientific will-o-the-wisp has abandoned the task of
narration and fails to tell any story; or fails to tell a story of
consequence. Lacking that story, we are left without a
compass, however much we may be told about the price of
mutton in the age of Philip II or the ritual cat-hangings of
old Paris. In the absence of historical stories, too many actors
even on the public stage today are content to make up their
small part of the human story with near indifference to
anyone else's plot or its continuity. This is the true arrogance
of historical illiteracy. If we are still restless about, say, the
legacy of Vietnam, is it not out of failure to tell ourselves a
sufficiently deep and inclusive story about it?

If I seem to hover all around the point without ever
stating it crisply and categorically, that is because the point
about storytelling, like the point of stories themselves, may
only be illustrated approximately and not baldly stated. I
choose this self-involved way to reflect on the centrality of
narration because for me what I call the third stage—the

stage at which we accept story as truth—renews something quite basic. As in the well-known lines of Eliot's "Little Gidding,"

> . . . the end of our exploring
> Will be to arrive where we started
> And know the place for the first time.

The mania for measure as the test of truth has permeated every old study today and lowered its sights and ambitions deplorably. Every day we late twentieth century people are tempted to rub along with the small truths that may be had in such abundance, and with such transitory certainty, by counting, weighing and measuring. These small truths are valuable in their way but they do not point the way out of that dark wood of which Dante spoke. It was a poet of antiquity who alone could guide him as the shadows lengthened—at least as far as the edge of Paradise, where no pagan could enter. It is Ariadne's tresses, better than compass or sextant, that leads through the Labyrinth.

14. Teaching Values

The latest war cry in education is "values education." The reasons are obvious. There is a feeling that it is harder these days for children to discover and internalize the elementary old virtues—honesty, loyalty, consideration of others, generosity, truthfulness: whatever one's list would consist of—harder, anyway, than it was at some earlier stage of American history. One hears it suggested that our children behaved better when our society was more homogeneous or rural or less affluent; or before kids had cars; or before the revolution in feminine expectations took Mom out of the kitchen; or when judges exercised less supervisory authority. Or even before the Beatles. There are many theories of decay; and many of them suggest more about the theorist than about the worry.

Social historians are wary of golden ages, theories that assume some absolute moral decline from one age or generation to another. But the history of the twentieth century warns us against complacency. Societies do sometimes go off the tracks. Some, of uncomfortable memory, have done so. The difficulty is that the debate about values needs qualification and complication.

If, for instance, you examine the history of the Nazi movement, you might discover that some of its young enthusiasts in the Hitler Youth believed that National Socialism and its satellite ideologies represented a purifying revolt against social immorality and chaos. Nazism, incredibly, was seen as a refreshing departure from the libertinism of the Weimar era; it was in some ways the "values education" enthusiasm of its day and place. The young Germans of the 1930s who came under the spell would have been staggered by the suggestion that they were being conditioned to condone, even collaborate in, far more monstrous "immoralities" than sexual license or pornography or atonal music or Relativity theory or Bauhaus furniture styles. They thought they were learning to be good boys and girls. They thought that the rallies and marches, the wholesome fresh-air exercises that were so much a feature of the Hitler Youth, guaranteed clean living. And so in a sense they did—a form of clean living remarkably isolated from the central realities and struggles that were taking place in Berlin. To remember this simply reminds us of the paradox of social moralities. They aren't always what they seem.

Today, American public schools are under renewed pressure to become vehicles of instruction in sound morality. No doubt good behavior—socially acceptable and civil behavior—is an important goal of good schooling. So should self-discipline be. But the question is how directly they can be "taught."

Values education cannot, I think, be a proximate goal of the schools—for many reasons. In the first place, there is little agreement as to which "values" are to be preferred, nor are we at one as to how, if at all, one goes about teaching them.

May values not be taught in a propositional fashion, as if they were axioms in some mathematical or geometrical system? It would be odd if they could be. Values are acquired in a school setting by a mysterious osmotic process whose key feature is what I would call dramatic empathy. That is true because schoolchildren are, like all of us, human beings at various stages of intellectual, emotional and moral development (or arrest). And it is a complex and lifelong process.

My own pedagogical bias, for whatever it is worth, is that American society has dangerously devalued at all levels of education those old subjects of study—the humanities—that once formed the unquestioned core of what one was supposed to know in order to live a life as well as earn a living. Our curricula are now tilted towards training: instruction in useful or practical skills and techniques, from carpentry to, yes, thoracic surgery or how to write a newspaper story. Skills matter; so do techniques. But to confuse the teaching of skills with education is a fundamental error. From the point of view of transmitting values, it may be a dangerous error as well.

How can an educational system overwhelmingly geared to "practical" considerations be a hospitable environment for reflection about, for the absorption of, values? I go back to the Germans for a moment. Their schools, the public educational system designed by dedicated Prussian schoolmasters, was one of the wonders of the nineteenth century. Illiteracy, which still flourished in many other advanced European nations in that time, was close to being wiped out in Germany. The flaw, it now seems, was the rigid stratification of the system. Those who were thought fit for training were trained; they constituted the vast majority, the hewers of wood and drawers of water. A smaller elite enjoyed the benefits of advanced study of literature, history, the arts and sciences. This two-tier system naturally produced a two-tier society with an antidemocratic crust overlying a lumpish and apolitical mass. The Prussian system illustrates the paradox of the utilitarian view of education: Make it too practical and the results may be disastrously impractical.

Not only are we now tilting towards training at the expense of education; those who still teach the humanities seem to me, looking at it from the outside, to have lost their nerve. Humanists have lost their faith in the power of good stories—using the term broadly—to speak for themselves to the student's head and heart. I am no authority on learning theory; indeed, I know almost nothing about it. But of one thing I am confident: No one's behavior was ever much altered, degraded or improved, by exposure to admonitions. The Garden of Eden was the first, not the only instance of the fascination of forbidden fruit and the vanity of "thou shalt nots." How then, if not propositionally, do we acquire and internalize values? I return to dramatic empathizing. It is not a complicated idea. It is what we do, and all we do, when we read or hear narratives that engage the moral imagination. In my high school days, George Eliot's *Silas Marner* was standard reading for ninth graders, Shakespeare's *Macbeth,* for a later year. *Silas Marner* is a story of ageless dilemmas and moral archetypes. A miser with a grudge against the world is redeemed by the innocence of a homeless child who wanders into his life. One *Silas Marner,* properly taught, is worth a bookshelf of admonitions. You may speak of the vanity of hoarding this world's treasures or the distorting effects of anger all you like. But to absorb those valuable lessons in "values" we must see, vividly displayed in dramatic terms, the consequences of defying them. Similarly, *Macbeth* may not be a cure-all for the universal human disease of ambition. It is surely, however, a better antidote, if there is one, than a bookshelf of homilies against covetousness.

And another random example. In Scott Fitzgerald's *The Great Gatsby* one is shown—not told; the distinction is of critical importance—a very great deal about values. Gatsby, who has risen from obscurity by shady means, has a wide streak of idealism in him. He has constructed for himself a yearning heroic myth based on his impression of the glamorous and powerful. The crushing irony of this is clear when Fitzgerald, with consummate artistry, introduces a few of Gatsby's friends from the fast lane—Tom and Daisy Buchanan, for instance—and one is shown (not told) what careless, cruel people they are, beneath the veneer of bogus gentility.

Any good story will do. And for these purposes, goodness in a story lies in its capacity to resonate for people of all sorts and conditions and ages. Teach or tell a good story well and some of it is bound to rub off. Let us, then, revive the good old stories—I don't mean just the fictional ones— and tell them well; and we shall have done much of what we realistically may hope to do for the transmission of values in the schools. Ultimately, everyone forms his value system for himself. Why else have stories always been the primary means for the transmission of traditions of civility? Why else did the most sublime ethical teacher of whom we have record teach in parables, rather than by passing out little rulebooks and asking his followers to memorize the rules?

But don't take my word for it. In Bruno Bettelheim's marvelous book, *The Uses of Enchantment,* he argues for the revival of a specific form of narrative—the folk fairy tale—in the education of small children. His reasons are interesting and compelling. They have to do above all with the graininess and complexity of these stories, their approximation to the real world in all its variety and hard edges. Bettelheim says with authority what I have been trying to say:

> . . . . Nothing is more important than the impact of parents and others who take care of the child; second in importance is our cultural heritage, when transmitted to the child in the right manner. When children are young, it is literature that carries such information best. . . . [But most children's] books are so shallow in substance that little of significance can be gained from them . . . Just because his life is often bewildering to him, the child needs to be given the chance to understand himself in

this complex world. . . . To be able to do so, the child must be helped to make some coherent sense out of the turmoil of his feelings. He needs ideas on how to bring his inner house into order, and on that basis be able to create order in his life. He needs . . . a moral education which subtly, and by implication only, conveys to him the advantages of moral behavior, *not through abstract ethical concepts but through that which seems tangibly right and therefore meaningful to him.* . . . There is a widespread refusal to let children know that the source of much that goes wrong in life is due to our very own natures—the propensity of all men for acting aggressively, asocially, selfishly, out of anger and anxieties. Instead, we want our children to believe that, inherently, all men are good. But children know that they are not always good; and often, even when they are, they would prefer not to be. . . . The dominant culture wishes to pretend, particularly where children are concerned, that the dark side of man does not exist, and professes a belief in optimistic meliorism. . . .

Dr. Bettelheim puts the values-education issue in precisely the right perspective: the perspective of honesty about our mixed and problematical nature. The advantage of good literature is that it, too, is on all fours with that nature. Why, one wonders, is this view so widely disregarded—not, of course, by seasoned educators but by the noisier advocates of the values-teaching fad? The reason, perhaps, is that the discussion is not rooted in an even-handed and disinterested quest for sound moral education but in a self-interested clash between competing political visions. Inappropriate to schools, these aim not at the improvement and refinement of moral awareness but toward indoctrination in some preferred system or ideology. For that reason alone it is sure to fail, as it should, but not before distracting us from more basic tasks of education.

15. Universal Rules of Evidence?

In his mischievous but delightful *Eminent Victorians,* Lytton Strachey tells how Cardinal Newman, in the course of editing a series of biographies of the saints, asked the historian James A. Froude to write about St. Neot:

> While [Froude] was composing it, he began to feel some qualms. Saints who lighted fires with icicles, changed bandits into wolves, and floated across the Irish Sea on altar-stones, produced a disturbing effect on his historical conscience. But he had promised his services to Newman and he determined to carry through the work in the spirit in which he had begun it. He did so; but he thought it proper to add the following sentence by way of conclusion: "This is all, and indeed rather more than all, that is known to men of the blessed St. Neot; but not more than is known to the angels in heaven."

We are not angels; and our knowledge is of men. Yet even with that limitation we like to think that what we know we really do know. We like to think that there came a time in recent centuries when the sort of credulity that permitted people to believe in St. Neot's unusual mode of passage across the Irish Sea yielded and "fact" was enthroned. Some would date this change from the Renaissance of the fifteenth or the scientific revolution of the seventeenth century. Some see its definitive arrival, for instance, in the decline of the trial by ordeal—that is, when the truthfulness of witnesses was no longer tested by determining whether God would permit them to be consumed by fire or drowned by water. Some would say that it was when the sun replaced the earth at the center of the universe. Some would say that it came when philosophers began to worry about *how* we know things—the representative figure being Descartes musing in his warm room, beginning with a skepticism so deep as to question his own materiality. Or perhaps it was when that inveterate wise man, Dr. Johnson, kicked a lampost in Boswell's presence to "refute" Bishop Berkeley's doubts about the reality of the physical world.

But even if no historical point may be specified for this transition—and probably none could be—all of us are interested in the rules by which we know what is true: how we determine that something is fact and not fancy.

Legal rules of evidence constitute perhaps the most familiar system of disciplined fact-finding; and most of us are at least acquainted with that familiar evidentiary process. Indeed, with the litigiousness of American culture today, it is inescapable. We know that it imposes rules about the competence of witnesses, rules of cross-examination, rules about the admissibility of evidence, rules governing the weight to be assigned to "expert" testimony, rules forbidding the partiality of jurors. There are of course other such systems, including that scientific method so highly valued—yet so difficult to define—in our time.

By whatever rules, however, modernity involves some systematic attentiveness to reputable rules of evidence. And that is critical; for notwithstanding the burgeoning of human knowledge since about 1400, the abiding certainty is that knowledge is obsolescent. It wears out and is discarded. Time makes ancient creeds uncouth, as the hymn says; it also overtakes "facts" as well—even those that once seemed very much up to date. Each generation, in Froude's amusing words, knows "rather more than all," about many things; and it is the more than all that is the usual casualty. Every day, some received assumption about the world bites the dust. *The New York Times* reported on its front page recently that physicists now question a central postulate of their science, the belief that there is no such thing as absolute motion.

Consider medical knowledge, than which no body of knowledge seems more volatile. It was not long ago that our grandparents laughed at Galen, who believed that illnesses sprang from an imbalance of the bodily humors—even as their own physicians applied leeches. Speaking of the abiding limits of medicine, the historian Cecil Woodham-Smith describes the last illness of Queen Victoria's father: "There now began a mighty struggle between the duke's magnificent constitution and the medical science of his age." (The duke's constitution was not equal to the fight.)

In his splendid history of the Panama Canal, *The Path between the Seas,* David McCullough recounts the struggle of Dr. William Gorgas to persuade superiors on the Canal Commission of the truth about yellow fever. The carrier was a mosquito which, uniquely, breeds in fresh water. Yellow fever owes nothing at all—as conventional medical opinion held at the time—to the influence of foul air exuded by upturned jungle soil. Dr. Gorgas was told at one point that he was "wild" on the subject of mosquitoes. He should put such nonsense out of his mind and get the dead cats out of the Panama City gutters.

In short, many a confident certainty will be overtaken, though usually not before it does harm. And this is to say nothing, mind you, of those trivial absurdities so charmingly deflated by Bertrand Russell in his essay, "An Outline of Intellectual Rubbish"—for instance, the resistance of eighteenth century theologians to lightning rods, which were imagined to be inventions of the Devil. I am thinking of far more reputable notions of fact: knowledge that seems to each age, in its turn, established as securely as inquiry and proof can make it.

All of which—you will have anticipated the next step— raises the obvious point. It is a cinch that succeeding ages will amuse themselves at many of our fixed beliefs, turning on our certainties the same indulgent smile we turn on Victorian medicine or eighteenth century sermons against lightning rods. It isn't given to us to visualize the overthrow of our own familiar universe of knowledge. But surprises are in store; and even the most scrupulous systems of inquiry— especially, one is tempted to say, those of science—will be shown to have produced mistaken conclusions.

Given that we have no foresight in the matter, what are the likely candidates for laughter in the next age? I would name two.

One would be those bodies of alleged social knowledge based on statistical measurement. Computers, so useful in the exact sciences, have now bewitched the inexact sciences. Fields as subject to human whim and vagary as history, economics and political science aspire to an exactitude and a form of knowledge they cannot attain, in the nature of the case. This has led to a great deal of foolishness. Recently, a noted southern historian was astonished to find, in a new "history" of slavery, the assertion that in the Old South a majority of plantation overseers were black. Decades of delving in the available archives had not prepared him for any such idea; his every intuition told him it could not be right. When he checked, so he told me, he discovered that this "fact" rested on nothing more substantial than a statistical assumption that enabled the computer to chew and digest its data.

Another fashionable branch of inquiry that may be

vulnerable to time's mockery—as full of confident subjectivity as the other is of confident objectivity—is the application of psychoanalysis to history and biography. In an article in the *Wall Street Journal,* Mr. Alan Otten recently reviewed, with a chortle or two of skepticism, the fall issue of the *Journal of Psychohistory,* which is devoted to psychoanalytic musings about President Carter. At a surprisingly early point, Jimmy Carter joins a presidential throng (including Washington, Jefferson, Jackson, Lincoln, Wilson and Nixon) on the couch of the psychohistorians, as they call themselves. One article suggested that the Democrats fell behind Mr. Carter in 1976 because of "a group fantasy desire for rebirth and a return to the mother-child relationship with a unifying leader." Reading this, Mr. Otten wondered what might be wrong with "the common-sense explanation that the Democrats knew they had to be united to win." Probably nothing; but the obvious never satisfies psychohistorians. Indeed, they are committed to the view—a legacy from Father Freud himself—that visible motives are misleading while real motives are usually invisible. Ordinary historians are trained to be modest about evidence. If it is missing, they confess ignorance or confine themselves to common-sense speculation, clearly identified as such.

A shortage of evidence is no embarrassment to psychohistory; indeed, it can be an advantage. Consider an amusing instance. One of the minor puzzles about Thomas Jefferson is that no letters between Jefferson and his mother are known to exist. An orthodox historian, not feeling himself licensed to go beyond the (missing) evidence, concludes either that they exchanged no letters or, which is more likely, that all letters were lost or destroyed. The psychohistorian finds the absence of letters irresistible grist for speculation: Jefferson or his mother had something to conceal, or disliked one another, but in any case the relationship must have been troubled in some abnormal way. The point is clear. History and psychohistory differ fundamentally. The latter can be interesting and it may even be true. But not because it uses evidence in a way that historians would regard as responsible, or even reputable.

If history is by and large a tale of people who knew "somewhat more than all" there was to know, much of it false, we must obviously regard much of our knowledge as provisional. Yet from the rules of evidence common to all disciplines, certain common rules of inquiry seem to endure from age to age, and in a sense to transcend a historical landscape littered with discarded certainties. No one has the wisdom to distill from all the known modes of inquiry one universal evidentiary system, proof against fallacy, but it might be fun to try.

Here are a few rules that would make my own list:

1. There would be that quality of mind or temperament that the poet John Keats called "negative capability": an ability to entertain contradictory and even incompatible beliefs without anxiety: not for a show of tolerance but in recognition of the multiplicity of truth.

2. There must be documentation, in both the narrow and the broad sense—not merely concrete evidence, the "smoking gun" of the murder scene—but the resolve to trace an item of information or belief to its sustaining foundation.

3. There would be some wariness of the pitfalls that lurk in "systems" and "models" of all kinds, grand schemes that purport to unify great bodies of diverse and untidy information. (This marks me, I know, as a "fox" in the great division of intellectual styles set out in Isaiah Berlin's *The Hedgehog and the Fox.*)

4. There would be a nodding acquaintance, and preferably more, with the rules of logic; some working skill at seeing what is implicated or not implicated, entailed or not entailed, by a given set of postulates. We need not, and of

course cannot, settle the question of whether logical systems are culturally determined, elegant human artifices, or mirrors of the very structure of our minds.

5. There would be some facility for distinguishing and discriminating, for seeing differences when it is easier or more convenient to see likenesses and similarities.

6. Finally, but not least, there would be some care and precision in the use of language—a comprehensive rule against its privatization, against its reduction to esoteric jargons whose function is to safeguard some citadel of specialized knowledge against neutral scrutiny.

We imagine, most of us, that we are proof against the fanaticisms and superstitions, the absurdities of the age; and we are usually right. The real trap lies in the secure and fashionable certainties, and history suggests that we are likely to tumble headlong into it even as we retreat in confident horror from the things we hardly need to be told are wrong. My universal rules of evidence might provide a bit of insurance. How much, I am—needless to add—not sure.

16. Heroic Biography

When Dumas Malone, the great Jefferson biographer, died in December of 1986, I found myself pondering what historians are apt to consider a hazardous subject: heroic biography.

It is not a recognized term of historical art. Indeed, insofar as it hints even slightly at the sly inflation of the biographer's subject for patriotic or nationalistic ends, it would be thought an illegitimate pursuit. We would be stepping into the shoes of the great neoclassical painter David, with his glorification of Napoleon and the imperial court.

Let us, however, use the term provisionally, as a convenient label for a certain sort of biography of the great and near great, a style of biography that we expect to satisfy both curiosity and the thirst for inspiring example. Obviously, I do not have in mind the sort of biography that Lytton Strachey famously attacked in his preface to *Eminent Victorians*—"those two fat volumes . . . with their tone of tedious panegyric, their lamentable lack . . . of detachment." Rather, it would fall somewhere in the broad realm between hagiography, which should be reserved for saints, and demonology, which should be reserved for the truly villainous. We think of Mason Weems, the nineteenth-century collector of charming myths about Washington, and William Herndon, scouring backwoods Kentucky and Illinois for tales of the martyred Lincoln, as examples to be avoided. They tilt toward hagiography, as H. L. Mencken, with his tongue-in-cheek depiction of Washington as an intoxicated *roué* and land-grabber, tilts toward burlesque. Where, then, is the balance to be struck?

I think we find a satisfying answer in Malone's six-volume *Jefferson and His Time*. Jefferson was clearly a heroic presence for Malone, who pursued his great subject for forty years. Yet Malone made no effort to conceal frailties and contradictions. Read Malone on Jefferson's narrowing view of states' rights in old age, or on his vindictive pursuit of Aaron Burr, or on his quarrels with John Marshall. No prettification there. Yet the overall effect of this wonderful work is to evoke those mythic strengths that make the author of the Declaration of Independence so imposing a presence in our national imagination. It would be a fortunate republic, lacking the unifying mystique of royalty, whose heroes and founders all in due course found their Dumas Malone.

The foregoing reflections lead naturally to a more general question: Does the biographer who takes on a national hero, a member of the pantheon of founders, incur some special obligation? A responsibility to handle the alabaster gingerly, to avoid the tarnish of mockery and iconoclasm? When the late Fawn Brodie published her best-selling one-volume Jefferson biography some fifteen years ago, she in effect accused the Jefferson scholars—Malone and others—of doing precisely that: playing watchdog to the pantheon and sacrificing the subtle, ambiguous stuff of truth to that role. Her most sensational charge, for instance, was that Thomas Jefferson, lonely after the early and tragic death of his wife, sired several illegitimate children by a slave woman, Sally Hemings. In her view, and in the view of those who swallowed her reading of the evidence, it was clear that a "Jefferson Mafia" had shirked the prime obligations of scholarship and conspired to keep Jefferson's character inviolate.

The suggestion was nonsense. There was no such conspiracy; only a very different—I would say more responsible—attitude toward some very shaky historical evidence. Yet the episode helps to illuminate the question I pose. And at the most obvious level one would have to say that Brodie was, in principle, quite right. It is not the right function of biographers, however exalted the patriotic standing of their subjects, to falsify them for any reason. In the Tudor age, British monarchs (especially Elizabeth I and her father before her) licensed and limited the manner in which artists might represent them. The result was a style in royal portraiture that, when the realistic influence of Holbein faded, tended to a pale abstraction and idealism of imagery. In the Soviet Union, even today, there is the Great Soviet Encyclopedia to which one may turn to discover the precise state of any historical reputation at any time. Republics neither have, nor assert, such controls. An American "great encyclopedia" enshrining some official orthodoxy about the nation's great is as unimaginable as a Soviet Lytton Strachey, poking saucy fun at Lenin.

The result is that the more complex the figure, the wider the variety of interpretations. Merrill Peterson had shown, in *The Jefferson Image in the American Mind,* how every age and political sect recreates the Sage of Monticello to its own specifications; and yet on the whole without lasting harm. One of the founders, Benjamin Franklin, undertook to codify, as it were, his personal image and reputation. He did it in his autobiography, one of the American classics and a rich source of votive myth and imagery. Yet if it was his intent to enshrine himself as a plaster wise man, he failed. He did not prevent later biographers, from Phillips Russell in the 1920s to more recent ones, from tracking him into the salons of eighteenth-century Paris, where the ladies of the salons are shown to be swooning over the doctor's rustic coonskin cap and stroking his bald head.

And what of the greatest national icon of all, George Washington? Like many generations of American school-children, I studied in public school classrooms from whose walls the *pater patriae* glared sternly down. That memorable Gilbert Stuart portrait, with its particularly reproving set of the mouth, was everywhere. I certainly knew the stories of the cherry tree and of spinning the coin across the Rappahannock. It would be many years before I encountered—in one of Daniel Boorstin's "American Experience" volumes—the story that the general's famous expression is not a reflection of character or mood so much as of Washington's discomfort with a new and ill-fitting set of false teeth. He happened to be trying them out when he sat to Stuart. That is the story, anyway, and of such are made the trivial and harmless dissonances that all of us encounter in the lore of the founders and other national heroes—and relish, too; for there is something in us ordinary folk that seeks the consolation of knowing that our heroes have their foibles too.

But turn the question around, ask it another way, and we get a rather different answer. Does a democratic republic, notwithstanding its presumed immunity to the cult of personality, not need heroes as much as more hierarchical societies? And if we do, as I think is the case, how shall the need be served without sacrifice of scholarly integrity?

I have cited the example of Dumas Malone's Jefferson. Douglas Southall Freeman's Washington (though perhaps not so good as his Lee) is a model; so is that brilliant cameo of Washington by Samuel Eliot Morison, "The Young Man Washington," with its endearing evocation of "the last person you would ever suspect of having been a young man." Beveridge's *John Marshall* would rank with them; and there are others.

Two expectations are, I think, to be satisfied in heroic biography. One, the more obvious and in some ways the easiest, is inspiration. Each of us will have his idea of what that is. For me it is the evocation of Washington's magnanimity—for instance, toward the egregious young "Citizen" Genet, the French revolutionary envoy who, landing at Charleston, so annoyed Washington with his inflammatory Anglophobe speeches. But when Genet's former colleagues turned against him in Paris and put a price on his head, Washington generously permitted him to stay on and settle down in New York as a gentleman farmer. I like to think, too, of John Marshall, in the pre-Supreme Court years, when almost alone among Federalists he opposed the hysterical and repressive Alien and Sedition Acts. I like to think of Jefferson, with that queer blend of vanity and modesty, deciding with a twinkle in his eye to omit all his political offices from the obelisk that marks his grave on the Charlottesville hillside.

If the Civil War was our Iliad, the lives and characters of the founding generation constitute our Aeneid, our founding myth. Modern scholarly biography is a long way from classical epic; yet the function of the heroic biographer is at least allied to the function Vergil assumed when he undertook to link imperial Rome to the fall of Troy. After all, history and its subspecies, biography, are precisely humanistic disciplines; and it is not outrageous to expect them to be, in appropriate measure, humanizing. As autonomous pursuits, independent of the response they evoke, they are likely to be sterile, worse than useless.

But if we may expect inspiration in some sense, there is no escape from complexity. After Freud, the ambiguities of human character, the willfulness of impulse, must be considered even when we deal with heroes. But this, while it can be overdone, is no barrier to heroism properly understood. James Madison, who was crucial to the founding of our government, was deeply imbued with the Calvinist view of human nature, the lurking dangers of the will to power and the need to contain it institutionally. He was no romantic; nor were most of the realists who wrote our Constitution. Dr. Freud would have had little of fundamental importance to tell the American founder who wrote in *Federalist* 51: "But what is government itself, but the greatest of all reflections on human nature? If men were angels, no government would be necessary."

It is no slight art to evoke greatness in biography— heroism within the limited meaning I have assigned it. Suetonius and Tacitus showed long ago how easy it is to evoke villains in high places, how the Neros and Caligulas can be portrayed believably in the starkest blacks and whites. Heroic portraiture demands a more varied palette, a more subtle and inclusive line. Dumas Malone showed how it can be done. May his tribe increase.

17. Roots: An Essay in Personal History

My most influential mentor died suddenly one Sunday morning, aged eighty-five, as he sat reading his newspaper at the nursing home. None of us chooses the hour or setting of this unwelcome summons, yet his had an uncanny fitness. There was, for one thing, the mastery of his stubborn, often willful spirit over physical frailty. Merely to read the morning paper, as he always did, cost great effort. He would be wheeled to a dining room table, and the journal would be spread before him. A nurse would return periodically to turn the pages his once powerful farm boy's hands had become too arthritic to handle.

This careful, observant scrutiny of a world he could no longer even barely affect, let alone control, suggested too his unquenchable curiosity. Early on the morning of his funeral, a few days later, I watched a long freight train crawl through the small North Carolina town whose schools he had administered for forty years. I thought: He was the only man I knew who could have told you what those odd-shaped cars were built to carry, whether they still did and, if so, where the cargoes were mined and made. For good measure he could have named the founders of the rail lines—rascals in his book, most probably—and told by what imposture against the public interest they had prospered.

His information was vast and seemed especially so to a boy. It pained him that I could rarely identify the cover crops that whizzed past the car windows as we pursued vacation routes through the southern countryside. "What is that, sonny?" I would look up blankly from my book. "Oats?" "No, clover." A few summers ago, he sat patiently listening as a babbling mob of newsless children and grandchildren on vacation idly guessed where the United States had recently shot down two Libyan planes. The Gulf of . . . of . . . ? Persian Gulf? "Sidra," he finally said. Others guessed; he knew.

That he was stricken over his newspaper suggests another great fact about him—that as to public matters he was never neutral. Perhaps it is not impious to wonder, in fact, what folly in the papers of July 7 stirred the fatal agitation. Until I was no longer a young man, his views weighed with me because they were his, rarely unemphatic, and usually wise.

In mid-1964, as the mess in Southeast Asia worsened, he followed my editorial errors—they were, after all, publicly committed, for all to see—in pained silence, as was his custom. But one day he brought himself to say in the kindliest way that I must surely realize that Vietnam would be our ruin, as it had been of the French. Even Douglas MacArthur, of all people, could see that.

No, I assured him; his worries were misplaced. We would gently bomb these people for a while and they would come to terms. The Bundy brothers had it all worked out. No small peasant society could long endure the benevolent displeasure of the world's strongest power. Wait and see, he said; and read your Walter Lippmann.

There seems to have been something genetic in this lavish investment of feeling in public issues. His father before him had been a militant Populist party leader in west-central

North Carolina until, as he put it, "the Democrats caught up" by nominating William Jennings Bryan. One day during the crazy presidential campaign of 1972, I tried calmly to tell him that while of course there could be no question of my voting—ever—for Richard Nixon, McGovern seemed to me to be saying such silly things that I might just not vote. "If I ever become so indifferent," he roared, "just bury me." I voted.

Oddly, these gusty political passions were a sort of hobby, incidental to his consuming interest in the nurturing and education of children. Incredibly, his farmer/school-master/politician father had sent ten children through college, and most of them, including my father, had proceeded on to advanced degrees. Education was so central to his family's vision of the world that to be without it, or to treat it lightly, was unimaginable. And by the way, to know was to know exactly. Once he ran through a geometrical demonstration with me as I sat, only half comprehending, by his reading chair. "See, sonny?" he asked. "I think I do," I responded. "In geometry," he said, "proofs are not a matter of opinion. They are either right or wrong." He felt that way about many things—not only math and science but history, behavior, and politics. Especially behavior. He conceded little to the twilight. His funeral services were, as he had wished, unadorned and ecumenical, with a few psalms and prayers and the last lines from Bryant's *Thanatopsis* express-ing the rational faith and hope of a public man. Quite without his leave, we ventured to add Luther's great hymn, "A Mighty Fortress," as seemed appropriate for a seventh-generation Carolina Lutheran.

The death of fathers is an old theme and some weeks of fond reflection yield no striking variations for me. But rising above the pain and indignity of his long decline, there is a fresh sense of the honor—and luck—of having had such a man as my teacher and friend.

II

The call I had dreaded, yet somehow imagined that I did not dread, came about ten o'clock one October morning three years later. My mother had died a few minutes earlier in the hospital where she had been a patient for a month.

My wife and I had said our farewells to her there on a sunny Saturday morning ten days earlier. The Carolina autumn sun streamed cheerfully into her small room where she sat, a frail and trembling but unbowed presence, a blanket hiding the small arms bruised by the monitoring devices that measured her life signs. Yet no one had ever seemed to me less diminished by machines. Only a day or two earlier her young doctor had approached me as I sat at her bedside, her small hand grasping my index finger in a child's way. He murmured sadly and quietly of "classic pneumonia" and did not need to add that for a frail woman in her eighty-ninth year the outlook was grim. As he said this, the lip of this good and disciplined man trembled. For no one ever entered her orbit without feeling its special grace.

The news of her death itself was not shocking; it was even expected. As we made ready to drive south—calling a few family members around the country, arranging to postpone work, packing clothes—I found myself strangely serene, just, I told myself, as she would have wished. For she had always gone to extravagant lengths to spare pain and anxiety to others. Even as we drove that afternoon through the matchless blaze of Virginia and Carolina autumn foliage, I began to wonder when and even whether seemly grief would come. Grief I had known before, usually for younger friends cut down too soon. But it had been her habit to make others feel as if her own fortunes were perfectly attuned, as if by the hand of nature, to the convenience of those she loved. Even as we left her there in the hospital those ten days earlier, really at death's door, she sang out that perky "Don't worry about me" that I had heard a thousand times, child and man. There might be secret bitterness or regret or self-pity in it for others; but when she said it one felt its unmistakable genuineness: Don't worry, don't grieve, only remember the good times. Yet for whom might one grieve, I wondered silently as the miles passed, if not for this radiant and gallant woman from whose very flesh one had been formed?

The grief eventually came, suddenly and overwhelmingly, and its strange nature requires some unraveling. But that was later. We gathered that night of her death at her house—our house, the house of my boyhood, built in 1935 on a schoolmaster's pay—my wife and I, my brother and a few old friends. It was a quiet evening, leavened by a few glasses of wine and fond reminiscence—and by the admirable funeral instructions she had thoughtfully provided. All these had been neatly entered in her graceful hand in the notebook she kept at her bedside, marked "Important Plans." Those of us who were closest to her knew what kind of "plans" these were—she was a master of elegant euphemism—but we rarely spoke of them. I had once read as far as her amusing injunction, "Age not to be given to newspapers"—concealing her years was one of her few vanities. But not far beyond. No life was more affirmative than hers, even as it stretched its apparently unclouded way into her late eighties, unbroken even by my father's lengthy decline. The mood she established around her made death seem a remote and boorish impertinence, a bad-mannered intruder lurking somewhere in the shadows, perhaps, but not to be acknowledged in polite company. The other instructions were in character—the arrangement of roses on the casket ("closed at all times . . . no brown or black for me") and the comfortable words of religion she loved. All in character, I say, for flowers, along with music and children and poetry, were her defining symbols, none more than roses. And no one had been a more resolute foe of all that was solemn, pompous, funereal and grave. Even the lines of poetry from Longfellow and Kipling that she wanted read in church were not about death but about the legacies we leave behind, and what artistry would be like in a universe of perfection.

But there in the "Plans" notebook, along with some family reminiscences she had been writing from time to time, I discovered some quite astonishing things—astonishing not in their eloquence, though they were eloquent, but rather in their theme and tone. They revealed that my mother had been leading what I can only call a double life. This small, cheerful woman, so radiant and equable, so insistently optimistic, so accomplished at the gesture that put others at ease, so devoted a connoisseur of happy, silly rhymes and teasing stories and Victorian sentiment, of flowers and children and bouncy music—this woman had clearly been thinking at times about far darker things. I was astonished. Could this be the woman I had known for fifty-four years? I could still picture her at the piano long years before, playing Percy Grainger's lilting tunes—especially "Country Gardens"— or "Washington and Lee Swing," or "The White Cliffs of Dover" (whose bluebirds told all) or dozens of other perky tunes. She wrote once that her creed was "Life is music, but only if the notes are touched lightly and in tune." Yet this high-flying spirit had, it seemed, walked along the valley of the shadow of death more than once. In her quiet hours she had been wrestling with that shadow. More than once she had copied from the small devotional book she kept at her bedside lines like, "the cold shadow of sorrow falls alike upon those of high and humble lot." Yet, she reflected, life without sorrow would lack nobility; it would be "hard, not gay but garish, devoid of tenderness and sympathy and sensibility." These somber yet consoling meditations she had mixed and varied with her own thoughts, not once but again and again—in the blank leaves of her books, and on this or that scrap of paper.

I thought how she must have struggled with the darker mysteries she had so carefully shielded me from as a child (I was an adult before I attended my first funeral) and I felt a great surge of grief. The grief was for her and her quiet struggle, of course, but until a few weeks earlier she had rarely been ill and she had seemed in high spirits the weekend before her death. It was more, perhaps, grief for my own superficiality, for all the jolly but routine hours I had passed with her in the years since my father's death, knowing that an appointment or a waiting flight would soon rescue me from the sensed but unspoken loneliness. It was grief in part for that larger loneliness that all of us must sooner or later endure, so wonderfully captured in the Emily Dickinson poem she read many times: "Because I could not stop for death, he kindly stopped for me." All of us surmise one day—a very long day—that the horses' heads are toward eternity; but until life gives truth to them, they are only words on the page. And now I was seeing how they had been given life in my mother's private meditations.

Reading these papers very early on the morning after the day she died, I sat alone for a long time, feeling for the first time the void she had left and wondering from what secret sources this surge of desolation had welled up. What was it rooted in, and how had I managed to miss the story all these years?

The story is poignant and interesting, though it has a triumphant ending; and it begins well over a century ago in the central Georgia countryside which, to the irritated amusement of my father, she called "home" even after sixty years in North Carolina. Its beginning lies in that stretch of country between Augusta and Macon, with its small towns and villages and old cotton plantations. I remember that country as an incomparably happy vacation refuge of my boyhood, so far in mood and style from the North Carolina haunts of the sober, learned, admirable, always serious and decorous Yoders. The native places of her people—these Logues and Laseters, these Bruces and Rivieres and War-thens—were places of spacious landscape and big airy houses in the country, filled with merry, laughing, tippling, fun-loving people, cavaliers in their southern way. And it was from them that her temperament and manners flowed. She had been born the youngest of five children to the marriage of Joseph Henry Lumpkin Logue and Ida van Della Laseter. She had been a frail baby and credited her survival to the care of two country doctors, her mother's brothers and the genetic sharers, perhaps, of a rich medical heritage among the male descendants of the marriage. But it was precisely here, in this happy place, that the pattern of light and dark had first begun to form. It is a tale, I think, of the hereditary nature of our inner lives.

My mother's grandfather, Calvin Logue—Captain Calvin Logue, that is, commander of Company B of the 22nd Georgia Infantry of the Confederate army—had been the magnate of his county. His handsome memorial obelisk—one that would have fascinated William Faulkner almost as much as the statue of his grandfather and perhaps even inspired a Satoris story—stands in the square of Gibson, the town he "founded" before riding off to be killed in the campaigning around Richmond in mid-August 1864. He left my grandfather, an only son with two sisters and a Con-federate widow to guard the family legacy, such as it was after Sherman and the devastation of war were through with it. The family place lay on Sherman's route; and according to family legend (whether true or not or half true hardly matters), Sherman's soldiery came one evening when the family were at dinner, barging right through the house from back door to front, swatting and slashing at the furnishings with their swords and muskets as they passed. In the mind's eye that scene—it could not have been long before my great-grandfather's death at Deep Bottom on the James River—was the warp of a pattern.

The ruin was great, to family and land alike, and my fatherless grandfather's response was to meet it with practically lifelong drunkenness and a sort of village-atheist bitterness about the formal religious assurances which were, of course, the sustenance of his wife and children and most of his neighbors. What it created also was a desperate and humiliating insecurity in my mother's early life, though she never spoke openly of it to me—I learned the story from others. And yet as her own example proved, the results were miraculously constructive. In her fascinating sketch of Ronald Reagan's boyhood, Gail Sheehy has noted how the triumphant adult survivors of alcoholic parents are often people of unconquerably sunny outlook. They have survived a hell of unpredictability and insecurity that most of us escape and if they come through it they know enough of the dark not to be dominated by it. When I read Sheehy's words some months ago, I suddenly realized with a start that she was writing about my mother no less than about the president of the United States.

But what is fascinating to me about all this is not the too familiar tragedy of alcoholism or of family fortune or happiness dissipated by it, but the heroic after-effect on my mother and her brothers and sisters. All of them emerged from it as wonderfully cheerful, gay, generous and productive people—not only in medicine and education and business but, more importantly, in the art of living well and gracefully. That childhood and its pain somehow transmuted character into something surpassingly resilient and nurturing.

But not all the darkness gets lost. As I sat reflecting on the painful thoughts she had had in old age, in the valley of the shadow, I also faced an unflattering reality about myself. I had not really known my mother as well as I thought I had. She had contrived to disclose only the cheerful and buoyant side. I had known that she was very brave. When she was only thirty-nine and my father forty, he had suffered a life-threatening spinal injury and only narrowly escaped death, sentenced to more or less constant pain thereafter. She stood against it without gloom or self-pity. In this as in all else she was relentless in her emphasis on what was sunny, flowery, hopeful. Her house, like that of my favorite aunt, her sister, in Augusta, told the story. They were both museums of the fine and the flimsy, bound in undifferentiated association by a single thread: each piece, valuable or junky, stood for some occasion or person or gesture that had touched her to the depths of her bounteous capacity for sentiment.

She and I had often met on our shared common ground, a love of poetry. But because we came of different eras and schoolings, it was almost the chance encounter of two continents temporarily abutting. She had grown up in the era of memorization, when an English major at her school, the Georgia State College for Women at Milledgeville, meant getting by heart great reams of "great poetry" of the kind one finds in Victorian anthologies. She had gone there at sixteen, the youngest student, and emerged three years later an accomplished pianist with a head stuffed to the limits of memory with poems and orations and declamations, sublime and silly and in between. Seventy years later, she could correct me on a Shakespeare soliloquy, or Kipling, and could endlessly recite "Twenty Froggies Went to School" and "The Courting of Miss Mousie." But here was the mystery, as I had seen it all the years. Many of these great lines she knew so well came from *King Lear* and *Hamlet* and *Macbeth*— came, in short, from what were, after all, sobering contemplations of the abyss. And I had imagined that she had never cared to bother with such things because they were so discordant with her steady and resolute cheerfulness. I was deeply, foolishly wrong.

And so as I sat there at the dining room table on a bright October morning, looking through her commonplace book, I thought about the strange destinies that link generations— link them in love and understanding, to be sure, but sometimes in stark incomprehension of one another. Her private meditations on what she called "the cold shadow of sorrow"—of which I had never once heard her speak, even at times of family death and tragedy—were shattering to contemplate. I could see in her lonely ordeal, so thoughtfully concealed for our convenience and comfort, one of the oldest of all the truths of our condition. The ethereal and radiant must, after all, draw their energy from a serene reckoning with all that is earthbound, mortal, fearful and even desolate. Ariel and Caliban are inseparable twins, air and fire with earth and water. She had seen it as clearly as I ever fancied I had, but she had never spoken of it. I learned again, but far more vividly than ever, that the real tragedy is what we learn too late. But that is an old story, told many times over, a banality.

For years I have been reading and rereading and talking to others about one of Henry James's masterpieces, the story called "The Beast in the Jungle." It is about a man called Marcher who is sure that he has some special but unidentified destiny, crouching in wait for him like a beast in the jungle. He finds a friend to "watch" with him, yet mistakes the nature of his relationship with her. His self-absorption in an imaginary future blinds him to the present possibilities of love; and it is only in the final harsh focus of her death that he sees the truth he has missed and is devastated by it. As I grew older, and a bit more accustomed to our universal mortality, I had begun to be mercilessly condescending about poor old Marcher, his foolish egotism and blindness.

And yet, as Henry James would surely have warned, we are all of us Marchers; it is a universal, not a special, fate. And that bright October morning I suddenly realized that I stood convicted, also, of Marcher's sin. I had missed an opportunity to reach across that great barrier of cheerfulness that she had arranged, so considerately, for our security and comfort, to share and acknowledge the darkness.

But would it really have been right, even if I had been more discerning than I was? When we are children, the most dreadful thing to imagine is the physical disappearance of a parent. As we come gradually to see that life is spirit or it is nothing, we grow accustomed to the the idea that the body, much as we love it and cling to it, must in the end be a great irrelevance; that it is only spirit that will be left to light the great darkness.

My mother had long since made her serene way to that supreme truth and, I think, scattered the evidence of her search behind to remind us that we too must find our way to it. I felt a certain bitter regret at what I had missed in her. But is it ever really possible, even with those we know and love best, to share that reckoning with the shadow? My mother must have begun to wrestle with it long before as a sensitive child and she had understood as more than pretty words that "after a time," as she wrote, "one lights a candle called Patience." The glow of that candle was what all of us saw in her last days, illuminating with unbowed spirit that frail, fragile, failing, shrunken body, bruised with the devices of modern medical technology, when her wish still was that we, continuing the traditions she lived by, get on with our lives.

18. Washington:
A Personal Perspective

Some years ago, a friend who was then teaching at the University of Texas asked her freshman English class to write a theme on H. L. Mencken's sassy little essay, "Pater Patriae." George Washington, according to Mencken,

> . . . was the Rockefeller of his time, the richest man in the United States, a promoter of stock companies, a land-grabber, an exploiter of mines and timber. . . . He was not pious. He drank whiskey whenever he felt chilly, and kept a jug of it handy. He knew far more profanity than Scripture, and used and enjoyed it more . . . He took no interest in the private morals of his neighbors. Inhabiting these states today, George would be ineligible for any office of honor or profit. . . . He would be on trial in the newspapers for belonging to the Money Power. . . . He would be under indictment by every grand jury south of the Potomac; and Methodists of his native state would be denouncing him (he had a still at Mount Vernon) as a debaucher of youth, a recruiting officer for insane asylums.

One of her students wrote one of those classics that tend to be tacked on departmental bulletin boards. Its indignant-writer suggested that this writer, "Pater Patriae," must surely be a communist—perhaps even an enemy of the oil-depletion allowance—to write such shocking things about the Father of our Country.

Mencken was not the first, and won't be the last, to make mildly iconoclastic sport of the reputation of George Washington, nor my friend's student the last to react oversolemnly to the game. But maybe the best way to get through to the complex humanity of Washington is to admit, despite the bombast, how much truth there is in what Mencken says. Washington did enjoy the company of pretty women, and he was, to say the least, no prohibitionist. His command of barracks-room language was often noted with admiration. And he did, to his considerable profit, speculate heavily in western lands—though there any useful resemblance to John D. Rockefeller ends. Whether, as Mencken merrily speculated (he was writing in the Red-scare and Temperance-ridden year of 1918), Washington might today be hounded by grand juries or excluded on moral grounds from public office is, to be sure, unknowable. But in our priggish and blue-nosed age, the possibility cannot be dismissed out of hand.

But all of this, however amusing, is so far from capturing the essence of Washington as to approach triviality—with one exception. "He was not pious," declares Mencken, and so far as we can tell, that is exactly so. And it is, I think, a fact of some consequence for those of us who seek to understand Washington. In his recent biography, James Thomas Flexner tells us that in the year 1768 Washington "went to church on 15 days, mostly when away from home, and hunted foxes on 49": an admirable balance. Washington was reverent when reverence was appropriate; but in his personality there seems not so much as an atom of that cloying religiosity that sentimentalists from Weems onward have sought to discover.

Indeed, in what is in some ways the most humanizing of Washington portraits, Samuel Eliot Morison observes—and is surprised—that even when he attended church Washington routinely refused Communion, "never joined Martha," as Morison puts it, "in the beautiful and comforting sacrament of the body and blood of Christ." Flexner ventures to doubt that Washington believed in any sort of afterlife. His, in short, was the simple, natural and benevolent deistic creed of the eighteenth century gentry, refreshingly free of dogma, cant and zeal. But one is not surprised to observe that the fruits of his faith were impressive. As dozens of incidents show, he was a remarkably benevolent and forbearing man, whose tolerance of other views, religious and otherwise, exceeded even the enlightened expectations of his age—and likewise his acts of charity. We all will have our Washingtons, I suppose, but in mine the absence of narrow pietism goes hand in hand with the magnanimity.

I think we may find another clue in what little we know—essentially what Douglas Freeman was able to find out—about the situation of that remote Washington ancestor, the Rev. Lawrence, sometime fellow of Brasenose College, Oxford. In 1643 the earlier Washington was deposed from his parish living by ascendant presbyterians or puritans. Might that hint at what prompted the parson's son, John, to move to Virginia some sixteen years later? Might it, more specifically, account for the latitudinarian views of their descendants? So far as we can see, there was small patience among the Washingtons, then or later, for religious enthusiasm. In 1750 Freeman finds the later Lawrence Washington, George's beloved half-brother, observing that "this colony was greatly settled in the latter part of Charles the First's time and during the usurpation by the zealous churchmen; and that spirit which was then brought in, has ever since continued, so that except a few Quakers we have no dissenters . . . " The result, he said, was that in contrast to

Pennsylvania, immigration had been stinted and Virginia accordingly left underpopulated. The least to be inferred from this is that in the view of Lawrence Washington, and presumably of his devoted and admiring half-brother, "zealous churchmen" and their enthusiasms should not be permitted to stand in the way of civic progress.

Finally, on the personal side, I think we do well to see in Washington the usual marks of the accommodating younger son. His mother, we know, was not far short of shrewish in the way she tried to control him and later pestered him for money and attention—to a degree that became embarrassing. His great model was Lawrence, schooled in England and connected by marriage to the Fairfaxes; and in Washington's youth Lawrence had achieved many of those marks of civil and military distinction that Washington craved: one of his few vanities. As Freeman remarks, Lawrence must have embodied for George the great world, as it appeared to the imagination of a gifted but provincial young Virginian of the mid-century. When this admired model was cut down by tuberculosis, it was natural that George would try to fill his shoes. And perhaps, without the formal advantages that might have come his way had his father lived, he was the more resolute in his own self-prescribed course of discipline and instruction.

II

As for the public man, dozens of the choices Washington made in office might be cited in support of his legendary wisdom. But let me mention three, no doubt familiar enough, that I believe illustrate his instincts.

Faced with the revolutionary situation of 1776 and after, Washington exerted a continuing influence for lenient dealing with the conservatives, some of them later "loyalists" or "tories," who parted uneasily with the English Crown.

This was not softness or sentimentality; it was a blend of policy and charity. There was the chance that if generously treated, these disaffected people would rally to the revolutionary cause. But even if they didn't, Washington understood the most fundamental truth of all revolutionary situations, which is that more often than not these upheavals devour those who conjure them up, and make a mockery, as well, of their instigating ideologies. He knew this, apparently by instinct, well before the Jacobins in Paris rubbed the lesson in nearly twenty years later.

Then, there was the Genet affair. The fiery young French emissary, sent to seek American aid in the revolutionary wars against Britain, foolishly presumed that because Washington's neutrality policy infuriated so many shallow Francophiles, it was fragile and not to be taken seriously; that it might be huffed and puffed aside by his inflammatory speeches; that he, Genet, could raise armies of liberation to attack Spanish Louisiana and outfit privateers to raid British shippers in American waters. And all with impunity.

Even Jefferson, the leader of the French party in Washington's administration, was outdone with Genet. That was the true measure of Genet's imprudence and presumption. I can imagine Washington observing the Frenchman's impertinences with mounting anger, yet not, I fancy, without amusement. As usual, Washington had measured the strategic stakes accurately. He knew what the result could be if the new nation were sucked again into the European quarrels from which it had struggled for twenty years to extract itself. Even the pro-French faction gradually came to see that things were getting out of hand with Genet. We know what the sequel was: Genet's recall was demanded; his masters in Paris scheduled him for execution. So Washington, despite the worry this upstart had caused him, permitted him to settle down in New York as a gentleman farmer. He prospered there and even married the governor's daughter. This act of unmerited clemency echoed the agony Washington is known to have felt in sending Major André, Benedict Arnold's co-conspirator, to his death.

Third, there is Flexner's speculation that Washington, had he still been president, would not have signed the Alien and Sedition Acts. There is much to support this notion, including Washington's tendency to value Jefferson's advice on constitutional precedent. And there is the collateral evidence that it was Washington who pushed the young John Marshall into politics; and Marshall was among the few Federalists who opposed the acts.

In fact, it is tempting to view Washington not only as the protector of American liberties but almost as a proto-civil libertarian. He was a more resolute and less thin-skinned defender of the press than Jefferson. He was as deeply committed as Madison to separation of church and state. And as the evils of slavery gradually dawned on him, he was the most active—and effective—of his great Virginia contemporaries in trying to do something useful about those evils. His heirs were paying pensions to ex-slaves as late as 1830.

At any rate, Washington for me seems one of those genuinely open-minded people who do prove all things before reaching conclusions; and it is a rare quality. One sees him ripening slowly like a great wine, so that in his mature years he could be admired even by the exacting Abigail Adams. "He is," she observed, "polite with dignity, affable without familiarity, distant without haughtiness, grave without austerity, modest, wise and good."

I have deliberately omitted the generalship, even though it was as a military man that he made his name. His military successes were, however, more those of character— of patience, fortitude, endurance, a sense of timing—than of Caesar-like dash or brilliance. In some ways, his greatest military accomplishments were things not done or prevented—stemming potential mutinies, restraing patriot zeal, curbing the Cincinnati, striving to avoid bloodshed in the face of the Shays and whiskey rebellions. Flexner, describing that most moving of all moments at Newburgh— when the general took out his reading glasses, saying, "Gentlemen, you will permit me to put on my spectacles, for I have not only grown gray but almost blind in the service of my country" and his assembled officers wept—quotes Jefferson: "The moderation and virtue of a single character probably prevented his Revolution from being closed, as most others have been, by a subversion of that liberty it was intended to establish."

What else is to be added? Just this, perhaps. With Washington, as with all great men, one is finally obliged to suspect uniqueness. It is not a popular idea in our age when everyone seems to be, or wants to be, cut from the same cookie-cutter. Washington doesn't fit the matrixes of historical orthodoxy. Yet the more one examines the details of his life, the less he seems the remote, marmoreal statue of legend and the more he seems to look upon us with that benevolent, friendly face in the Houdon life mask. This was the Washington that friends, family, soldiers, neighbors and servants knew, the finished edition of the rawboned and ambitious youth of Ferry Farm. The Enlightenment treasured benevolence as a supreme value, and in him that difficult ideal seems to have found true expression.

Even in our advanced post-Freudian age of pinched and guarded assessments of human character, there is a great deal in the legendary figure Lord Byron called "Cincinnatus of the West . . . the last, the best . . . whom envy dared not hate . . . to make men blush there was but one."

Notes and Acknowledgments

THE UNMAKING OF A WHIG was initially delivered in a slightly different form as one of the Bicentennial "Text and Teaching" lectures at Georgetown University, September 29, 1988.

Page 107: " . . . a prefatory word . . . " "Whig, 1657 . . . An adherent of the presbyterian cause in Scotland in the 17th century. . . Applied to the Exclusioners who opposed the succession of James, Duke of York, to the Crown, on the ground of his being a Roman Catholic . . . Hence, from 1689, an adherent of one of the two great parliamentary parties in England . . . " *The Oxford Universal Dictionary on Historical Principles*, 3d ed. (Oxford, 1955), p. 2415.

Page 109: " . . . a Midwestern senator . . . " Quoted in Eric Goldman, *The Crucial Decade* (New York), 1956.

Page 111: "An age-long experience . . . " See "The Search for Southern Identity," in Woodward, *The Burden of Southern History* (Baton Rouge: Louisiana State University, 1960), p. 21.

Page 112: " . . . the warnings of Reinhold Niebuhr" See especially Niebuhr and Heimert, *A Nation So Conceived: Reflections on the History of America from its Early Visions to its Present Power* (New York: Scribner's, 1963).

Page 112: "the standard edition . . . "Herbert Butterfield, *The Whig Interpretation of History* (London: G. Bell and Sons, 1951).

Page 113: " . . . the simplest version . . . " Personal correspondence with the author, 19 September 1988. John Maurice Evans is professor of English, Washington and Lee University.

Page 113: The Inaugural Lecture may be found in J.E.E.D. Acton, First Baron Acton, *Essays on Freedom and Power*, ed. Gertrude Himmelfarb (London: Thames and Hudson, 1956), pp. 25 ff.

297

Page 114: " . . . the profession was still very young . . . " See John Kenyon, *The History Men* (Pittsburgh: University of Pittsburgh Press, 1984), passim.

Page 114: " . . . the Germans, led by Ranke . . . " Leopold von Ranke (1795-1886). See "Ranke: The Respectful Critic," in Peter Gay, *Style in History* (New York: Basic Books, 1974).

Page 115: " . . . Butterfield has been described . . . " by Kenyon, op. cit., p. 261.

Page 117: " . . . I had stayed up straight through one fog-filled night . . . " Willie Morris, *North Toward Home* (Oxford, Miss.: Yoknapatawpha press, 1982), p.195.

Page 118: " . . . a famous remark of Keynes. . . . " " . . . The ideas of economists and political philosophers, both when they are right and when they are wrong, are more powerful than is commonly understood. Indeed the world is ruled by little else. Practical men, who believe themselves to be quite exempt from any intellectual influences, are usually the slaves of some defunct economist. Madmen in authority, who hear voices in the air, are distilling their frenzy from some academic scribbler of a few years back. . . . Soon or late, it is ideas, not vested interests, which are dangerous for good or evil." John Maynard Keynes, *The General Theory of Employment, Interest and Money* (London: Macmillan, 1954), pp. 383-84.

Page 120: Walter Laqueur, *The Terrible Secret: Suppression of the Truth about Hitler's "Final Solution"* (Boston: Little Brown, 1980).

Page 121: " . . . the great Dutch historian . . . " See Pieter Geyl, "Ranke in the Light of the Catastrophe," in *Debates With Historians* (New York: Meridian Books, 1958), p. 28.

*   *   *

THE AMERICAN USES OF THE PAST was delivered, in an earlier form, as the Phi Beta Kappa Address at Wake Forest College and appeared in the *Virginia Quarterly Review* 41.1 (Winter 1965). Revised, March 1989.

*   *   *

THE MADISONIAN PERSUASION was initially given as a paper at the "James Madison Days," a bicentennial commemoration in honor of James Madison at Madisonville, Kentucky, June 19, 1987 and subsequently appeared in *Kentucky Bench and Bar* 51.4 (Fall 1987).

* * *

THE CENTRALITY OF INSTITUTIONS was a lecture at the winter Carolina Symposium, University of North Carolina, Chapel Hill, 1979. Revised, February 1989.

* * *

WHOSE CONSTITUTION IS IT? Reprinted from *The Embattled Constitution: Vital Framework or Convenient Symbol,* ed. Adolph H. Grundman (Malabar, Fla.: Krieger Publishing Company, 1986).

* * *

PRIVACY: THE SEARCH IN THE SHADOWS was prepared for "Constituting and Reconstituting America: Two Hundred Years of American-European Dialogue," a colloquium at the New School for Social Research, New York City, October 25, 1986.

Page 163: " . . . in the *Olmstead* wiretapping case . . . " *Olmstead v. U.S.,* 277 U.S. 438 (1928). In his dissent, Brandeis said in part: "Subtler and more far-reaching means of invading privacy have become available to the government. Discovery and invention have made it possible for the government, by means more effective than stretching upon the rack, to obtain disclosure in court of what is whispered in the closet," a remarkably far-sighted observation. He added with equal prescience: "Advances in the psychic and related sciences may bring means of exploring un-expressed beliefs, thoughts and emotions."

Page 165: *Bowers, Attorney General of Georgia v. Hardwick, et al.,* (1986).

Page 165: "Justice White rejected . . . " "The Court," wrote Justice Byron White (majority opinion, page 9) "is most vulnerable and comes nearest to illegitimacy when it deals with judge-made constitutional law having little or no cognizable roots in the language or design of the Constitution. That this was so is painfully demonstrated by the face-off between the executive and the Court in the 1930s, which resulted in the repudiation of much of the substantive gloss that the Court had placed on the Due Process Clause of the Fifth and Fourteenth Amendments . . . "

Page 165: "The most revealing disputes . . . " Other notable privacy cases have dealt with the right to abortion (repeatedly), hair styles and lengths, and psychological testing as a precondition of government employment.

Page 165: "Tocqueville's shrewd observation . . . " "Scarcely any political question arises in the United States that is not resolved, sooner or later, into a judicial question." Alexis de Tocqueville, *Democracy in America* (New York: Vintage Books, 1945), p. 288.

Page 165: "Chief Justice Hughes' famous quip . . . " "We live under a constitution, but the constitution is what the judges say it is."

Page 166: "all of scores of citations . . . " Author's personal inspection at the U.S. Supreme Court library.

Page 167: "as against the government . . ." In the *Harvard Law Review* article these privacy rights were to apply, rather more sweepingly, "as against the world." The emphasis was on threats other than those from government: "Shall the courts . . . close the front entrance to constituted authority and open wide the back door to idle or prurient curiosity?" Still a very pertinent question.

Page 168: *Griswold v. Connecticut,* 381 U.S. 479 (1965). Further Note, 1989: This essay obviously was written before the privacy issue in general and the *Griswold* case in particular became—at least ostensibly—a critical issue in the 1987 Senate Judiciary Committee hearings on the nomination of Judge Robert Bork to the Supreme Court. No issue in the Bork controversy more clearly illustrates the general confusion than the issue of sexual privacy. Judge Bork, contrary to a widespread impression, perhaps deliberately spread by his opponents, expressed no hostility to privacy as such. He did reiterate his view that the Constitution establishes no generalized right of privacy. It is conceivable, as argued above, that other specified rights (for instance, against "unreasonable searches and seizures") may entail important privacy values. But nowhere is privacy itself mentioned, let alone guaranteed in the constitutional text—the omission is simply an indisputable fact. What a judge makes of this omission is where the real judicial difficulty begins. One may perhaps tease a general right of privacy out of "emanations" of the specified rights, as Justice Douglas did in *Griswold;* or one may invoke the natural law tradition, as did Justice Harlan. But a judge who infers general rights from specific ones in effect creates new rights by judicial fiat; and that was the essence of Judge Bork's complaint. Even if judges are by some customs licensed to do this—and clearly they are—what judges may invent at whim they may also retract at whim, a larger power over the scope of our liberties than some would be prepared to grant. If a judge invokes a natural law tradition older than the written Constitution, he must explain why his own grasp of the unwritten tradition is worthier of constitutional standing than others just as plausible and as strongly rooted in historical evidence—the more so when some claimed right of privacy (as in the *Hardwick* case) collides with historical evidence that certain sexual acts, however more tolerant society's attitudes may be today, have traditionally been considered *contrary* to natural law. No such disciplined framework of discussion was ever acknowledged by Judge Bork's critics, let alone invoked in an intellectually honest and straightforward fashion.

Page 169: "put economic pressure on . . . " *NAACP v. Alabama*, 377 U. S. 288 (1964).

Page 170: " . . . recently published diaries reveal . . . " Mrs. Black describes the justice's persistent effort to educate his "boys" (law clerks) in the fallacies of what he called the "shocks-the-conscience" school of natural-law jurisprudence. *Mr. Justice and Mrs. Black: The Memoirs of Hugo L. Black and Elizabeth Black* (New York: Random House, 1986).

Page 170: " . . . strenuously argued for years . . . " As early as his noted dissenting opinion in *Adamson v. California* (1947), Hugo Black assailed the infusion of natural law theory into the construction of protected constitutional liberties, saying, among other things: " . . . The 'natural law' formula . . . should be abandoned as an incongruous excrescence on our Constitution. I believe that formula to be itself a violation of our Constitution, in that it subtly conveys to courts, at the expense of legislatures, power over public policies in fields where no specific provision of the Constitution limits legislative power . . . "

Page 172: " . . . at some 'canonical moment' . . . " The term is from Ronald Dworkin's *Law's Empire* (Cambridge, Mass. & London: Belknap Press of Harvard University Press, 1986). Of his imaginary interpreter of law, "Hercules," Dworkin writes (p. 348): "Hercules' method . . . rejects the assumption of a *canonical moment* at which a statute is born and has all and only the meaning it will ever have. . . . He does not identify particular people as the exclusive 'framers' of a statute and then attend only to their hopes or expectations . . . "

Page 172: Hamilton, *The Federalist*, no. 84: " . . . I go further, and affirm that bills of rights . . . are not only unnecessary in the proposed Constitution, but would even be dangerous. They would contain various exceptions to powers not granted; and, on this very account, would afford a colorable pretext to claim more than were granted. For why declare that things shall not be done which there is no power to do? Why, for instance, should it be said that the liberty of the press shall not be restrained, when no power is given by which restrictions may be imposed?" *The Federalist* (New York: Modern Library, 1937), p. 559. As secretary of the Treasury in Washington's cabinet, and an energetic advocate of what came to be called the "loose construction" of federal powers, Hamilton soon supplied a compelling answer to his own question.

* * *

THE STATE OF THE CONSTITUTION, 1987 originated as a talk at the National Archives, Washington, D. C., and appeared in Robert S. Peck and Ralph S. Pollock, eds., *The Blessings of Liberty: Bicentennial Lectures at the National Archives* (Chicago: American Bar Association (ABA) Press, 1987).

* * *

THE MYTH OF THE FOURTH ESTATE was a constitutional bicentennial lecture at the Chautauqua Institution, Chautauqua, N. Y., June 1987. Revised, January 1989.

* * *

HARRY TRUMAN AND THE LESSONS OF HISTORY: Annual banquet address, Friends of the Library, University of North Carolina at Greensboro, 1978. It appeared in a condensed form in the *Washington Star* and was further revised, January 1989.

* * *

W. J. CASH AND "THE MIND OF THE SOUTH" was written (for French translation) as an afterword to the reissue of *L'esprit du sud,* the French version of *The Mind of the South* (Paris, 1941). The new edition is being edited by the distinguished anthropologist Jean Malaurie for Terre Humaine: Civilisations et Sociétés, and published by Librarie Plon, Paris.

Page 209: Geyl, *Napoleon: For and Against* (New Haven, 1963).

Page 210: Woodward, in *American Counterpoint* (Boston, 1971), pp. 261-283.

Page 211: Genovese, *The World the Slaveholders Made,* paperback ed. (New York, 1971), pp. 137 ff. An interesting European perspective on the ethos of the Southern planters is to be found in Raimondo Luraghi, *The Rise and Fall of the Plantation South* (New York and London, 1978).

Page 212: *The Education of Henry Adams,* quoted in Cash, *The Mind of the South,* 5th printing (New York, 1957), pp. 98-99.

Page 215: Cash, op. cit., page 46: "Moreover, there was the influence of the Southern physical world—itself a sort of cosmic conspiracy against reality in favor of romance."

Page 215: Herbert Butterfield, *The Whig Interpretation of History* (London: G. Bell & Sons, 1951) p. 107: "For him [the Whig historian] the voice of posterity is the voice of God and the historian is the voice of posterity. And . . . he tends to regard himself as the judge when by his methods and equipment he is fitted only to be the detective."

Page 216: Genovese, op. cit., page 144: "The popular practice (among historians) is to treat the proslavery advocates and the slaveholders generally as men whose ideas deserve only patronizing dismissal and who are of historical interest only as subjects for amateur psychological analysis."

Page 216: Joseph L. Morrison, *W.J. Cash: Southern Prophet* (New York: Knopf, 1967).

Page 221: See especially, T. Harry Williams, *Huey Long* (New York, 1969).

* * *

FUNDAMENTALISM and PIETY AND POLITICS constituted, in a slightly different form, the 27th annual Finch Foundation lectures in theology at High Point College, March 18 and 19, 1987.

* * *

THE STORYTELLING ANIMAL, in another version, was the Reynolds Lecture at Davidson College, January 28, 1988; it is dedicated to the memory of my friend Charles Lloyd, late professor of English there.

Page 247: " . . . the novelist Reynolds Price has suggested" Price, *A Palpable God* (New York: Atheneum Press, 1978), p. 3.

Page 247: Conrad, "Henry James," in *Notes on Life and Letters* (London, 1924), cited in Peter Brooks, *Reading for the Plot* (New York: Vintage Press, 1985). Other valuable discussions of storytelling as truthtelling include Eric Auerbach, *Memesis: The Representation of Reality in Western Literature* (Princeton: Princeton University Press, 1953); Robert Alter, *The Art of Biblical Narrative* (New York: Vintage Books, 1981) and Randall Jarrell, "Introduction," in *The Anchor Book of Stories* (New York: Doubleday, 1958).

Page 247: Shakespeare, *Hamlet*, 2.2.308.

Page 250: C.K. Ogden and I.A. Richards, *The Meaning of Meaning* (Cambridge: Cambridge University Press, 1923).

Page 250: "the authoritative text . . . " Cleanth Brooks, *The Well Wrought Urn* (New York: Harcourt, Brace, 1947), esp. Appendix One: "Criticism, History, and Critical Relativism."

Page 250: William Butler Yeats, "The Second Coming."

Page 250: See Colin Campbell, "The Tyranny of the Yale Critics," *New York Times Magazine*, February 9, 1986. "A deconstructionist is not a parasite but a parricide . . . a bad son demolishing beyond hope of repair the machine of Western metaphysics" (quoting Prof. J. Hillis Miller).

Page 253: Peter Taylor, *A Summons to Memphis* (New York: Knopf, 1986).

Page 254: On Tolstoy's view of history, the classic study is Isaiah Berlin, *The Hedgehog and the Fox* (London: Weidenfeld & Nicholson, 1953). For the parody of schoolbook history, see pp. 21-23.

Page 255: "the price of mutton in the age of Philip II or the hanging of cats in Old Paris . . . " See Fernand Braudel, *The Mediterranean and the Mediterranean World in the Age of Philip II* (New York: Harper & Row, Torchbooks, 1975), vol. 1, pp.517 ff. Robert Darnton, "Workers Revolt: The Great Cat Massacre of the rue Saint-Severin," in *The Great Cat Massacre and Other Episodes in French Cultural History* (New York: Viking Press, Vintage Books, 1985), pp. 75ff.

Page 255: "with indifference to anyone else's plot . . . " The metaphor is borrowed from Ronald Dworkin's discussion of the ethics of legal interpretivism in *Law's Empire* (Cambridge, Mass.: Havard University Press, 1986). See especially chapter 7, pp. 228 ff.

* * *

TEACHING VALUES originated as a column in the *Washington Post* and other newspapers, expanded as a talk to a summer seminar for Montgomery County, Md., teachers, July 1988.

* * *

UNIVERSAL RULES OF EVIDENCE? was the Phi Beta Kappa Address, Alpha Chapter of North Carolina, University of North Carolina at Chapel Hill, winter 1977. It appeared in a somewhat different form in the *Washington Star*.

* * *

HEROIC BIOGRAPHY initially appeared in *Humanities*, the bimonthly review of the National Endowment for the Humanities, 8.2 (March/April, 1987), pp. 9-11.

*   *   *

ROOTS: AN ESSAY IN PERSONAL HISTORY originated, in part, as a column for the *Washington Post* and other newspapers, August, 1985.

*   *   *

WASHINGTON; A PERSONAL PERSPECTIVE was the opening address at a conference at Shenandoah College, Winchester, Va., on "George Washington and the Virginia Back Country," commemorating the 200th anniversary of Washington's inauguration as first president, April 1989.

INDEX